THE SCHOOLS AND
INTERNATIONAL UNDERSTANDING

The University of North Carolina Press, Chapel Hill, N. C.; The Baker and Taylor Company, New York; Oxford University Press, London; Maruzen-Kabushiki-Kaisha, Tokyo; Edward Evans and Sons, Ltd., Shanghai; D. B. Centen's Wetenschappelijke Boekandel, Amsterdam.

THE SCHOOLS

AND

INTERNATIONAL UNDERSTANDING

BY SPENCER STOKER, Ph.D.

*Professor of Education in the
Texas State College for Women*

CHAPEL HILL
THE UNIVERSITY OF NORTH CAROLINA PRESS
1933

PREFACE

FROM THE close of the nineteenth century belief in the value of the schools as a medium for promoting international understanding has become increasingly evident. Since 1919 sustained concerted effort has been made through the higher and lower schools to further international understanding. The present study proposes to analyze the nature, the method, and the development of this effort up to 1930.

The study deals primarily with objective evidence. It is believed that this evidence points clearly to an increasing unity of action and to a growing attitude of confidence in the utilization of the schools in a program of world understanding. The problem of the study is to determine what is being done through the schools to substantiate this belief.

SPENCER STOKER

Denton, Texas, 1 November, 1932

TABLE OF CONTENTS

PART II

EFFORTS TO PROMOTE INTERNATIONAL UNDERSTANDING THROUGH THE LOWER SCHOOLS

INTRODUCTION

The International Aspect of Ancient Education.—International education in the sense in which the term is most commonly employed today is a comparatively recent development. It is the result of a recognition of the interdependence of nations and an acknowledgment of the social danger and the intellectual narrowness inherent in intense nationalism. Internationalism in education existed, however, in ancient times; in fact, the national point of view in education was a late development, superseding an earlier international point of view.

The system of education that prevailed in the city of Athens after the Macedonian invasion may be cited as an instance of the international character of ancient education. With the loss of political independence, Athens gradually ceased to require compulsory training of her young men.[1] The national training had been largely for military purposes; and when Athens ceased to need soldiers or statesmen, education became more philosophical and scientific.[2]

Patriotism no longer received stimulation; the sophists, many of whom were foreigners, did most of the teaching,[3] and students of many races and beliefs came pouring into Athens. "Strangers flocked thither from distant countries," W. W. Capes says. "Not only from the isles of Greece, and from the coasts of the Ægean, but, as Hellenic culture made its way through the East, students even of Semitic race were glad to enroll their names upon the college registers, where one may still see them with marks of their several nationalities affixed."[4]

---

[1] W. W. Capes, *University Life in Ancient Athens*, pp. 3-6.
[2] E. H. Reisner, *Historical Foundations of Modern Education*, p. 76.
[3] Capes, *op. cit.*, p. 1.　　　　[4] *Ibid.*, p. 7.

The Athenian sophists took pride in the number of their students and in the cosmopolitan range of their influence. "It was with natural pride," Capes says in his study of university life in Athens, "that the great Sophists pointed to the proof of their world-wide reputation in the numbers who streamed to them from every land. Libanius, in one of his orations . . . says that he is too modest to aver that he has filled the three continents and all the islands, as far as the pillars of Hercules, with rhetoricians, but that he certainly has spiritual children—for so he likes to call them —in Thrace, Constantinople, and Bithynia, in the Hellespont, Ionia, and Caria; some few even among the Paphlagonians and Cappadocians. Far more were in Galatia and in Armenia, and most of all in Cilicia and Syria. 'If you cross the Euphrates, and visit the cities which lie beyond it, you will find some not unworthy members of our brotherhood. Phoenicia besides, and Palestine, and Arabia owe me some gratitude'."[5]

Himerius, another famous Sophist, was always careful in his addresses to his freshmen "to note their birthplace and to add some flattering word of reference to the historic glories or the present importance of their race, while dwelling on his pleasure at being brought into such wide-spread relations."[6] In fact, there were so few native born students at Athens that the purists complained that the multitude of strangers had corrupted the purity of the Attic tongue and that the old dialect could be heard only from a few hermits.[7]

Later as a result of the patronage of Alexander the Great, in whom Aristotle had influenced devotion to Greek culture, a world center of learning similar to that of Athens grew up about the famous library and museum of Alexandria. Here learned Greek, Hebrew, Egyptian, Roman, and Oriental philosophers assembled, some of them sup-

---

[5] Capes, *op. cit.*, pp. 79-80.   [6] *Ibid.*, p. 80.   [7] *Ibid.*, p. 54.

ported at royal expense, and the learning, philosophy, and religion of East and West met.[8]

In the period of the Roman Empire the Greek teachers and philosophers perpetuated the Greek culture and philosophy. Rome took over, to a large extent, the libraries of Greece, and continued the institutional side of Greek higher education,[9] thus continuing the cosmopolitan aspect of the higher institutions of Greek learning.[10]

The International Aspect of Medieval Education.—With the decline of the Roman Empire and the advent of the medieval period, the Roman Church, which for almost a thousand years dominated practically all intellectual endeavor, was at first the great internationalizing force in education. The schools were monastery schools, and later cathedral schools, where churchmen did the teaching according to the directions of the heads of the institutions, who were in general controlled by one point of view rather than divided by many points of view. This meant that, generally speaking, in every country of the civilized world, all who received formal educational training in schools were given practically the same instruction both in content and in intellectual and spiritual outlook. Thus in a certain sense international education prevailed,—not for promoting international understanding and good-will between peoples, but for the strengthening and development of the Church.[11]

With the advent of feudalism in the eighth century, followed by the crusades of the eleventh and twelfth centuries, modern nationalism finds the roots of its origin; and contemporaneous with the slow development of national governments were the decay of the church schools and the appearance and growth of the medieval university. The latter institution, the medieval university, continued the international aspect in medieval education, not so much through

---

[8] Paul Monroe, *A Textbook in the History of Education*, pp. 169-172.

[9] Monroe, *op. cit.*, p. 172.

[10] *Ibid.*, pp. 193-208.   [11] Reisner, *op. cit.*, p. 241.

uniformity in educational thought as through stimulation of student migration similar to that of early Greece.

"In and after the thirteenth century," writes Norton, "the place or school in which a university existed was almost always called a *studium generale*, i.e., a place to which students resorted, or were invited, from all countries."[12] Monroe describes the student bodies of medieval universities as "heterogeneous masses of students, drawn from all over Europe at a time when territorial lines were very indefinite and national distinctions were more those of a genetic than of a territorial and political character."[13] Philip the Fair, in 1313, referred to the international character of the medieval universities when on one occasion, recognizing the honor due to students, he said, "It is right . . . to have a great respect for the labors, the vigils, the drudgery, the deprivations, the pains and perils encountered by the students in order to acquire the precious pearl of science, and . . . it is just to consider how they have left their friends, their relatives, and their country, how they have abandoned their goods and their fortunes."[14]

The fact too, that certain privileges ignoring national boundaries proceeded from the medieval university is a further instance of its international nature. "Universities as corporations were given, among other privileges," Norton says, "the right to confer upon their graduates the license to teach 'anywhere in the world' without further examination."[15]

In the *studium generale*, or medieval university, the internationalizing influence of the Church was perpetuated to a certain extent, for the schools of theology of the medieval university in some degree carried on the work of the mon-

---

[12] A. O. Norton, *Readings in the History of Education*, p. 7.
[13] Monroe, *op. cit.*, p. 319.
[14] Quoted from G. Compayré, *Abelard and the Origin and Early History of Universities*, p 101.
[15] Norton, *op. cit.*, p. 80.

astery and cathedral schools which were falling into decay. Thus the theological doctrines of the medieval church, disseminated among cosmopolitan groups in the medieval university, continued to be an internationalizing influence in education.

Theology, however, was no longer the unique interest in education. Students sought the medieval universities to pursue the studies of law and medicine and other newly encouraged fields of intellectual interest. International uniformity in learning existed, nevertheless, in another form. In spite of the appearance of liberal tendencies which centered around various intellectual lights, scholasticism dominated university thought and teaching; all universities acknowledged Aristotle as the source of authority; thus uniformity was given to subject matter taught, regardless of the geographical location of the institution. Scholasticism allowed no place, moreover, for the language of the locality or the history of the national group. Latin was the universal language of the educated class.

After scholasticism, the renaissance continued the international attitude in education, in that it gave unity to the intellectual world through common interest in the original Latin and Greek writings of Rome and Greece. Thus again the intellectual world had a common cultural interest. The universities were stubbornly reluctant in accepting the new spirit, but in time the humanists were in the ascendancy, and the intellectual world became devoted to the form and content of the humanities.

The Rise of Nationalism in Education.—The words *form* and *content* indicate a significant alignment with respect to the future of learning and the international point of view in education. The wing of scholars that emphasized the form of Greek and Latin supported the universal character of education after the fashion of the scholastics. The wing of scholars that pursued the content of the humanities laid the foundation for national education by stimulating a questioning attitude and rejecting fixed authority. This attitude was abetted by the Reformation.

First of all, the Reformation divided the Church, which had been the chief agency of international uniformity in education during the middle ages. This created differences of opinion in which the populace could share, thus fostering fundamental convictions which definitely caused factions of thought. In the second place, the doctrine of the reformation required individual responsibility before God and also accepted the content of the Holy Scriptures as the only genuine source of the will of God. To be able to read and understand the Bible was therefore indispensable to every individual. The result of such a conception of individual responsibility was the translation of the Bible into the vernacular and the gradual ascendancy of the several vernaculars over a common international language.

These results of the reformation were important. The division of the church and the development of the written vernacular, added to the inherently nationalizing force of feudalism, effected a change in the political point of view. Nationalism became well rooted. The intellectual vehicles and wares became local and were rapidly used to strengthen national security.

The German states and the American colonies were the first modern countries that made education strictly a state or national affair. In 1642 laws were passed in Massachusetts and in Prussia establishing a basis for the idea that education is a function of the state and is therefore to be administered by the state. The succeeding century was the great transition period. During this century national education received attention from practically all the governments of Europe,[16] paving the way for the complete sway of the national ideal in educational thought in the nineteenth

---

[16] E. P. Cubberley, *History of Education*, Chapter XXII.

century. Definite national theories of education and programs of administrative control were products of the nineteenth century.

"From the late eighteenth century," Monroe says, "common culture has become the dominating element in the conception of nationality. This has resulted in the recognition of two fundamental and correlated truths: First, common culture is a trait which transcends social, religious, and economic distinctions, and its recognition transfers the seat of national existence from dynasties or bureaucratic legal institutions supported by military force to the masses of the people. Second, the discovery was made that common culture is an artificial product and can be manufactured. This process of manufacture is by education. From one point of view, then, the nineteenth century is the period of national development, working toward the democratic interpretation of nationality and using educaiton as a means."[17]

Germany, as Monroe points out, was the first nation to manufacture education and apply it to the determination of nationality, but other nations followed shortly.[18] In France in the early years of the nineteenth century, Compayré points out, education became the function of the state, to serve the ends of the state.[19] Education was nationalized.

---

[17] Paul Monroe, "Education and Nationalism," *Essays in Comparative Education*, pp. 3-4.

[18] *Ibid.*, pp. 3-4.

[19] "La loi du 11 mai 1806, complétée, par les décrèts du 17 mars 1808 et de 1811, instituait une corporation enseignante, unique et entièrement dépenante de l'État. 'Il sera formé un corps chargé exclusivement de l'enseignement et de l'éducation publique dans toute l'étendue de l'empire.' L'instruction devenait ainsi une fonction de l'État, au même titre que la justice ou l'organisation des armées. Talleyrand avait demandé que les professeurs fussent nommés par le roi. Condorcet avait proposé que les maîtres de chaque degré d'instruction fussent choisis par les maîtres du degré supérieur, Daunnou voulait confier à l'Assemblée legislative cette délicate mission. Napoléon décrète que le pouvoir exécutif nommera dorénavant à tous les emplois de l'instruction publique ceux qu'il en jugera dignes." G. Compayré, *Histoire Critique des Doctrines de l'Éducation en France*, II, 332.

History served to develop national consciousness. The national point of view extended even to points of general culture. For example, in the latter part of the nineteenth century, when there was a popular tendency in France to disregard the humanities because they did not apparently contribute to material national advantage, a French educator argued in favor of them as that education that produces men "most capable of perpetuating from generation to generation that permanent national spirit which constitutes the true 'national will'."[20]

Ideals of national culture thus gradually displaced the cultural unity of the preceding centuries. Yet out of this growth of national interests came an interest in international welfare which in its development underwent a change in point of view. Along with the strengthening of nationality by the spread of democracy came the acquisition of material wealth and the increased development of international commerce. As the citizen grew wealthy under the protection of his government he was interested in material national strength as a guarantee of the safety of his investments. Internationalism concerned him chiefly as it affected commercial welfare.

International Educational Organization in the Nineteenth Century.—Gradually, however, propaganda for international understanding assumed a less commercial aspect. Laymen and statesmen of various states became solicitors for greater international understanding; philanthropists created foundations for the purpose of mitigating national strife; unofficial and official organizations initiated various programs of propaganda to create a better international attitude.

---

[20] Alfred Fouilée, *Education from a National Standpoint*, translation by W. J. Green, 1892, p. 9.

"If the theory of evolution, applied to problems in pedagogy," Fouilée says, "has so far only led to very general and often rather vague conclusions, it is because the middle term between humanity and the in-

From the middle of the nineteenth century the international perspective developed steadily. According to a publication of the Central Office of the Union of International Associations, non-commercial international organizations began in 1840, and by 1912 there were more than four hundred of them representing almost every phase of human interest.[21] In the decade between 1840 and 1849 there were only nine International Congresses of all sorts. Between 1850 and 1859 twenty International Congresses were held; between 1860 and 1869, one hundred and seventy-four; between 1870 and 1879, more than three hundred and fifty; between 1880 and 1889, about twice as many; between 1890 and 1899, twice as many still; and between 1900 and 1909, more than eleven hundred and twenty.[22]

In this atmosphere of growing interest in internationalism a desire for international intellectual coöperation was evident. A survey of the lists of international organizations before 1900 shows that the last half of the nineteenth century witnessed the development of international organization in practically every field of learning.[23]

In the last half of the nineteenth century professional teachers also began to meet in international congresses. In addition to a number of international meetings of special

dividual—nationality, to wit—has not been introduced. I am now going to reëstablish that middle term. It is not enough, in fact, for the development of the individual to be, with Comte and Spencer, in harmony with the development of the whole of humanity; it must also be more particularly in harmony with national development, of which it is a summary, and to which it contributes." Later, he continues, "To sum up—the classics, which are supposed to be 'ancient,' should be conceived as national, aiming at the maintenance of the national spirit, the national language, the national taste, and finally the national influence." (*Ibid.*, pp. 103, 135).

[21] Office Central des Associations Internationales, *Publication No. 25a*, Brussels, 1912, pp. 11-12. The Union of International Associations was established in Brussels in 1910 for the purpose of coördinating existing international associations. (*Publication No. 60*, 1914, p. 67).

[22] Office Central des Associations Internationales, *Publication No. 25a*, table opposite p. 12.

[23] See *Ibid.*, No. 25a, pp. 43-90, and the League of Nations *Handbook of International Organizations*.

groups interested in some particular aspect of teaching,[24] at least seventeen international education congresses of general character were held between 1851 and 1915, chiefly in connection with international expositions.[25]

At the Education Conference in London in 1851 only four countries were represented: Germany, France, England, and the United States. Succeeding meetings until the outbreak of the War showed increasing interest. At the meeting in Philadelphia in 1876 thirteen foreign countries were represented and most of the states of the United States. At the meeting in Chicago in 1893 most of the countries in the world were represented. The Congress at Paris in 1900 remained in session two months, and twenty conferences considered

---

[24] Among these are the International Kindergarten Union, 1873; International Congress in Commercial Education, 1886; International Bureau of New Schools, 1899; International Bureau of Teachers' Federations, 1905 ("to improve teaching and education by the promotion of People's Schools, to establish bonds of international friendship and solidarity between members of the teaching staff"); International Commission of Congresses for Family Education, 1905; International Commission on Teaching Mathematics, 1908; and the International Moral Education Congress, 1908.

[25] Monroe's *Encyclopedia of Education* names and discusses briefly the following thirteen congresses, held in connection with world expositions except where indicated in the table:

1851 London	1885 New Orleans (International Cotton Exposition)
1855 Paris	
1867 Paris	1889 Paris
1873 Vienna	1893 Chicago
1876 Philadelphia	1900 Paris
1878 Paris	1904 St. Louis
1880 Brussels	1910 Brussels (International Congress of Education)

In addition may be cited the International Congresses in London (1884), Le Havre (1885), Brussels (1901), and San Francisco (1915). See *International Conference on Education, London, 1884,* Four Volumes; "International Congress of Education at Le Havre," *Education,* 178, December, 1885; Bureau of Internationale de Fédérations Nationales du Personnel de l'Enseignement Secondaire Public, *Dix Années de Vie Internationale* (1919-1929), publication of the Bureau International des Fédérations Nationales du Personnel de l'Enseignement Secondaire Public, 1929, p. 1; "San Francisco Conference, 1915," *Report of the Commissioner of Education, 1915,* pp. 611-613.

practically every phase of educational activity.[26]

At several of the international educational congresses the idea of an international federation of national associations of teachers was proposed.[27] At length, in 1905, an international federation of elementary teachers was organized. This was the International Bureau of Associations of Teachers (Bureau International des Associations d'Instituteurs). In 1910 it had a membership of 408,000, representing national associations of teachers of seventeen countries,[28] but at the close of the war it did not resume activity.

A second international federation of teachers' associations developed out of the suggestions advanced at the Congresses in Brussels in 1901 and 1910 in favor of an international federation of secondary teachers. The International Bureau of National Associations of Secondary Teachers was established in 1912 by representatives of Belgium, France, and Holland. It held its first annual meeting in 1913, and resumed its activity at the close of the war.[29]

These ventures in international educational coöperation are important because they contributed to the establishment of a basis for breaking down national isolation in matters of educational theory and practice.

A further venture in organization for intellectual cooperation in the nineteenth century is found in the international organization of students. Dr. Julius Lips, in discussing the background of the International Confederation

---

[26] Monroe, *Encyclopedia of Education,* International Congresses on Education.

[27] "Le Bureau International des Fédérations d'Instituteurs," *La Vie Internationale,* 1912, vol. 5, p. 205; Fédération Internationale des Associations d'Instituteurs, *Bulletin,* No. 1, 1927, p. 1; Bureau International des Fédérations Nationales du Personnel de l'Enseignement Secondaire Public, *Bulletin International,* June, 1929, pp. 17-18.

[28] Office Central des Associations Internationales, *Annuaire de la Vie Internationale,* 1910-1911, pp. 1673-1674.

[29] Bureau International des Fédérations Nationales du Personnel de l'Enseignement Secondaire Public, *Bulletin International,* No. 25, June, 1929, "Historique du Bureau International," pp. 17-18.

of Students,[30] cites as the first modern international student conference the meeting in 1842 in Lund, attended by students of Denmark, Sweden, and Norway. It was followed in 1843 and 1845 by conferences in Upsala and Copenhagen. In 1848 a committee of German and foreign students met in Breslau in response to the invitation of a committee of German students, but again no fixed organization resulted. Later international conferences in Brussels (1884), Bologna (1888), Montpellier (1890), Lausanne (1891), and Madrid (1892) gave evidence of interest in the idea of international organization of students.[31]

In the last decade of the nineteenth century two international federations of national student groups developed. The first was founded on creed. The World Federation of Christian Students, formed in 1895 by the union of national groups from the Scandinavian countries, Great Britain, the United States, and Germany, was probably the first realization of the idea of a permanent federation of national student organizations.[32]

Three years later came a proposal for an international student confederation unrestricted by race, color, or religion. In 1898 the idea of a world-wide student organization

---

[30] See below, p. 26.

[31] Julius Lips, *Die internationale Studentenbewegung nach dem Kriege*, pp. 1-3. The work is a discussion of the first two years of the International Confederation of Students (1919-1921). See below, p. 26.

[32] See below, p. 24. Attempts at international organization of Catholic students had preceded this. A report of the Catholic student organization Pax Romana (see below, p. 25) makes the following statement in a report in 1929:

"Si les catholiques n'ont pas réalisé la première union internationale etudiantine, il semble du moins qu'ils en ont eu les premiers l'idée. L'utilité d'une telle union était, en effet, déjà présentée en 1887, par un étudiant suisse, le baron Georges de Montenach, qui devint le Pièrre l'Ermite de cette nouvelle croisade. Une confédération internationale d'étudiants catholiques se fonda à Rome, en 1891, à l'occasion d'un pèlerinage de la jeunesse catholique. Le projet échoua malheureusement dans la suite, mais l'idée n'en continuer pas moins à germer, jusqu'au jour récent où elle fut reprise et incarnée dans Pax Romana." (*La Coöpération Intellectuelle*, July, 1929, p. 437.)

founded upon the principle of the universal solidarity of mankind occurred to a young Italian of Turin, who addressed an emotional appeal to Italian students. The support of Italian students having been enlisted, an international conference (groups of Belgian, French, Dutch, Hungarian, Italian, Roumanian, and Swiss students) met in Turin November 11-12, 1898, and formed the International Federation of Students. They adopted "Corda Fratres" as their motto in token of the ideal of brotherly love.

At its meeting in The Hague in 1909 plans were made for union with the Cosmopolitan Clubs, student groups established upon a similar ideal: "Above all is humanity." These clubs had begun in the United States in 1903, and in 1912 numbered twenty-six groups in the United States and a small number in South America, England, and Germany. At an international conference in Ithaca, in 1913, the plans for coöperation between the Corda Fratres and the Cosmopolitan Clubs were ratified, thus making a truly international organization of students.[33] At this congress also a program of more practical activity for mutual understanding and closer relationship among students of foreign nations was outlined. In particular it called for the international study of student problems, the establishment of national student bureaus to promote coöperation and through them the more extended exchange of students and professors.[34]

The period of the development of international education and student congresses was also a period of development in international student migration. Accurate statistics compiled systematically over a period of years are wanting;

---

[33] See Louis P. Lochner (Secretary of the Association of Cosmopolitan Clubs), "Internationalism among Universalites," *World Peace Foundation Pamphlets*, Vol. III, No. 7, Part I, July, 1913, p. 7; Louis P. Lochner, "The Cosmopolitan Club Movement," *International Conciliation*, No. 61, December, 1912, pp. 1-14; and Lips, *op. cit.*, pp. 2-8.

[34] Lips, *op. cit.*, p. 8.

but according to information presented in a recent study undertaken by the Y. M. C. A. Commission on Survey of Foreign Students in America, even fragmentary records of foreign student enrollment in several nations give decisive evidence that the last half of the nineteenth century was a period of increasing activity in international interchange.[35] For Germany more definite information is available. According to statistics compiled by the United States Commissioner of Education in 1904-1905, foreign student enrollment in German universities, to which foreign students gathered in greatest numbers, increased from 477 (or 4.02 per cent of the total enrollment) in 1835 to 3,097 (or 8.00 per cent) in 1904.[36]

About the beginning of the twentieth century the encouragement of international interchange of both students and professors began to be advocated as a means of promoting international good-will. Educators advanced the idea of educational reciprocity as a new and significant move in international friendships,[37] and in a few instances organized interest and private resources sought to facilitate it. In Europe university offices began to be established to facilitate inter-university relations with foreign countries.[38] In 1910 a conference of American States held in Buenos Aires recommended university interchange to the governments of America as a means of promoting mutual good-will among American States. The recommendations proposed interchange of university professors, establishment of scholarships

---

[35] W. R. Wheeler, H. H. King, A. B. Davidson, *The Foreign Student in America*, pp. 3-38.

[36] *Annual Report of the Department of Interior, Report of the U. S. Commissioner of Education*, 1904, Vol. II, pp. 2335-36.

[37] See, for example, Charles F. Beach, Jr., "Educational Reciprocity," *North American Review*, 183:611-612, October, 1906; Kaneko Kentaro, "For a Better Understanding between the East and the West," *Independent*, 63:251, August 1, 1907; L. S. Rowe, "The Possibility of Intellectual Cooperation between North and South America," *International Conciliation*, April, 1908, No. 6, pp. 3-15.

[38] See below, pp. 8 ff.

for the purpose of encouraging student intercourse among the several states, and the holding of a university congress to consider equivalence of studies.[39]

International scholarships, which were apparently almost unknown before the beginning of the twentieth century,[40] began to be established in the first decade of the century for the promotion of international friendships through university contacts. The Rhodes scholarship fund established in 1902 seems to have been the first significant foundation of the kind. This was established by the will of Cecil John Rhodes, who believed that a good understanding among England, Germany, and the United States would secure the peace of the world, and that, in effecting such international understanding, education formed the strongest tie. It provided for liberal scholarships at Oxford to be held by young men of Germany and the English speaking countries.[41]

This was followed nine years later by a similar foundation in America of less extensive resources. The American Scandinavian Foundation received in 1911 about $500,000 for the purpose of promoting friendships between the Scandinavian countries and the United States. It was to be used in strengthening educational interrelations through student exchange, translations, and the exchange of information. The scholarship fund, which at present because of post-war donations supports about fifty traveling fellows annually, was limited in the beginning years to some half a dozen scholarships.[42]

In 1909 the Chinese Government decided to follow the

[39] Pan-American Union, *Fifth International Conference of American States, Special Handbook for the Use of Delegates*, p. 144; *Sixth International Conference of American States, Special Handbook for the Use of Delegates*, p. 96.

[40] Institute of International Education, *Ninth Annual Report of the Director*, 1928, pp. 10-11.

[41] J. Kennedy, "Rhodes Scholarships," *School and Society*, June 28, 1919, No. 9, pp. 763-767.

[42] The Scandinavian Foundation, *Sixteenth Annual Report*, pp. 3-4.

suggestion of the President of the United States by using
the returned portion of the Boxer Indemnity Fund to promote educational relations between China and the United
States. This fund has subsidized the sending of some sixty
or more Chinese students to the United States each year.[43]

One venture in international interchange in the first decade
of the twentieth century is of interest in that it anticipates
efforts at international coöperation in interchanges belonging to the period following the world war. This is the Association for the International Interchange of Students,
established in 1909. The term "student" was interpreted
broadly by the Association to include "graduates, professors,
lecturers, and others."[44]

The Association, which originated in England, began
with interchange between Great Britain, Canada, and the
United States, with the hope of extension to other countries
as soon as circumstances permitted.[45] It was sponsored by
a committee of public officials, university officials, and business men.[46] Working primarily in the interest of affording
technical and industrial experience abroad, it proposed "to
promote interest in imperial, international, and domestic
relations, and in civic and social problems; and to foster a
mutual sympathy and understanding imperially and internationally."[47] In the course of a period of about two years

[43] Sixtieth Congress, Second Session, House of Representatives, *Document No. 1275; Proceedings of the First Pan-American Congress on Education, Rehabilitation, Reclamation and Recreation, held at Honolulu, Hawaii, April 11-16, 1927.* U. S. Department of Interior, 1927, p. 59.

[44] *First Annual Report of the Association for the International Interchange of Students,* 1909-1910. Edited by Henry W. Crees, London, 1910, p. 8.

[45] *Ibid.,* p. 7.

[46] See list of members, *ibid.,* pp. 2-6, and the list of the adherents of the North American Section, pp. 14-16.

[47] *First Annual Report of the Association for the International Interchange of Students, 1909-1910,* p. 7.

One purpose of the organization was to interest English university faculties in technical and industrial courses. Section I, points 5 and 6, of the statement of General Objects (pp. 7-8) reads thus:

it arranged two educational tours for small groups, secured traveling scholarships for five students,[48] and facilitated travel and study for a number of applicants.[49]

Among the resolutions adopted at the International Conference of the Association at the close of its experimental period, June, 1912, were the following:

"That the Conference further desire to recommend the inclusion of countries other than the British Empire and the United States in the scheme of work as and when opportunities offer.

"That the Conference recommend that every effort should be made to develop the facilities for the International Exchange of Professors.

"That upon the permanent establishment of the Association in London, steps should be taken to bring the work of the Association to the more immediate notice of the Universities and other Institutions of higher education of the world. And, further, that every effort should be made to obtain permanent endowment for one or more similar bureaux to be opened on the Continent of North America to serve the interests of Canada and the United States under the direction of the Association."[50]

There is no evidence that these resolutions were realized; the period of experiment seems to have resulted in no permanent organization.

"5. To afford technical and industrial students facilities to examine into questions of particular interest to them, in manufactures, &, by observation in other countries, and by providing them with introductions to leaders in industrial activity.

"6. To promote interest in travel as an educational factor among the authorities of Universities, with a view to the possibility of some kind of such training being included in the regular curricula."

[48] Three English (Armstrong College) and two American (Throop Polytechnic, Pasadena, California).

[49] Thirty-six during the first year; a larger number the second year. See *First Annual Report*, pp. 37-40, 43; *Second Annual Report*, pp. 18-30; *Third Annual Report*, pp. 161 ff.

[50] *Third Annual Report*, 1912, p. 49.

Finally, by the close of the nineteenth century, there appeared an interest in peace movements in the lower schools. The Education Congresses at the close of the century showed interest in the possibility of making the schools a force in developing universal understanding and peace. M. Léon Bourgeois, speaking at the Educational Congress of Paris in 1889, emphasized the fundamental importance of the school in the following appeal:

"It is quite evident to everyone that the School, the humble primary school, is the basis of public peace, universal peace. Throughout the entire world, all of the friends of justice, truth, and liberty must rally about the school and, through it, bring about the triumph of the cause of liberty."[51]

By the beginning of the twentieth century peace societies had begun to organize peace propaganda in the schools. Attempts were made to arouse sentiment against the glorification of war in text-books[52] and to initiate Peace Day celebrations in the schools.[53] By the close of the first decade school peace leagues existed in several countries.[54]

The war of 1914 stopped the operations of the international associations, save the activities carried on between geographical sections that were more or less remote from the war area. Yet the war, too, made its contribution to the movement. It gave to governments and to all thinking individuals proof of the interdependence of man and nations, and of the almost certain spread of war to originally neutral states.

---

[51] Bureau international des Fédérations d'Instituteurs, *Session de 1913, réunion de Bruxelles*, p. 39. (Translated by the author.)

[52] *Fifth Universal Peace Congress*, Chicago, 1893, p. 294; *Teaching of History in the Public Schools of the United States with Special Reference to War and Peace*, 1906, Report of a Committee of Three appointed in accordance with the Annual Meeting of the American Peace Society, May 18, 1905; *The Peace Year Book*, 1912, pp. 101-102.

[53] *The Peace Year Book*, 1912, pp. 98-99, 100, 107.

[54] *Ibid.*, pp. 98, 101-102.

At the close of the war new energy was devoted to the cause of peace and understanding between nations. The result has been that the decade since the World War has witnessed phenomenal interest in means of securing international peace. Much of this interest has centered on the schools as a medium for international understanding.

PART I

EFFORTS TO PROMOTE INTERNATIONAL
UNDERSTANDING THROUGH THE HIGHER
SCHOOLS AND UNIVERSITIES

CHAPTER I

ORGANIZATION FOR PROMOTING INTERNATIONAL UNIVERSITY RELATIONS

INTEREST in the possibility of securing world amity and international coöperation through the schools and universities had been evident before the World War. It became a particularly active interest after the war on the part of societies already in existence devoted to such interests, and on the part of new organizations that sprang up during the war, and in particular after the war, for the purpose of reestablishing broken relations or cementing new international contacts. The fact, too, that throughout Europe intellectual life was felt to be endangered, resulted in a movement towards greater international intellectual solidarity because of mutual needs. Moreover, the change in governments and the creation of new states as a result of the war were occasions of increased interest in international intellectual coöperation.

The number of agents—national and international, private and official—devoting all or a part of their interest to promoting understanding among nations through schools and universities is legion. Sentiment in favor of developing in the youth of the world a new mental attitude conducive to world peace and understanding has steadily increased. Foundations have been established and institutions set up for education along international lines. Numerous international organizations originally of non-educational function have interested themselves in international educational relations. Finally, national governments, coöperating especially with educational organizations and with the aims of the League of Nations, have lent their support to international education contacts in the interest of international understanding.

NATIONAL UNIVERSITY OFFICES AND INTERNATIONAL RELATIONS

International Meeting of Directors.—One of the important national institutions for establishing international understanding and promoting international contacts through higher education is the national university office or similar organ, acting in coöperation with the universities. Most of these are of post-war origin. Some—the Danish, French, Greek, Hungarian, Italian, Netherland, Polish, and Spanish offices—are partially or wholly supported by State subsidy.[1] The international activity of these organs has been furthered through the League of Nations Committee on International Intellectual Coöperation.

From its beginning the League of Nations Committee on Intellectual Coöperation has considered the question of internationalizing the universities, chiefly through the encouragement of international professorial and student interchange and encouragement of international courses. At its initial session in 1922, a proposal was considered for convening an international conference of universities for the discussion of this question, but was dismissed for the time as impracticable under the prevailing conditions.[2] A proposal submitted at the second session for the creation of an International Uni-

---

[1] League of Nations Institute of Intellectual Coöperation, *Handbook of University Exchanges in Europe*, 1928, pp. 41, 54, 139, 142, 162, 172, 180.

[2] League of Nations Committee on Intellectual Coöperation, *Minutes of the First Session*, pp. 25-29. The proposal was made on the following basis:

"1. The League of Nations, being the central organization for the coordination and control of international relations, is entitled to be informed of relations between universities, although it may not interfere with university teaching or infringe the sovereign rights of States.

"2. Anything which contributes towards the institution of more intimate and more constant relations between the higher teaching establishments of the different nations would constitute a powerful aid towards peace-

versity Information Bureau to serve a similar purpose met with greater success,[3] and led to an important development in national university offices.

The International Committee on Intellectual Coöperation in 1923 stated that it was impossible to continue its work in university relations unless an international university office was formed. In reply the Fourth Assembly authorized the Committee to convert its secretariat into an international university office. The Assembly suggested the following activities:

"(a) Communication of the recommendations of the Committee on Intellectual Coöperation for their information to the competent authorities and particularly to the national university information offices.

"(b) Publication of any information which it may receive, especially from national university information offices, where such offices exist, in regard to the equivalence of studies and diplomas recognized by different countries, the curricula of universities, especially university courses relative to modern nations, the teaching of modern languages, literatures and civilizations and international vacation courses.

"(c) Preparation of a meeting between the University Sub-Committee and delegates of the international students' associations with a view to examining methods of extending the ex-

---

ful relations between nations and would be a strong guarantee of civilization.

"3. In inter-university relations there are three aspects relating to: (a) professors; (b) students; and (c) studies and their results (diplomas and degrees).

"4. In each of these fields the League of Nations is authorized to make practical suggestions to universities and Governments, with a view to improving inter-university relations and to making them frequent, regular, and profitable." (*Ibid.*, p. 26).

[3] *Minutes of the Second Session*, pp. 33-34, 68-69. The idea had been advanced at the first session. (*Minutes of the First Session*, p. 43, No. 9; *Minutes of the Second Session*, p. 33, note.) The proposal adopted provided for a bureau to collect and distribute information about university studies and personnel and international relationships (cquivalence, international congresses, vacation courses, and exchanges of students, professors, and publications. *Minutes of the Second Session*, pp. 68-69.)

change of students, with the concurrence of their universities.

"(d) Establishment of relations with all the organizations existing in various countries for the purpose of rendering exchanges of professors more frequent."[4]

In accordance with the first two of these recommendations of the Assembly, a circular was sent to directors of national university offices and similar institutions,[5] announcing the establishment of the International University Information Office, and requesting information and coöperation.[6] At length, July 7-9, 1926, the International Committee on Intellectual Coöperation, acting through the International Institute of Intellectual Coöperation,[7] convened in Paris the first meeting of the Directors of National University Offices and similar institutions.

Since the initial session, the meeting of the Directors of National University Offices has been convened annually by the Institute. Its representation has indicated consistent interest on the part of a number of European offices and a United States office. The questions chiefly considered by the

---

[4] League of Nations, *Official Journal, Special Supplement No. 13, Records of the Fourth Assembly, Plenary Meetings,* 1923, p. 109.

[5] "This circular was addressed to the National University Offices in all countries in which an office of this kind exists (British Empire, France, Germany, and Switzerland), as well as to all institutions of a similar kind, (the *Fondation Universitaire* in Belgium; the *Junta para Ampliacion de Estudios* in Spain; the Institute of International Education, and the two offices of the American University Union, as far as the United States are concerned; the *Institute Inter-Universitario Italiano* in Italy; the General Committee for International University Questions in the Netherlands; and the Secretariat of the Chancellor of Universities in Sweden)." In other countries it was sent to the National Committee on Intellectual Coöperation or to Rectors of the various universities. (Report on the Fourth Session of the University Sub-Committee of the Committee on International Intellectual Coöperation, "Organization of the International University Information Office," *Bulletin of the International University Information Office,* 1924, Nos. 1 and 2, pp. 5-6.)

[6] *Ibid.,* pp. 5, 6, 16, 17.

[7] The Institute had meanwhile been established, in 1925, and the activity of the International Office for University Information had been transferred to its University Relation Section. (*Bulletin for University Relations,* 1926, No. 1, p. 1.) See below, p. 35, note 101.

meetings—in addition to questions of organization (the inter-relation of the National Offices, their relation to the International Institute, and the desirability of creating new Offices)—have been these: the international migration and exchange of professors, secondary teachers, and students, the international dissemination of information concerning vacation courses and regular academic courses, and the equivalence of studies and degrees.[8]

The meetings of the Directors of the National University Offices have been attended by delegates of thirteen organizations representing thirteen European States and three American organizations, acting as a unit, representing the United States. These are the Fondation Universitaire (Belgium), the Danish University Information Office, the Office National des Universités et Écoles Françaises, the German Akademisches Auskunftsamt,[9] the Universities Bureau of the British Empire,[10] the Greek National Office for University Information,[11] the Hungarian International University Office, the Italian Inter-University Institute, the Netherlands Committee of International University Relations, the Polish University Office, the Roumanian University Office, the Junta para Ampliacion de Estudios (Spain), the Swiss Central Universities Office, and, for the United States,

---

[8] League of Nations, International Committee on Intellectual Coöperation, *Bulletin of the International University Information Office*, 1924, No. 1, p. 6, etc.; No. 2, pp. 119-120; No. 4, p. 222; *Bulletin for University Relations*, 1926, Nos. 4-5, p. 351; 1928, No. 1, p. 35; No. 2, p. 77, No. 3, p. 174. *Minutes of the Eighth Session of the International Committee on Intellectual Coöperation*, 1926, pp. 81 ff.; *Minutes of the Ninth Session*, 1927, pp. 79 ff.; *Minutes of the Tenth Session*, 1928, pp. 77 ff.; *Minutes of the Eleventh Session*, 1929, pp. 93 ff.

[9] Represented only at the 1927 and 1928 sessions. *Minutes of the Eighth Session*, pp. 80-81, list of delegates, 1926; *Minutes of the Ninth Session*, p. 80, list of delegates, 1927; *Minutes of the Tenth Session*, p. 77, list of delegates, 1928.

[10] Represented only at the 1929 session. *Minutes of the Eleventh Session*, p. 93, list of delegates, 1929.

[11] Represented only at the 1928 and 1929 sessions. See notes 9 and 10 above.

the American Council on Education, the Institute of International Education, and the American University Union.

In addition, the Akademischer Austauschdienst of Germany should be mentioned as a national office which, though not represented in the meetings of Directors, has acquired the importance of a national university office in the function of inter-university exchanges.

Origins of National Offices.—Most of these are, as was stated above, organizations established since the World War for the definite purpose of disseminating abroad information concerning the university life of the country represented, and of furthering international intellectual contacts in the field of higher education. Only four existed before 1914.

The Akademisches Auskunftsamt was established at the University of Berlin in 1904. Since its foundation it has served in coöperation with the similar offices at Giessen and Cologne as state information bureau of Germany in questions concerning national and foreign students and studies.[12] The Junta para Ampliacion was established in 1907 as a State Institute, free from party interests, for the promotion of language, history, and art studies. The purpose embodied in its principles of foundation were to encourage scientific interest for its own sake, to keep in touch with scientific progress in other countries, and to make use of Spanish culture to enhance the prestige of Spain in Spanish America, "in order that she may become one day the guide and mouthpiece in Europe of all the Spanish race." [13] The Office National des Universités et Écoles Françaises was founded in 1910 for the development of French culture abroad.[14] The

---

[12] *Die Hochschulen Deutschlands,* publication of the Akademisches Auskunftsamt, Berlin, 1926, pp. 60-61.

[13] League of Nations Committee on Intellectual Coöperation, *Bulletin of the University Information Office,* 1924, No. 1, p. 45.

[14] Its university and school relations with foreign nations are controlled and encouraged officially by the Services des Oeuvres françaises à l'étranger and the Service d'Expansion universitaire et scientifique, attached respectively to the Ministry of Foreign Affairs and the Ministry

Universities Bureau of the British Empire was founded in 1912 by the delegates of the Congress of Universities of the Empire for the purpose of summoning a congress every five years and of keeping the universities of the Empire in touch with each other during the interval.[15] The international activities of these organizations have greatly increased since the war in efforts to promote a broad interest in the intellectual life of their respective countries and to develop or reëstablish international interchange relationships.

The other organizations sending representatives to the Meetings of Directors of National University Offices are post-war institutions, several having evolved out of situations definitely conditioned by the World War.

The Belgian Fondation Universitaire had its beginning in a University foundation provided for during the war as a factor of national reconstruction. It was definitely established in 1920 to aid young Belgians without means and to develop scholarly production in Belgium. It has the international function of arranging exchanges of professors with foreign countries and granting scholarships to Belgian students for study abroad. The Cercle des Alumni de la Fondation Universitaire, established in 1923 under the auspices of the Fondation Universitaire for the purpose of maintaining relations among beneficiaries of the Fondation scholarships, serves as international university information bureau for Belgium.[16]

---

of Public Instruction. (Office National des Universités et Écoles Françaises, *Rapport sur l'Expansion Universitaire et Scientifique de la France et l'Activité de l'Office National des Universités en 1923 et 1924* by Charles Petit-Dutaillés, Director of the Office, Director General of Public Instruction, p. 5.)

[15] Second Congress of the Universities of the Empire, 1921, *Report of Proceedings*, p. xi.

[16] For the history of the endowment see the report of the Foundation in League of Nations International Committee on Intellectual Coöperation, *Bulletin of the International Office*, 1925, No. 2, pp. 81-85. See also League of Nations Institute of Intellectual Coöperation, *A Handbook of University Exchanges in Europe*, 1928, p. 29.

The American institutions representing the United States at the Meetings of Directors likewise had their inception in the need of meeting war conditions. The American University Union in Europe, had its beginning in 1917 as overseas college clubs established in London, Paris, and, for a time, in Italy, by a group of American colleges and universities, to care for the interests of American students in Europe. In 1919 its activities underwent radical change. The institutions supporting it made it a central office for liaison between European universities and students from American colleges and universities, to encourage international interchange of students and to facilitate in every way possible the studies of American students abroad.[17] In 1923, as a result of a general desire in America for closer coöperation among educational organizations, the Union became a part of the American Council on Education, established in 1918,[18] with which also the Institute of International Education became, at the same moment, closely affiliated.[19]

The latter organization, the Institute of International Education, was also conceived during the war. It was proposed as an organization to develop among people of the United States, through the medium of international educational coöperation, a better understanding of the problems and difficulties of other people. It was not established, however, until February, 1919, when a subsidy of $30,000 was granted by the Carnegie Endowment for the first year of

---

[17] League of Nations International Committee on Intellectual Coöperation, *Bulletin of the International University Information Office,* 1924, No. 1, pp. 50-52; *ibid.,* 1925, No. 1, pp. 13-16.

[18] An American organization composed of sixteen important educational associations as constituent members, twelve learned societies and foundations as associated members, and one hundred and ninety-four universities and colleges as institutional members. It was established to promote national and international coöperation in educational matters. (*The Educational Record,* Vol. 1, No. 1, January, 1920, pp. 30-38.)

[19] *Institute of International Education, Its Origin, Organization, and Activities,* New York, March 1, 1928, pp. 3-4.

the Institute's work.[20] The Institute later took over the international academic activities of the American Council on Education (receiving in turn from the Council the Laura Spelman Rockefeller memorial subsidy). It likewise assumed the direction of the American University Union in Europe, which in turn is the European representative of both the Institute and the American Council on Education.[21] Thus the three organizations function as a unit in the field of international educational relations.

The Swiss organ mentioned above also came into existence as a result of the unusual post-war conditions. The National Association of Swiss Universities, recognizing after the war the disadvantages of excessive decentralization, particularly in relations with foreign students and foreign universities, established in 1920 the Swiss Central University Office.[22]

Again, the Roumanian University Office, which had its beginning in 1923, though not formally recognized until 1927, grew out of post-war conditions. It was established as a result of the increase in the number of universities when Roumanian territory was extended after the war, and of the post-war needs of Roumanian students.[23]

Last, the Akademischer Austauschdienst, founded in 1925, grew out of efforts to reëstablish academic relations interrupted by the war. In 1924 the Staatswissenschaftliche Austauschstelle was created by the Heidelberg Institute of

[20] Ibid., pp. 1, 2. League of Nations Committee on Intellectual Coöperation, Bulletin of the International University Information Office, 1924, No. 3, report of the Director of the Institute of International Education, pp. 121-122.

[21] Institute of International Education, Eighth Annual Report of the Director, Eighth series, Bulletin No. 4, pp. 8-9; League of Nations Committee on Intellectual Coöperation, Bulletin of the International University Information Office, 1924, No. 1, p. 51.

[22] League of Nations Committee on Intellectual Coöperation, Bulletin of the International University Information Office, 1924, No. 1, p. 50, report of the Swiss Central University Office.

[23] League of Nations International Committee on Intellectual Coöperation, Bulletin for University Relations, 1928, No. 2, pp. 96-98, report of the Roumanian National University Office.

Social and Political Science. Its initial activity was the knitting of relations with the universities of the United States, in response to the desire expressed by certain important American universities to reëstablish academic exchange relations with Germany. Out of this organization the Akademischer Austauschdienst was developed and established in 1925, with the encouragement of the German Ministry of Education.[24]

The fourteen offices named above are organs which represent the interests of the universities and other higher institutions of culture in their respective countries,[25] and serve to bring them in touch with academic institutions abroad. They may be defined in general as organizations coördinating and developing university life in their respective nations, encouraging international recognition of the national university life represented in each case, and promoting through the influence of higher educational authorities the international migration of professors and students for the purpose of teaching or study. The several offices, however, judged by their reports to the University Information section of the International Committee on Intellectual Coöperation, vary widely in nature and scope.

Functions of National University Offices.—The Swiss and Hungarian Offices have functioned internationally chiefly as information offices. The Belgian, Danish, and Roumanian Offices, function also as international information bureaus, and to some extent actively promote international exchange of students. They direct their chief concern to the development of academic life at home and the material assistance

[24] Institute of International Education, *Sixth Annual Report of the Director*, 1925, pp. 25-26; League of Nations Institute of Intellectual Coöperation, *Handbook of Institutions for the Scientific Study of International Relations,* p. 56.

[25] For the academic nature of these organizations see League of Nations Institute of Intellectual Coöperation, *Handbook of University Exchanges in Europe*, 1928, pp. 28, 41, 54, 116, 139, 142, 150, 162, 172, 177, 180, 192.

of students in the national universities in each case. The Akademischer Austauschdienst aims at the promotion of academic collaboration with foreign countries, chiefly through reciprocal exchange scholarships for pupils, students, and younger research workers.[26]

Other offices report more comprehensive programs. The Italian Office was established in 1923 "to develop Italian culture and make it better known abroad and to promote intellectual relations between Italy and other countries by creating courses of literature for foreigners and Italians and by coördinating and improving such courses as already exist."[27]

The Universities Bureau of the British Empire, established originally as a liaison factor between the universities of Britain and her dominions, still functions chiefly as a means of coördination between British universities; but it has widened its interest to include other nations. It defines itself as "an association for the collection and propagation of university information from every part of the Empire, the distribution throughout the university world of information regarding vacation appointments and opportunities for advanced study and research, the facilitation of the migration of students and temporary exchange of professors and other teachers."[28] It has promoted the visits of delegations of British university professors abroad, has arranged a conference of Swiss and British universities,[29] and has promoted the visits and study of British professors and

[26] See p. 9, note 16; p. 11, notes 22 and 23; p. 12, note 24; p: 16, note 37; p. 17, note 43.

[27] League of Nations Committee on Intellectual Coöperation, *Bulletin of the International University Information Office*, 1925, Nos. 4-5, p. 198, report of the Italian Inter-University Institute.

[28] Second Congress of the Universities of the Empire, 1921, *Report of Proceedings*, p. 5; Universities Bureau of the British Empire, *Yearbook of the Universities of the Empire*, 1923, pp. 552-631.

[29] *Ibid.*, 1923, pp. 628-631.

students abroad and foreign professors and students in Britain.[30]

The Polish University Office encourages intellectual life in Poland, disseminates abroad information about Polish university life, and serves in Poland as information center concerning foreign university life. In addition it serves the Minister of Public Instruction in questions of professional scholarships, studies abroad, and vacation courses for foreigners, and prepares international conventions in these matters.[31]

The Junta para Ampliacion de Estudios, in addition to functioning as the State Information Bureau in academic matters, has been active in securing foreign lecturers in Spain and sending Spanish professors abroad, establishing funds for scholarships in Europe and America, and organizing holiday and winter courses for foreigners.[32]

Finally, perhaps two of the most active organizations of this type are the Office National des Universités et Écoles Françaises and the Institute of International Education. The former has since its establishment continually expanded in international functions. In particular it has actively pursued its major work of professorial and student exchange,[33] has effected the conclusion of educational agreements between France and foreign nations and established lists of equivalence, and has served as an organ for propaganda in the interest of French culture, establishing French institutes and

---

[30] *Ibid.;* Second Congress of the Universities of the Empire, 1921, *Report of Proceedings,* p. 5.

[31] League of Nations Committee on Intellectual Coöperation, *Bulletin for University Relations,* 1928, No. 2, p. 91, report of the Polish University Office.

[32] League of Nations Committee on Intellectual Coöperation, *Bulletin of the University Information Office,* 1924, No. 1, pp. 45-49.

[33] In this connection the university councils coöperate with the Office. (*La Rapport sur l'Expansion Universitaire et Scientifique de la France et l'Activité de l'Office National des Universités en 1923 et 1924,* p. 7.)

schools in foreign countries and closely supervising their interests.[34]

The chief international activity of the second, the Institute of International Education, has been to promote the interchange of professors and students between the United States and foreign countries. To this end it has been active in establishing contacts with foreign agents of similar nature. It collects and publishes accurate information concerning opportunities and requirements for higher study at home and abroad and concerning the opportunities for securing savants and lecturers in American Universities. It works to increase the number of scholarships and fellowships open for foreign study and to make known those already in existence. It also encourages the interest on the part of American university students in European summer courses.[35]

International Contacts Through Bureaus Abroad and Corresponding Offices.—These offices, serving as organs of liaison between the universities and higher schools of their respective nations and foreign nations, have been enabled, as was pointed out above, to enter into closer relations through the meetings of directors convened annually by the League of Nations International Committee on Intellectual Cooperation. At these meetings problems of mutual interest are discussed and reports are heard concerning the treatment of these problems in the various nations. In addition, practical international contact is secured by the establishment of bureaus abroad or by affiliation with similar existing offices for the purposes of information or exchange.

The Belgian Fondation Universitaire in its work of student and professorial exchange with the United States works

---

[34] League of Nations Committee on Intellectual Coöperation, *Bulletin of the International University Information Office,* 1924, Nos. 1 and 2, pp. 39-44, and the Annual Reports of the Director of the Office, 1923-1929.

[35] See below, pp. 84, 155, and the Annual Reports of the Director of the Institute.

in coöperation with the Committee for Relief in Belgium Foundation Incorporated, a foundation established in the state of Delaware in 1920 for the promotion of intellectual relations between the United States and Belgium.[36] The Danish Office in its work as international information bureau is affiliated with offices established in London (Anglo-Danish Bureau)[37] and Paris (Bureau franco-danois des Renseignements).[38] Each of these is subordinate, like the main bureau in Copenhagen, to a commisison of professors and students of the four Danish High Schools. Each was granted subsidy by the Danish Government at the same time that the office at Copenhagen was subsidized, 1921.[39]

The German Akademischer Austauschdienst in its work of student exchange with the United States relies upon the American-German Exchange directed by the Institute of International Education, not merely as an intermediary in the distribution of exchange scholarships, but also as a society for fostering good-will and confidence between Germany and America.[40] This, as was mentioned above, was its first venture in international academic relations.

Later, in 1926, when psychological conditions seemed ripe, the Akademischer Austauschdienst entered into academic relations with England through the Anglo-German Academic Board, a committee of English university professors established in that year, including representatives of the Universi-

---

[36] League of Nations Committee on Intellectual Coöperation, *Bulletin of the International University Information Office*, 1925, No. 2, p. 82, report of the Belgian University Foundation.

[37] *Ibid.*, 1925, No. 6, p. 275, report of the Danish University Information Office.

[38] For a brief description of its activity see League of Nations Committee on Intellectual Coöperation, *Bulletin for University Relations*, 1926, No. 2, pp. 72-73.

[39] League of Nations Committee on Intellectual Coöperation, *Bulletin of the International University Information Office*, 1924, pp. 38-39; League of Nations Institute of Intellectual Coöperation, *A Handbook of University Exchanges in Europe*, 1928, pp. 41, 79, 106.

[40] League of Nations Committee on Intellectual Coöperation, *Bulletin for University Relations*, 1928, No. 1, p. 44.

ties of Oxford, Cambridge, Manchester, and London.[41] The two collaborate for the purpose of arranging university exchanges. In 1927 the Akademischer Austauschdienst established a permanent corresponding office in London, the Anglo-German Academic Bureau. Its functions are to promote further development of academic relations with England, to arrange exchanges of students and teachers, to aid German university men coming to England (particularly students of language attending the vacation courses), and to serve as information office concerning questions of study in Germany. In addition steps have been taken to reëstablish relations with France.[42]

The Hungarian Office functions as international information office. It gives information concerning Hungarian university life to the Hungarian Student Centers (Collegia Hungarica) established by the Hungarian Government in 1923 and 1924 in Berlin, Vienna, and Rome, and to the Bureau franco-hongrois des renseignement universitaire in Paris (1927). The former, the Collegia Hungarica, were established to supervise the interests of Hungarian students abroad and to serve as Hungarian university information offices abroad. The latter serves as information bureau to promote closer academic relations between Hungary and France.[43]

The English Bureau maintains close relations with the American, Danish, and French offices through their respective branches in London. These branches—the American University Union in Britain, the Anglo-Danish Student Bureau, and the Bureau du Royaume Uni of the Office National des Universités et Écoles Françaises—are quartered

---

[41] League of Nations Committee on Intellectual Coöperation, *Bulletin for University Relations*, 1928, No. 1, p. 45.
[42] League of Nations Institute of Intellectual Coöperation. *Handbook of University Exchanges in Europe*, 1928, pp. 106-107.
[43] League of Nations Institute of Intellectual Coöperation, *Handbook of University Exchanges in Europe*, 1928, pp. 24, 94, 142, 149; *Bulletin for University Relations*, 1928, No. 2, p. 90.

in the same building with the English Bureau.[44]

The French Office has been particularly active in establishing corresponding bureaus abroad. In 1923 it had established bureaus in New York and London[45] and was represented in Madrid, Barcelona, and Florence by the French Institutes in those places, and in Switzerland and Holland by a French professor at Fribourg and Amsterdam respectively, acting unofficially.[46] In the report of 1923-24 the Office announced the establishment of a corresponding bureau for collaboration with Jugoslavia, to begin in 1925, the bureau to be composed of three French professors serving in the Universities of Belgrade, Zagreb, and Ljubliana.[47] In 1928-29, bureaus were established in Luxembourg and Poland.[48]

In addition the Office maintains close collaboration with the Institute of International Education of New York and with foreign university offices in Paris.[49] Among these are the American University Office, the Comité Franco-Autriche (which was founded by the Office in 1923 as a bureau for the exchange of information and publications, and has its secretariat at the Office),[50] and the bureau for university relations with Germany (established by the Office in 1927 at the suggestion of the Ministers of Public Instruction and

---

[44] *Bulletin of the University Information Office,* 1924, Nos. 1 and 2, p. 37.

[45] The New York Office was liquidated in 1926 because of lack of funds occasioned by the drop of the franc. The interests of the Office in New York were assumed then by the professor of French of Bryn Mawr in charge of the French scholarship holders, and closer collaboration was established with the Institute of International Education. (*Assemblée générale de l'Office National des Universités et Écoles Françaises et Rapport du Directeur sur l'Activité de l'Office des Universités en 1926,* April 2, 1927, pp. 7-9; *ibid.,* 1928-29, p. 4.)

[46] *Rapport sur l'Expansion Universitaire et Scientifique de la France et l'activité de l'Office National des Universités en 1923 et 1924,* p. 2.

[47] *Ibid.,* pp. 1, 2.

[48] Assemblée Générale de l'Office National des Universités et Écoles Françaises, *Rapport du Directeur sur l'Activité de l'Office des Universités en 1928-1929,* p. 4.

[49] See above, p. 10.

[50] *Rapport sur l'Expansion Universitaire et Scientifique de la France et l'Activité de l'Office National des Universités en 1923 et 1924,* p. 19.

Foreign Affairs and in accordance with a decision of the
Comité de Direction of the Office).[51]
Likewise active in establishing contacts in other countries
is the American Institute of International Education. One
of its chief functions has been the establishment of corresponding agents in foreign countries. This has been ac-
complished chiefly by means of personal contact through
the director's visits abroad in 1919 and 1925 and through
the visits of foreign professors to the New York Office since
its foundation. As a result, the Institute is represented
abroad, for purposes of interchange of professors and students and exchange of information concerning university
matters, by the branches of the American University Union
in London, Paris, and Rome, the American Institute of
Education in Vienna, the Akademischer Austauschdienst in
Berlin, the Hungarian and Czechoslovakian Ministers of
Public Instruction, the Office National des Universités et
Écoles Françaises, the Direttore General delle Scuole Italiane
all'Estero, and, in Switzerland, the Schweizerischer
Schulratsprasident and a committee of the rectors of the
Swiss Universities. It is also the official representative in the
United States of the Office National des Universités et Écoles
Françaises, the Akademischer Austauschdienst, and the
Centro de Estudios Historicos.[52] In addition it coöperates
with numerous organizations in the United States interested
in international educational activities, and with a number
of societies established for the purpose of promoting inter-
course, not primarily educational, between the United States
and the respective countries which they represent.[53]
In this group of national institutions one finds an im-

[51] *Rapport du Directeur sur l'Activité de l'Office des Universités*, 1927,
p. 22.
[52] League of Nations Committee on Intellectual Coöperation, *Bulletin of
the University Information Office*, 1924, Nos. 1 and 2, p. 46.
[53] See Institute of International Education, *First Annual Report of the
Director*, 1920, p. 7, Representatives and Correspondents Abroad; p. 10,
The Institute as Headquarters for Educational Organizations; *Sixth An-*

portant factor in international university relations. Representing the interests of their national universities at home and abroad, and entering into international affiliations through the annual meetings of their directors and through coöperation with special bureaus established for academic collaboration with other nations, they constitute an important force in promoting inter-university relations.

INTERNATIONAL STUDENT ORGANIZATION

Committee of Representatives of International Student Organizations.—At the same time that the International Committee on Intellectual Coöperation entered into relations with the national university offices, it entered also into relations with the international student organizations, which have interests similar to those of the university offices. As a result these organizations have been brought into coöperation with one another in a manner similar to that employed in the meetings of the directors of national university offices.

International student organizations had their modern origin in international student conferences of the nineteenth century. Two federations of students had reached international scope before the war: the World's Student Christian Federation and the "Corda Fratres" organization.[54] The latter in 1919 joined the International Confederation of Students (Confédération Internationale des Étudiants) established in that year.[55]

After the war a number of new international student associations arose, five of which established themselves as truly international in scope. These are the International Confederation of Students mentioned above, the International

---

nual *Report*, 1925, pp. 5-32; *Institute of International Education, Its Origin, Organization, and Activities*, pp. 5-6; *Ninth Annual Report*, pp. 11-12.

[54] See above, pp. 16-18.

[55] League of Nations *Handbook of International Organizations*, 1926, p. 106.

Federation of University women (a graduate organization), the International Universities League of Nations Federation, Pax Romana, and the World Union of Jewish Students. In addition to these may be mentioned the international student movement known as International Student Service (Entr'aide Universitaire Internationale), which, though without formal membership, enlists the support of students of some forty countries.[56] These international student and graduate organizations, functioning through an active central committee, represent the point of view and the international aims of the students of the world.

At the first session of the International Committee on Intellectual Coöperation, in 1922, a communication was read from the International Confederation of Students, suggesting that students should be directly associated with the work of the Committee.[57] At the second session, July, 1923, in connection with the discussion of the international exchange of students, the Committee adopted a resolution favoring a joint meeting of the Committee and representatives of international student federations.

The resolution read:

"(1) The Committee on Intellectual Coöperation is of the opinion that the exchange of students can be organized and developed very largely by the students themselves, and particularly by the international students' associations. It is of the opinion that an agreement among these associations would be desirable; the object of such an agreement would be to coordinate their efforts on practical lines, to supply each other with information and to prevent overlapping, but in giving effect to these recommendations, none of these associations

---

[56] League of Nations Committee on Intellectual Coöperation, *Bulletin for University Relations*, 1926, No. 2, p. 79, report of International Student Service.

[57] League of Nations Committee on Intellectual Coöperation, *Minutes of the First Session*, p. 43.

should be forced to modify its plan of work or abandon its special aims. The Committee has chiefly in view the four following associations with which the Universities Sub-Committee is at present in touch: the International Students Federation,[58] the Universal Federation of Students' Christian Associations, the Pax Romana, and the Inter-Federation of University Women. The Committee accordingly invites the Sub-Committee to make arrangements for a joint meeting between the Committee and the delegates of these four associations; it will draw up beforehand the programme for this meeting in agreement with the associations, and will submit it to the Committee."[59]

This joint meeting was held December 4, 1923. The Sub-Committee on University Relations represented the International Committee. The European Student Relief urged through its executive secretary that the increase in number of international student organizations might result in serious duplication and unwise complication. It submitted a program which recommended a meeting of representatives of the most important international student organizations for the purpose of adopting a unified plan of procedure, and suggested a rather lengthy list of subjects that the proposed committee of international student organizations could deal with.[60] The Sub-Committee on Inter-University Relations agreed to prepare the agenda and invite the most prominent international student organizations to send delegates to Geneva for the meeting.[61]

---

[58] The organization is referred to as International Federation of Students, or International Confederation of Students. See League of Nations Committee on Intellectual Coöperation, *Bulletin of the International University Information Office*, 1924, No. 3, p. 159; 1925, No. 2, p. 112.

[59] League of Nations Committee on Intellectual Coöperation, *Minutes of the Second Session*, 1923, pp. 31-32.

[60] League of Nations Committee on Intellectual Coöperation, *Bulletin of the International University Information Office*, 2nd year, No. 6, November, 1925, pp. 265-270.

[61] League of Nations Committee on Intellectual Coöperation, *Minutes of the Eighth Session*, Annex C., July 26-29, 1926, pp. 74-78.

To the first meeting at Geneva, April 8-10, 1926, the
seven international student organizations mentioned above
sent representatives. The presence of League of Nations officials gave a semi-official character to this voluntary meeting
of student representatives.[62] The principle adopted sub-
sequently by the Sub-Committee has been to summon two
annual meetings at the International Institute of Intellectual
Coöperation:[63] one in the spring, attended by three delegates
from each association, for the discussion of general questions,
and one in the autumn, attended by one delegate from each
association, to consider measures for the practical application of the resolutions adopted at the spring meeting.[64]

At the first meeting and succeeding spring meetings the
Committee of Representatives have dealt with matters of
fundamental concern to all students interested in attending
foreign universities: the interchange of students, traveling
facilities for students, international identity card, equivalence of university degrees, and mutual assistance for
students.[65]

Of the organizations represented, one, the International
Universities League of Nations Federation, exists, as its

---

[62] M. G. de Reynold, a member of the Committee on Intellectual Cooperation (which is an organization of the League of Nations), presided
over the deliberations of this meeting of students. Present in an advisory
capacity were the heads of the sections of General Affairs and University
Relations, both of the International Institute of Intellectual Coöperation
(a League institution); a member of the International Labor Bureau of
the League of Nations; the Under-Secretary-General of the League
of Nations Secretariat; and the Secretary of the Committee on
Intellectual Coöperation, also of the Secretariat of the League of Nations.
League of Nations International Committee on Intellectual Coöperation,
Minutes of the Eighth Session, Annex 8, pp. 74-75.

[63] See below, p. 35, note 101.

[64] League of Nations International Committee on International Cooperation, *Minutes of the Eleventh Session*, p. 29.

[65] League of Nations Committee on Intellectual Coöperation, *Minutes of
the Eighth Session*, pp. 74-80; *Minutes of the Ninth Session*, pp. 71-79;
Minutes of the Tenth Session, pp. 88-99; *Report of the Eleventh Plenary
Session*, pp. 8-10.

name indicates, for furthering interest in the principles of
the League of Nations in university circles. It may be
identified in its aims and activities with the International
Federations of League of Nations Societies, discussed below,
of which it is a part. Three of the organizations—the
World Federation of Christian Students, Pax Romana, and
the World Federation of Jewish Students—are based on
creed or culture, and act in the interest of students internationally on a basis of the principles of creed or culture
which they represent.

World Federation of Christian Students.—The oldest of
these, the World Federation of Christian Students, founded
at Vadstena in 1895 by six students representing North
America, Great Britain, Germany, and Scandinavia,[66] and
numbering a membership of more than 300,000 students
in 1928,[67] was established to promote Christian faith and
to encourage friendly intercourse between the students of
all countries on a basis of Christian principles. In pursuing
its ideals, the Federation has been active in fostering international sympathy through international student relief
(especially during the period of reconstruction following
the World War),[68] through international summer schools,
camps, and conferences, and through the exchange of students—particularly the exchange of students of countries

---

[66] John R. Mott, *La Fédération Universelle des Associations Chrétiennes
d'Étudiants, les Origines, l'Oeuvre Accomplie dans le premier Quart de
Siècle, 1895-1920, l'Oeuvre Projétée,* p. 1.

[67] World's Student Christian Federation, *An Adventure in International
Friendship,* Geneva, 1929, p. 4.

[68] During the war it administered the work of the European Student
Relief. During the period from September 1, 1920, to July 1, 1924, it
collected from approximately forty countries ten and one-half million
dollars in cash and materials, and distributed this fund to students in
about twenty countries. In view of the handicaps arising from war
hatreds, difficult transportation, currency fluctuations, and import duties
following the war, this was a significant service in international coöperation, rendering aid where it was an indispensable prerequisite for the
intellectual work of thousands of students. See Ruth Rouse, *Rebuilding
Europe,* 1925.

where the work of the Federation is weak with students of countries where it is more advanced.[69]

Pax Romana.—Pax Romana, the International Secretariat of Catholic student associations, was established in Fribourg, in July, 1921. Its purpose is "to realize the full development of the Catholic ideal in all the domains of university, intellectual and social life by appealing to the best traditions of Christian history while endeavoring at the same time to comply with the demands of the present age."[70] In its practical activity to realize this aim it has concentrated on the international exchange of students, the Pax Romana "semaine" (a week at some university center, where, in lecture rooms and on excursions, students from various countries are brought into contact with each other), and the support of indigent students, especially Catholic students in countries ruined by the war.[71]

World Union of Jewish Students.—Similar in nature to Pax Romana is the World Union of Jewish Students, which was initiated by a conference in Vienna in 1923 and was formally established in May, 1924, at Antwerp, sixteen countries participating in its foundation. The Union has been active in organizing Jewish students for mutual benefit. It seeks, in coöperation with organizations of countries concerned, to obtain the removal of legal restrictions on Jewish students in certain institutions of learning. It supports institutions of self-help and relief, and encourages international exchange of Jewish students and contact of Jewish and non-Jewish students.[72]

---

[69] For the activities of the World Federation of Christian Students see John R. Mott, *op. cit.*

[70] League of Nations Committee on Intellectual Coöperation, *Bulletin of the International University Information Office*, 1924, Nos. 1 and 2, p. 69.

[71] *Ibid.*, pp. 68-69; *Ibid.*, 1926, No. 3, pp. 168-171; *La Coöperation Intellectuelle*, July, 1929, pp. 437-440.

[72] League of Nations International Committee on Intellectual Coöperation, *Bulletin for University Relations*, 1926, No. 2, pp. 86-88; *La Coöperation Intellectuelle*, July, 1929, pp. 440-442.

International Student Service.—The fifth of the international student organizations represented by the Committee of Representatives of International Student Organizations, International Student Service, grew out of the postwar European Student Relief Commission of the World Federation of Christian Students. Beginning with student relief activity in Vienna in 1920, the work expanded throughout Europe. In 1926 European Student Relief became an independent organization with its own constitution and adopted the name International Student Service (Entr'Aide Universitaire Internationale). It maintained collaboration with the World Federation of Christian Students. Its recent international activity has been directed chiefly toward the development of international work-student scholarships and international "self-help" schools, or "semaines."[73]

International Confederation of Students.—More important in their international activities are the remaining two associations represented in the Committee of Representatives of International Student Organizations: the International Federation of Students and the International Association of University Women, an association of graduate women.

The International Confederation of Students was founded at Strasbourg in November, 1919, by representatives of various student organizations who were attending the congress of the National Union of Students Associations of France. The countries represented were Belgium, Great Britain, Greece, Italy, Poland, Roumania, Czechoslovakia, Jugoslavia, and the United States.[74] In 1924 the members

---

[73] For an account of the work of European Student Relief see Ruth Rouse, *Rebuilding Europe.* For the organization and activity of the International Student Service, see League of Nations, *Bulletin for University Relations,* 1926, No. 2, pp. 77-82; *La Coöpération Intellectuelle,* July, 1929, pp. 420-428; *Student Service in Five Countries* (Publication of I. S. S., 1929), pp. 18-19.

[74] International Confederation of Students, *Yearbook,* 1927-28, p. 1.

of the Federation numbered twenty-eight, representing nearly 500,000 students.[75] In 1929 the membership had reached thirty-five national federations, aggregating approximately 700,000 students.[76]

The International Confederation of Students, an organization which states as its main object "complete and intimate understanding between the students of the world,"[77] was organized in response to the need for coöperation among intellectual workers after the war. A period of about five years was spent largely in establishing its organization, in encouraging the development or creation of national unions of students, and in breaking down to some extent the antipathy existing between students whose countries had recently been at war with each other.[78] After the Congress of Warsaw, in 1924, the Confederation entered upon a more active program to realize the aims laid down in its statutes:

"1. To create ties of friendship and esteem between the students and intellectual workers of the whole world;

"2. To organize a permanent liaison between the student associations of all countries;

---

[75] *Ibid.*, p. 7.

[76] Confédération Internationale des Étudiants, *Annuaire*, 1929, pp. 109-121: list of national unions; dates of admission; membership (twenty-five full members; nine free members; one associate member).

[77] International Confederation of Students, *Yearbook*, 1927-28, p. 6.

[78] For an historical summary of the development and work of the International Confederation of Students, see the *Yearbook*, 1927-1928 and 1929, and *La Coöperation Intellectuelle*, July, 1929, pp. 414-420. For a detailed discussion of the development of the confederation and the question of membership of the German student union, Deutsche Studentenschaft, during the first two years of the existence of the Confederation, see Julius Ernst Lips' discussion of the Confederation from its beginning until 1921, *Die Internationale Studentenbewegung nach dem Kriege*, Leipsig, 1921. The question of German membership remains one of the questions of debate, the German union being founded on a racial basis and the members of the International Confederation of Students representing national states. From 1924 to April, 1926, the Deutsche Studentenschaft collaborated with the Confederation as associate member. In 1929 it again was joined to the Confederation as associated member.

"3. To coördinate their activities in the University world;

"4. To study international questions relating to higher education and to the intellectual and material life of students.

"These activities are to be entirely independent of any religious faith or any political party."[79]

In realizing these aims the Confederation has undertaken, among other activities, the assembling of information regarding colleges, universities, and student organizations. It is also conducting an inquiry into the equivalence of degrees, the nature of instruction in law and medicine, and the conditions governing professional practices in the various countries. Its chief work, however, has been to assist students in universities and other higher institutions of learning, to secure the adoption of an international student identity card, and to facilitate foreign travel and study.[80]

International Federation of University Women.—The International Federation of University Women, a graduate organization, was founded in July, 1919, by a resolution passed by women graduates of Great Britain, Canada, and the United States. The resolution proposed "to promote understanding between university women of different countries; to promote the exchange of lecturers and scholars of different universities; to coöperate with the national bureaus of education; and by these means to strengthen those foundations of international fellowship which must form the basis of the League of Nations."[81] Before 1920, Great Britain, the United States, Canada, Sweden, and Holland were the only countries in which university women were organized. In 1922, sixteen national associations were affiliated with the International Federation of University Women; in 1924, twenty; in 1926, twenty-three; and in

---

[79] International Confederation of Students, *Yearbook,* 1927-1928, p. 11.

[80] International Confederation of Students, *Yearbook,* 1927-1928, pp. 1-18, 51-71; 1929, pp. 79-106.

[81] International Federation of University Women, *Report of the First Conference,* July, 1920, p. 3.

1929, thirty-three,[82] the thirty-three national groups including a membership of about 47,000.[83]

The Federation declares three ideals: the development of international friendship by personal intercourse, internationalism in learning (which, among other things, would make the universities of the world places where scholars from any country could go and study), and the development and enrichment of education.[84] In pursuing these it has worked primarily in the interest of its own members, and has concentrated on the endowment of the international fellowships, the establishment of international halls of residence, the international exchange of secondary school teachers, the promotion of international contacts between traveling members, the promotion of interest in international vacation courses, and the study of equivalence of university degrees.[85]

The world federations of student associations, coördinated to a certain extent through a central Committee of Representatives of Student Associations, are an academic organization interested primarily in international contacts of students and graduates as a means of promoting international understanding and enrichment of intellectual life. Working through their national members, they seek to promote personal contacts in the university world through the establishment of international scholarships, the encouragement of interest in international schools and vacation courses, the accumulation and international dissemination of information about the university world, the investigation of equiva-

---

[82] For the names and dates of admission to the International Federations, see *Report of the Fifth Conference*, July, 1929, pp. 14-19.

[83] *La Coöpération Intellectuelle*, July, 1929, p. 429.

[84] International Federation of University Women, *Report of the First Conference*, 1920, p. 11; *Report of the Fifth Conference*, 1929, p. 51.

[85] See the Reports of the Conferences, 1920-1929. Besides the interests mentioned above, the Federation studies the possibilities of careers for graduate women, encourages the teaching of the League of Nations and international coöperation in the schools, coöperates with the policies of the Committee on International Intellectual Coöperation and with other organizations having interests similar to its own, and encourages the trans-

lence of studies and means of facilitating student travel, and the encouragement of the foundation of international residence centers. In these aims they parallel the interests of the national university offices discussed above, which represent the international interests of both the professorial and the student world.

INTERNATIONAL COMMITTEE ON INTELLECTUAL COÖPERATION

Origin.—Especially significant among organizations interested in intellectual understanding between the nations of the world is the League of Nations, acting through an advisory educational committee. This advisory education committee, the Committee on International Intellectual Cooperation, was appointed by the League in response to a general demand.

While the Peace Congress was in session in Paris during the first months of 1919, it received from national and international delegations, requests to include an international bureau of education in the plans for the League of Nations. In reply the Congress expressed interest in plans for international education, but reported that the work of the Congress would probably be confined to the adoption of general outlines, leaving detailed organization and administration to be worked out later.[86] The Covenant of the League of Nations adopted by the Congress made provision, however, for the creation of new committees on international problems as need should arise;[87] and from the very beginning of the League's activities it became evident that a committee on education was necessary.

At its meeting in June, 1920, the Council of the League

---

lation of books of cultural interest of the various nations as a means of encouraging international understanding.

[86] *The League of Nations and Intellectual Coöperation,* 1927, publication of the Information Section of the Secretariat of the League of Nations.

[87] *Covenant of the League of Nations,* Article 24.

of Nations received resolutions from the Directors Council of the French Association for the League of Nations requesting the League to include at an early date a permanent organization for intellectual work analogous to the International Labour Office.[88] A few months later the first session of the Assembly of the League of Nations also sent resolutions to the Council concerning international education, strongly endorsing the Council's interest in international intellectual activity and inviting it to define more specific aims in the field of international education.[89]

A further request on the subject came to the Council shortly afterwards from the Union of International Associations asking that an international conference be called for the purpose of organizing intellectual labor. Similar requests came from the Association of the League of Nations and

---

[88] The resolutions suggested as a basis for discussion a scheme prepared by M. Julian Luchaire and M. Charles Garnier. Accompanying the resolutions was the scheme, "Draft Convention for the Promotion of International Understanding and Collaboration in Educational Questions and Science, Literature, and Art," prepared by the two authors mentioned. For the text of the Draft Convention, see Annex A, *Official Journal of the League of Nations*, 1st year, No. 7, p. 446.

[89] They read thus: "The Assembly of the League of Nations, approving the assistance which the Council has given to works having for their object the development of international coöperation in the domain of intellectual activity, and especially the moral and material support given to the Union of International Associations on the occasion of the Inaugural Session of the International University and of the publication of the List of Recommendations and Resolutions of the International Congresses: Recommends that the Council should continue its efforts in this direction, and should associate itself as closely as possible with all measures tending to bring about the international organization of intellectual work.

"The Assembly further invites the Council to regard favorably the efforts which are already in progress to this end, to place them under its august protection, if it be possible, and to present to the Assembly during its next session a detailed report on the educational influence which it is their duty to exert with a view to developing a liberal spirit of goodwill and world-wide coöperation, and to report on the advisability of giving them shape in a technical organization attached to the League of Nations."

(League of Nations, First Assembly, *Records of the Plenary Meetings*, 1929, Annex E, p. 771.)

from M. Appell, Rector of the University of Paris, asking for the formation of an International Bureau of Education.[90] Six months later, September, 1921, the League formally proposed to include in its activities a program of international coöperation in education. This proposal is embodied in the following statement prepared by the League Secretariat and approved by the Council:

"The League of Nations cannot pursue any of its aims, either the general aims of coöperation as laid down in the Covenant, or even the more precise aims assigned to it by certain provisions, such as the campaign against the use of dangerous drugs, and against the traffic in women and children, without, at every moment, encountering educational problems, and without being obliged to ask for active help from those engaged in education in all countries. . . . It [the Council] is unanimously of the opinion that the League of Nations should include in its program the coördination of Intellectual activity and international coöperation as regards education."[91]

After a further exchange of opinion between the Council and the Assembly, [92] it was agreed that the Council should appoint a committee of twelve, which should include women, for the purpose of examining international questions regarding intellectual coöperation. As a result, a committee consisting of a cosmopolitan representation of eminent scholars and educators was announced in the course of the year 1922.[93]

During its first meeting, at Geneva, August 1-5, 1922, the Committee received, through the Secretariat of the

---

[90] *Official Journal of the League of Nations,* 2nd year, March-April, 1921, No. 12, p. 179.

[91] *Ibid.,* December, 1921, Nos. 10-12, p. 1111.

[92] *Official Journal of the League of Nations,* 3rd year, February, 1922, No. 2, p. 111; League of Nations, Second Assembly, *Records of the Plenary Meetings,* 1921, p. 309.

[93] *Official Journal of the League of Nations,* 3rd year, No. 11 (Part II), *Minutes of the Twentieth Session of the Council,* November, 1922, p. 1184.

League of Nations, communications from forty-eight recognized national and international organizations, in which they either pledged support and coöperation, offered schemes or suggestions, or described the phases of their work which they thought would be of interest to the League of Nations Committee.[94] Among these were requests for the establishment of an International Bureau of Universities and for direct association of students with the Committee. Each of these, it has been noted above, was soon realized.[95]

The request made to the League of Nations asking for the formation of a committee on international education, and the subsequent requests and suggestions submitted to the Committee when created, are evidences that the need of such an organization was widely recognized. The activities of the Committee during the six years since its appointment have justified its existence.

Agenda.—The agenda adopted by the first session included the question of international coöperation in the realm of higher education as a means of strengthening and enriching intellectual life and promoting international understanding. The chief points proposed for discussion were the investigation of conditions of intellectual life in countries where it was endangered by war, coöperation of national universities and other higher institutions of learning in the organization of intellectual work to be undertaken by the Committee, international interchange of professors and students, international scholarships, an international university, international courses, and equivalence of studies.[96]

One of the first problems attacked by the members of the Committee was an inquiry into the intellectual life of the Central European countries. The countries that received the

---

[94] League of Nations Committee on Intellectual Coöperation, *Minutes of the First Session,* August, 1922, pp. 41-46.

[95] See above, pp. 28-29, 51-52.

[96] League of Nations Committee on International Intellectual Coöperation, *Minutes of the First Session,* pp. 8-12, 22-23, 25-29, 31-32.

most attention were the ones that were suffering most as a result of the war. Information was obtained on the spot by members of the Committee, by means of questionnaires, and by reports of local educators. The greater portion of the second meeting of the Committee was devoted to hearing and discussing reports relative to conditions among the teaching personnel in the educational institutions of the countries studied.[97] As a result of the investigations and reports of the Committee, relief was given to university work in war-stricken districts. Books and university publications were sent to the libraries from other nations, and assistance was rendered the students' relief organizations in ameliorating living conditions of professors and students.[98]

The work of the Committee in enlisting the interest and support of the universities of the world through the establishment of an International University Information Bureau and annual meetings of directors of national university offices has been pointed out above. From its beginning the Committee has considered, chiefly through its sub-committee on inter-university relations, the international interchange of professors and students, international scholarships, international courses, and equivalence of studies. The result has been that the attention of national governments and national Ministries of Education, as well as national universities has been directed to the importance of these questions.[99]

In carrying out its program the Committee has been aided by the several National Committees of Intellectual Coöperation,[100] and has had as its organ, since 1925, the Inter-

[98] League of Nations Committee on Intellectual Coöperation, *Minutes of the Second Session*, pp. 18-22; *Official Journal of the League of Nations*, 4th year, No. 3; *Minutes of the 23rd Session of the Council*, March, 1923, pp. 254-255.

[97] League of Nations Committee on International Intellectual Coöperation, *Minutes of the First Session*, pp. 8-12, 22-23, 25-29, 31-32.

[99] See the Minutes of Sessions of the Committee on Intellectual Coöperation, reports of the Sub-Committee on Inter-University Relations.

[100] In view of the difficulty of the continuance of intellectual work in the various countries affected by the war, the International Committee on

national Institute of Intellectual Coöperation. The latter was created by the French Government and placed under the auspices of the League to serve the International Committee on Intellectual Coöperation, but has been supported by other nations as well.[101]

Intellectual Coöperation drew up a scheme for the formation of National Committees on Intellectual Coöperation in the several countries. (League of Nations Committee on Intellectual Coöperation, *Minutes of the Second Session,* 1923, pp. 19, 21.) In accordance with the scheme, the meeting of the third plenary session of the Committee, December 5-8, 1923, was attended by delegates from twenty-one national committees that had been formed or were in the process of formation. The national committees were, in general, to act as intermediaries between the intellectual organizations in their respective countries and the International Committee of the League; to assist in the latter's investigations concerning conditions of intellectual life; to inform the League of urgent requests made by intellectual institutions in their respective countries for "books and instruments, traveling facilities, and inter-university exchanges," and to unify intellectual agencies in their respective countries. In 1929, there were 35 National Committees. (League of Nations Committee on International Intellectual Coöperation, *Bulletin of the International University Information Office,* 1st year, January-April, 1924, Nos. 1 and 2, p. 78; *Official Journal of the League of Nations,* 10th year, December, 1929, No. 12, pp. 1917-1921.)

While it is evident from the report of the third conference of representatives of the National Committees, July, 1929, that perfect understanding and coöperation have not existed between certain national committees on the one hand and the International Committee on the other (chiefly perhaps because of the diversity in constituency and national functions of the several committees), and that lack of resources have frequently hindered desirable activity, the meeting gave evidence on the whole of general coöperation and increasing activity on the part of national committees. (League of Nations International Committee on Intellectual Coöperation, *Meeting of Representatives of the National Committees,* July 18-20, 1929.) In addition to serving as liaison committees between the intellectual life of their respective countries and the work of the International Committee, the interests of the National Committees have centered about the facilitation of scientific research, exchange of publications, international interchange of professors and students, international scholarships, and instruction in the schools of the aims of the League. (*Ibid.,* third and fourth meetings; *Bulletin of the International University Information Office,* 1924, pp. 166, 220; 1925, pp. 121, 163.)

[101] The early activity of the Committee on Intellectual Coöperation was embarrassed for lack of adequate financial support. In 1924 when the situation became critical, the Fifth Assembly of the League passed resolutions endorsing the work of the Committee and soliciting national moral and financial support of it. As a result, the French Minister of Education

The International Committee on Intellectual Coöperation represents officially the interest of the League of Nations and its member states in the field of international intellectual coöperation. It has been an organ of propaganda and co-ordination in the interest of international academic relations. It has investigated existing conditions and, through its recommendations to the Assembly and Council, has enlisted the support of governments, public educational authorities, national committees on intellectual coöperation, and university officials in the importance of higher institutions of learning as a medium of international understanding. It has coördinated activities in the university world towards inter-university relationships, particularly through the annual meetings of directors of university offices and international federations of students. In turn, the League

notified the Committee that the French Government was ready to establish and support an International Institute of Intellectual Coöperation at Paris to be under the direction and control of the League of Nations. Later a similar letter from the French Government was submitted to the Council of the League of Nations. In 1925 the Council and the Assembly approved the establishing of the International Institute of Intellectual Coöperation at Paris. Accordingly the Institute was established and began work in 1925. Article No. 5 of the Organic Statute of the Institute provided for the direction of its work by the International Committee on Intellectual Coöperation. The chief function of the Institute is to investigate questions referred to it by the Committee. (League of Nations Committee on International Intellectual Coöperation, *Minutes of the Fifth Session,* May, 1925, Annex 1, pp. 42-43; *Official Journal of the League of Nations, Minutes of the Thirty-fourth Session of the Council,* 6th year, July, 1925, No. 3, pp. 1015-1021; *Official Journal of the League of Nations, Records of the Sixth Assembly, Plenary Meetings,* Text of the Debates, Special Supplement No. 23, 1925, pp. 132-143. For the Organic Statutes of the Institute, providing for its organization, activities, and control see *The League of Nations and Intellectual Coöperation, Information Section, League of Nations Secretariat,* Revised Edition, 1927, pp. 49-52.)

Since its foundation other nations have contributed to its financial support, enabling it to enlarge its activities. In addition to 2,500,000 francs contributed annually by the French Government, over 700,000 francs are contributed by eighteen other governments. (League of Nations Committee on International Coöperation, *Tenth Plenary Session,* August, 1928, p. 54.) In 1929 the French Minister of War announced the agreement of the French Government to increase the French subsidy by a million francs. (*Minutes of the Eleventh Session,* 1929, p. 44.)

principles for which it stands have received reciprocal support.

INTERNATIONAL FEDERATION OF LEAGUE OF NATIONS SOCIETIES

Among the organizations encouraging the interest of higher institutions of learning in the principles of the League of Nations as a means of international understanding is one established for the sole purpose of supporting and making known the League. The International Federation of League of Nations Societies was organized in Paris, January, 1919, by national groups that had been formed almost simultaneously in several countries either during the war or during the peace negotiations following. It comprised in 1929, as affiliated members, thirty-seven national Associations of League of Nations Societies and, as associated members, five national Associations.[102] One of the regular functions of the Federation is to forward to the several organs of the League the demands expressed by the general public, and in particular by the yearly Assemblies of the Federation.[103]

United for the purpose of propagating and strengthening the League of Nations, the Federation has as its chief educational function the work of making known the accomplishments and ideals of the League of Nations. It proposes thus to improve the relations of organized people to one another, to increase the sense of the interdependence of nations, and to foster sentiment against war.[104] It has worked

---

[102] See the International Federation of League of Nations Societies *Bulletins*, 1924, Jan.-Feb., No. 1, pp. 2-5; 1928, Jan.-Feb., No. 1, pp. 4-7; 1929, Jan.-Feb., No. 1, pp. 15-48.

[103] *Ibid.*, 1925, No. 4, pp. 30-32.

[104] See International Federation of League of Nations Societies, *Ninth Assembly, Plenary Sessions, Resolutions*, July 5-8, 1925, pp. 30-31; *Ibid., XIIth Plenary Congress, July, 1928, Proceedings and Resolutions*, pp. 92-94; *Bulletin*, 1928, July-August, No. 4, pp. 17-22; *XIIIth Plenary Congress, May, 1929, Proceedings and Resolutions*, pp. 104-107.

especially to introduce League ideals into the syllabuses of various grades of instruction, to encourage revision of school texts,[105] to acquaint teachers and teachers in training with the ideals and activities of the League by means of lectures, special courses, and teaching material,[106] and to make possible their attendance upon international League of Nations summer schools.[107] In this connection it has actively supported the recommendations in the report of the Sub-Committee of Experts of the League of Nations International Committee on Intellectual Coöperation.[108]

In connection with the use of the schools above secondary rank for spreading propaganda concerning the League of Nations and for bringing about international *rapprochement*, the Federation has worked through its Education Committee and through its associations of university students to develop and coördinate University Departments or specialized institutions for the advanced study of international affairs;[109] to further interchanges and study tours;[110] and to encourage study of the League through university courses, lectures, model assemblies, and competitions.[111]

---

[105] See International Federation of League of Nations Societies *Bulletin*, Oct.-Dec., 1928, No. 5, p. 9; March-May, 1924, No. 2, pp. 11-23. See below, pp. 185 ff.

[106] International Federation of League of Nations Societies, *Ninth Assembly, Plenary Sessions, Resolutions*, July 5-8, 1925, pp. 30-31; *XIIIth Plenary Congress, Proceedings and Resolutions*, pp. 196-97.

[107] International Federation of League of Nations Societies, *Bulletin*, 1928, No. 2, pp. 12-15; No. 4, p. 21; No. 5, p. 49.

[108] International Federation of League of Nations Societies, *Bulletin*, Oct.-Dec., 1926, No. 4, p. 31; *XIIth Plenary Congress*, 1928, p. 94, a. See below, pp. 136-144.

[109] International Federation of League of Nations Societies, *Ninth Assembly, Plenary Sessions, Resolutions*, July 5-8, 1925, pp. 30-31; *Bulletin No. 13, Plenary Congress, Proceedings and Resolutions*, p. 104. See below, pp. 90, 95.

[110] International Federation of League of Nations Societies, *Ninth Assembly, Plenary Sessions, Resolutions*, July 5-8, 1925, pp. 30-31. See below, pp. 60-61.

[111] See below, pp. 94-96.

The organizations discussed above have represented national interests brought into international relations. The International Committee on Intellectual Coöperation is an International body which through its Sub-Committee on Inter-University Relations serves as an international investigative and advisory organ in matters of inter-university relations, and coördinates the efforts of national and international organs. The national university offices and similar institutions, coördinated through the annual meetings of directors, have acted on an international basis to promote inter-university relations. Similarly the national federations of students, linked in international federations, and further linked in coöperation through the annual meetings of representatives of the several international federations, have considered students' interests from an international point of view.

Other international organizations, such as the international organization of Institutions for the Scientific Study of Politics and the International Sociological Congresses have encouraged inter-university relations, including international academic exchanges, from the point of view of a particular cultural interest.[112]

OTHER ORGANIZATIONS PROMOTING INTELLECTUAL COOPERATION AMONG NATIONS

Binational Societies—In addition to the international organizations discussed above which further inter-university relations on an international basis, other organizations promote international university relations between two countries or small groups of countries.

A number of academic organs of binational interests were mentioned above as the corresponding bureaus of national

---

[112] League of Nations Committee on Intellectual Coöperation, *Minutes of the Tenth Session*, p. 86, resolutions of the Conference for the Scientific Study of Politics; *Bulletin of the International University Office*, 1924, No. 4, pp. 223-24, resolutions of the third Sociological Congress.

university offices. Of similar character are the following organizations established to promote academic exchanges or cultural relations in general between two nations. The Austro-English Interchange Committee of Vienna, for the exchange of students and secondary school teachers with England, and its corresponding committee, the Anglo-Austrian Society for the Interchange of Teachers and Students, were established in 1927 through the influence of the Austrian Government.[113] The Austro-French Academic Committee (Oesterreichisch-Franzoesisches Hochschulkomitee) was established in Vienna in 1926 for the promotion of exchanges of French and Austrian Students.[114] The Centre d'Études Néerlandaises and the Société des Amis du Centre d'Études Néerlandaises were established in Paris in 1923 and 1927 respectively for promotion of Dutch Studies in France and French Studies in The Netherlands.[115] The Centro Hispania was founded in Berlin in 1922 to promote scientific and educational relations between Germany and Spain.[116] The Instituto Alemao, a Portuguese university institution, was established in 1925 to promote cultural exchanges between Portuguese and German speaking countries.[117] The Centro de Intercambio Intellectual Germano-Espanol was established in 1924 to further scientific relations between Spain and Germany.[118] The Instituto Cultural Argentino-Norte Americano was established in 1928 "to promote reciprocal knowledge of the culture of the Argentine Republic and of the United States

[113] *A Directory of Societies and Organizations in Great Britain Concerned with the Study of International Affairs*, 1929, p. 30; League of Nations Institute of Intellectual Coöperation, *Handbook of University Exchanges in Europe*, 1928, pp. 23, 105; *London Times, Educational Supplement*, February 12, 1927, p. 76.
[114] League of Nations Institute of Intellectual Coöperation, *Handbook of University Exchanges in Europe*, 1928, p. 25.
[115] *Ibid.*, pp. 79, 87.   [116] *Ibid.*, p. 94.   [117] *Ibid.*, p. 174.
[118] *La Coöpération Intellectuelle*, July, 1929, p. 454.

of America, and to facilitate the consequent intellectual inter-change between the two countries."[119]

Other binational societies founded to promote friendly relations between two nations encourage academic or cul-tural relations as an auxiliary interest. The Anglo-Spanish Society, established in London in 1916, "to promote friendly and sympathetic relations between Spain and Spanish America and the British Empire, and to encourage the study of their language, literature, art, history, and customs, with historical research," names among other activities the inter-change of teachers and students.[120] In France, the Associa-tion Amicale et de Patronage Franco-Chinois, organized in Paris in 1923 to promote cordial relations between France and China, names among other functions patronage of Chinese students in France.[121] The Association France-Grande-Bretagne and its sister organ in England, established to strengthen the bonds of friendship between England and France, support university relations between the two coun-tries by giving assistance to French and English professors and students through the creation of scholarships.[122] Similar societies functioning binationally in the interest of these and other countries might be named.[123]

[119] Instituto Cultural Argentino-Norte-Americano, *Estatutos del Instituto Cultural Argentino-Norte-Americano*, Buenos Aires, 1928, pp. 1, 2; *Memoria y Balance del Primer ejercicio Terminado en 30 de Abril de 1929*, pp. 8-28.

[120] The Royal Institute of International Affairs, *op. cit.*, pp. 37-38.

[121] League of Nations Institute of Intellectual Coöperation, *Handbook of University Exchanges in Europe*, 1928, p. 72.

[122] League of Nations Institute of Intellectual Coöperation, *Handbook of University Exchanges in Europe*, 1928, p. 74.

[123] The Franco-Japanese Association in Japan (*Bulletin of the Inter-national University Information Office*, 1924, No. 2, pp. 133-134); the As-sociazione-Giapponese, 1927 (*Handbook of University Exchanges in Europe*, 1928, p. 147); the Nederlandsch-Amerikaansche Fundatie, 1923 (*Handbook of University Exchanges in Europe*, 1928, pp. 163-164); the Amis de l'Espagne, Roumanian-Spanish. (*La Coöpération Intellectuelle*, June, 1929, p. 354); the Kosciusko Foundation, Czechoslovakia-United States (*Bulletin for University Relations*, 1926, No. 4, p. 340). Each of these promotes uni-versity exchanges between the two countries concerned.

Multi-National Societies.—Along with these institutions may be mentioned others more comprehensive in scope, established for fostering friendly relations between several nations rather than two. One of these is the English Speaking Union, founded in 1918 to strengthen relations between Great Britain and her Dominions and America. Its Educational Committee arranges university interchanges between the countries represented.[124] Similarly the Norden, established to develop intellectual coöperation between the countries of the North,[125] encourages university and school exchanges between Norway, Sweden, and Denmark.

The Pan-American Union for inter-American relations has a Division on Intellectual Coöperation to promote educational relations among Latin American and North American countries. Recently it has established an Inter-American Institute on Intellectual Coöperation similar to the International Institute. An Inter-American Congress of Rectors, Deans, and Educators met in Havana in 1930 and formulated plans for the operation of the institute.[126]

The purpose of this chapter has been to point out the extent and the nature of the organization for international understanding through higher educational institutions. The organization has two aspects: organization to coördinate efforts in a universal program of inter-university relations, and organization to further mutual interests of two nations or a small group of nations. In conclusion mention should

---

[124] English-Speaking Union, *List of Members,* 1920, pp. 11-12.

[125] League of Nations Institute of Intellectual Coöperation, *Handbook of University Exchanges in Europe,* 1928, p. 169; *Bulletin for University Relations,* 1928, p. 231.

[126] The Pan-American Union, *Report of the Governments of the Republics, Members of the Pan-American Union, on the work of the Union since the close of the Fourth International Conference of American States,* covering the Period 1910-1923, pp. 11-15; *Report on the Activities of the Pan-American Union,* 1923-1927, pp. 5-12; *Documentary Information Compiled for the Information of the Delegates to the Inter-American Congress of Rectors, Deans, and Educators,* 1930, pp. 1-11; *Bulletin of the Pan-American Union,* June, 1930, pp. 594-595.

also be made of the extensive private interest which has developed in the twentieth century, resulting in endowments to promote intellectual contacts between nations and to further world peace through the medium of educational relations. Finally, the interest of governments in establishing educational relations with other nations is, as will be indicated later, a factor of importance in international understanding.

CHAPTER II

INTERNATIONAL STUDENT INTERCHANGE

THE EXTENSIVE international organization in the interest
of intellectual relations has developed for the purpose of
making it possible for them to continue and to develop more
effectively for international understanding. Among the
causes of the increase of interest in international intellectual
relations, was, as mentioned above, the realization in certain
quarters that the intellectual life of Europe was threatened,
and that active measures were necessary to protect it.

A series of investigations begun in 1922 by members of
the International Committee on Intellectual Coöperation
reported in general the following situation. In Germany and
Austria and Russian refugee circles there was painful
diminution of intellectual activity because of an economic
crisis which rendered it acutely difficult for students and
scholars to continue their work. In the neutral countries,
the indifference of governments and population in general
to questions of science and art was attended by a consequent
utilitarian tendency, which was partly, at least, the result
of economic crisis. In France a similar diminution in pure
science and art evoked the pessimistic opinion of the in-
vestigator that "never before had there been such reason
to fear a profound deterioration in the standards of culture."[1] In Italy, there was noted on the whole a renaissance
of interest in culture. In the countries of eastern Europe
there was a manifestation of intellectual interest, remarkable
in the face of the material difficulties, which in some quarters
were acute; there was also a spontaneous desire to establish

---

[1] League of Nations Committee on International Intellectual Coöperation, *Minutes of the Second Session*, p. 20.

intellectual contact with western Europe. Investigations concerning intellectual conditions in the United States and in the countries of Latin America reported an increasing interest in pure science and in international relationships.[2] A recognized field for the stabilizing of culture, the encouragement of disinterested intellectual pursuits, and the promotion of international understanding was the field of inter-university relations. In recognition of its importance the Secretariat of the League of Nations submitted the following point as one of the three aspects of the agenda to be undertaken by the newly constituted International Committee on Intellectual Coöperation: "the proper method of encouraging inter-university relations."[3]

The Committee, in turn in considering the question decided that there were three aspects of inter-university relations: exchange of students, exchange of professors, and studies and their results (diplomas and degrees).[4] Each of

---

[2] *Ibid.*, pp. 10-12, 22, 50-59; *Minutes of the Fourth Session*, pp. 15-16.

[3] *Minutes of the First Session*, p. 41. The other points were international bibliography and exchange of publications and international scientific relations.

[4] In discussing the agenda of the proposed International University Conference, the Committee adopted the following text:

"In inter-university relations there are three aspects, relating to: (a) professors; (b) students; and (c) studies and their results (diplomas and degrees).

"In each of these fields the League is authorized to make practical suggestions to universities and governments, with a view to improving inter-university relations and to making them frequent, regular, and profitable.

"For this purpose, the League has decided, in agreement with the various governments, to summon an International University Conference, to which will be submitted a programme; this latter will be explained and commented on in a report to be drawn up by the Committee on Intellectual Coöperation.

"This work will relate to the following three points:

(a) Exchange of professors;
(b) Exchange of students;
(c) Equivalent recognition of academic courses and degrees.

"The League of Nations lays down the principle that all measures intended to improve inter-university relations must also be calculated to

these aspects mentioned in the Committee's analysis of the question has received the consideration of organs and individuals concerned with international coöperation for the advancement of intellectual life and for the promotion of international understanding. The question of international student interchange has been, in particular, a point of active interest.

SCHOLARSHIPS

The important encouragement given to international student interchange by the establishment of scholarships has been one of the distinguishing features of international educational relations of the past decade. International scholarships—that is, scholarships offered by one nation for study in its universities by students of another nation—were comparatively unknown at the beginning of the twentieth century.[5] At present, partly as a result of the realization at the close of the war that students were no longer in a position to undertake study on private resources and partly as a result of the increasing interest of individuals, organizations, and governments in the value of student contacts, the number of international scholarships and national traveling scholarships has reached very considerable proportions.

In this respect, in the matter of private foundations for the benefit of foreign students, the United States has taken the lead. A study made by the American Council of Education in 1925 listed some one hundred organizations, societies, and foundations interested in university exchanges.[6]

---

maintain or to raise the standard of university studies and of higher teaching, this being in the League of Nations' own interests.

"The League of Nations considers that it is in the interests of civilization that higher teaching should strive to disseminate general culture and synthetic ideas, and should tend to discourage excessive over-specialization and professional utilitarianism." (League of Nations Committee on International Intellectual Coöperation, *Minutes of the First Session*, p. 26.)

[5] See above, p. xxiii.

[6] David A. Robertson, *Educational Record*, Vol. VI, No. 2, 1925, pp. 91-150.

In 1929 the number of American scholarships available to students of the United States for study abroad and to foreign students for study in the United States was 1,645. Of these 467 were offered to American students for study in foreign universities. The remaining 1,178 scholarships included those established expressly to enable foreign students to study in the United States and those open to foreign students and American students on the same terms. In addition an indeterminate number of tuition scholarships were available to foreign students.[7] The numbers quoted include a large number of reciprocal exchange scholarships arranged by the Institute of International Education since 1920. Beginning with France in 1920, the system of reciprocal exchanges has extended to Czechoslovakia, Germany, Hungary, Switzerland, Italy, Spain, and Austria.[8]

A comparison of the numbers given above with the information collected by the League of Nations International Institute concerning scholarships in European countries, indicates the lead of the United States in private scholarship foundations. There are listed, for example, only fifty-one British scholarship funds or prizes which offer opportunities for British Students to study in Europe and fifteen British funds open to foreign students (exclusive of

---

[7] Institute of International Education, *Fellowships and Scholarships open to American Students for Study in Foreign Countries*, 1929, 64 pp.; *Fellowships and Scholarships open to Foreign Students for Study in the United States*, 87 pp. See the analysis of these scholarships made by the Director of the Institute of International Education before the 30th annual Congress of the Association of American Universities, *Bulletin of the American Association of University Professors*, April 1929, pp. 289-291.

[8] Institute of International Education, Eleventh Series, Bulletin No. 2, *A Decade of International Scholarships*, pp. 7-10; *La Coöpération Intellectuelle*, "Échanges d'Étudiants," February, 1930, p. 74 The reciprocal exchange system does not involve a fixed number of exchanges annually. The number of foreign students who came to the United States in 1929 under the exchange agreements included 48 Germans, 18 Swiss, 12 Austrians, 10 Hungarians, 9 Czechoslovakians, 4 Italians, and about 20 French. The number of Americans exchanged was somewhat smaller.

the Dominions) for study in European nations.[9] In addition, the list of the Institute of International Education the same year names eight British scholarship funds open specifically to Americans.[10]

In France the number of scholarships of private foundation listed is equally limited in comparison with America. The university scholarships for American students, established on a reciprocal basis by the universities of Bordeaux, Grenoble, Lyon, Paris, Strasbourg, and Toulouse total some twenty in number.[11] In addition, university scholarship endowments for foreign students in France or for French students abroad are mentioned only for the University of Paris, which lists fifteen.[12] Besides these only six private organizations offering scholarships are listed.[13] The numbers, though applying only to European and American exchanges and doubtlessly incomplete, are at least suggestive in comparison with the American private resources available for scholarships. Other European countries have even fewer international scholarships of private foundations.

Scholarships, private or official, offered by South American countries are extremely limited in number. The documentary information compiled by the Division of Intellectual Coöperation of the Pan-American Union for the considera-

---

[9] League of Nations Institute of Intellectual Coöperation, *Handbook of University Exchanges in Europe*, 1928, pp. 128-138.

[10] Institute of International Education, *Fellowships and Scholarships open to American Students for Study in Foreign Countries*, 1929, pp. 46-52.

[11] League of Nations Institute of Intellectual Coöperation, *Handbook of University Exchanges in Europe*, 1928, pp. 56, 58, 59, 60.

[12] *Ibid.*, pp. 60-62.

[13] League of Nations Institute of Intellectual Coöperation, *Handbook of University Exchanges in Europe*, 1928, pp. 64, 69, 74, 80, 81: Biermans Lapôtre Endowment (1924), for students of Belgium or Dutch Limburg; Société des Amis de l'University of Strasbourg; Association France-Grande-Bretagne (37 scholarships in 4 years); Comité Catholique des Amitiés Françaises à l'Étranger Scholarships (between 1921 and 1930, 150 scholarships for study in France, amounting to 450,000 francs. (*La Coopération Intellectuelle*, February 1930, pp. 62-63); Comité Central de Patronage de la Jeunesse Universitaire Russe à l'Étranger (1923); Comité Français de l'Entr'aide Universitaire (1926).

tion of delegates to the Inter-American Congress of Rectors, Deans, and Educators in 1930 gives the following list of inter-American scholarships in Latin-American countries: Brazil 4 (Bolivian Medical students), Cuba 2 (nurses), Mexico 1 (Ecuadorian officer in aviation service), Peru 3 (agriculture and vocational subjects), Uruguay 3 (veterinary science).[14] It cites, in addition, the reciprocal exchange agreement of 1923, according to which Costa-Rica, Guatemala, Honduras, Nicaragua, and Salvador were each to grant six scholarships to each of the other Central American countries entering into the agreement,[15] and the agreement between the University of Buenos Aires and the University of North Dakota for reciprocal exchange of two commercial students.[16] In comparison, in the United States in 1929 seven university scholarships with stipends and some ninety tuition scholarships were available to Latin American students,[17] in addition to those to be offered from the $1,-000,000 Guggenheim Memorial Foundation established in

---

[14] Pan-American Union, Division of Intellectual Coöperation, *Documentary Information compiled for the Information of Delegates to the Inter-American Congress of Rectors, Deans, and Educators,* 1930, p. 36.

[15] For the text see *International Conciliation,* August, 1923, No. 189, pp. 77-80. The convention was to "take effect with respect to the Parties that have ratified it, from the date of its ratification by at least three of the Signatory States" and to remain in force until the first of January, 1924, "regardless of any prior denunciation, or any other cause," and from that date one year after the date on which one of the States bound notified the others of his intention to denounce it, in which case it should continue in force as long as the States not denouncing it remained three in number.

[16] This exchange agreement is not mentioned in the 1929 edition of *Fellowships and Scholarships open to Foreign Students for Study in the United States,* and its companion volume, *Fellowships and Scholarships open to American Students for Study Abroad.*
A statement in the information section of *La Coöpération Intellectuelle,* August, 1929 (p. 526), states that the parliament of Nicaragua has voted the creation of a number of scholarships for study at the University of Mexico, expressing the hope that the Mexicans would send an equal number of students to Nicaragua.

[17] Institute of International Education, *Fellowships and Scholarships open to Foreign Students for Study in the United States,* 1929, pp. 73-75.

that year for Latin American scholarships.[18]

In the European countries, however, the limited number of private foundation scholarships open to foreign students is offset by the large number of government scholarships, established for the most part since the war, and totaling in some countries very considerable expenditures.

France in 1929 distributed through the Ministry of Public Instruction a scholarship and reimbursement fund amounting to 350,000 francs, benefiting 440 students of twenty countries (313 of them Russian), studying in universities and technical high schools of France. In addition it distributed a special scholarship fund of 552,000 francs for Yugoslav students. The Ministry of Foreign Affairs offers scholarships to an indefinite number of students of eleven countries. Also government traveling scholarships, reserved for graduate students, are open to French students for study abroad.[19]

By a decree of March 11, 1923, the Italian Ministry of Education grants annually scholarships to the value of 200,-000 lire to foreign students desiring to study in Italy and Italian students wishing to pursue studies abroad. In 1928-1929 the 200,000 lire available for scholarships for foreign students benefited 80 students of fourteen countries.[20]

By Royal Decrees of January and November, 1921, at the suggestion of the Spanish American Republics, Spain appropriated the sum of 4,000 pesetas to be distributed by the Ministry of Public Instruction for scholarships for Spanish-American students in Spanish university faculties

---

[18] La Coöpération Intellectuelle, July, 1929, p. 444.

[19] League of Nations Institute of Intellectual Coöperation, Handbook of University Exchanges in Europe, 1928, pp. 52-53.

[20] Bulgaria (18), Jugoslavia (16), Roumania (13), Greece (12), Hungary (5), Corsica (4), Poland (4), Armenia (2), Syria (1), Palestine (1), Malta (1), Czechoslovakia (1), Lithuania (1), Germany (1). In addition, 74 special scholarships have been granted to Albanian students. (La Coöpération Intellectuelle, October, 1929, p. 634.

of engineering, architecture, and fine arts, and in the Normal Schools. In 1928 the scholarships were extended to Portugal, Italy, and the Philippine Islands. In 1929, 124,000 pesetas were expended in these scholarships, and in addition 20,000 pesetas for reciprocal scholarships.[21]

A further point of interest in European student exchanges made possible by government subvention concerns the countries of Eastern Europe. The attention of governments was directed to the importance of intellectual ties between Eastern and Western Europe by the reports of the investigation of conditions of intellectual life in Eastern Europe, referred to above.[22] Resolutions adopted by the International Committee on Intellectual Coöperation concerning intellectual life in Central and Eastern Europe, also directed attention to this point.[23] In 1925 the meeting of Directors of National University Offices passed resolutions concerning the desirability of reciprocal arrangements for exchange in general.[24] Recent reports show that a large number of traveling scholarships are arranged mutually by official agreements between countries of Eastern Europe and between these countries and countries of Western, Southern, and Northern Europe.

In 1929 Bulgaria was granting scholarships, either ac-

---

[21] Statement of the Director General of the Junta para Ampliacion de Estudios, *La Coöpération Intellectuelle*, August, 1929, pp. 482-483. In addition to these, other countries offering government traveling scholarships are Netherlands, Bulgaria, Belgium, Estonia, Finland, Latvia, Jugoslavia, Poland, and Albania. (League of Nations Institute of Intellectual Coöperation, *Handbook of University Exchanges in Europe*, 1928, pp. 27, 31, 43, 45, 46, 154, 159, 170, 195; *La Coöpération Intellectuelle*, November, 1929, p. 692.)

[22] See above, p. 44.

[23] League of Nations International Committee on Intellectual Coöperation, *Minutes of the Fourth Session*, p. 46. See below, p. 72.

[24] *Minutes of the Eighth Session*, p. 85, report of the meeting of Directors of National University Offices, resolution VII: "The Conference invites the International Institute to request the national offices to take the necessary steps to arrange a satisfactory system for the interchange of scholarships with foreign countries wherever such reciprocity is possible."

cording to reciprocal agreements or in a spirit of reciprocity, to students of Czechoslovakia and Poland; Czechoslovakia to students of France, Belgium, Denmark, Sweden, Bulgaria, Poland, Roumania, and Yugoslavia; Poland to students of Belgium, France, Bulgaria, Czechoslovakia, Roumania, and Jugoslavia; Roumania to students of Czechoslovakia and Poland; and Jugoslavia to students of England, France, Czechoslovakia, and Poland.[25] In addition Roumania in 1929 offered seventy-one traveling scholarships for study in Czechoslovakia, England, France, Germany, and Italy; Hungary offered one hundred and forty-eight traveling scholarships for study in Austria, Germany, France, Switzerland, Great Britain and Italy; and Lithuania awarded eighty-four scholarships for study in France, Germany, Belgium, Austria, Switzerland, Italy, and Czechoslovakia.[26]

The development of scholarship funds has aroused interest in the possibility of establishing foundation scholarships on a basis best calculated to serve international interests. In particular the need of more post-graduate scholarships of purely international character, awarded without reference to the nationality of the holder or locality of research, has been advocated as a means of best encouraging scientific research of international value. The Rockefeller Foundation has offered a notable example in this field. It appoints foreign representatives in several countries to nominate deserving candidates.[27] In 1925 the International Federation of University Women proposed the establishment of a Million Dollar Fund for international scholarships open to

[25] League of Nations Institute of Intellectual Coöperation, *Handbook of University Exchanges in Europe*, 1928, pp. 31, 33, 170, 176, 184, 195; *Bulletin of the International University Information Office*, 1925, pp. 142, 313.

[26] League of Nations Institute of Intellectual Coöperation, *Handbook of University Exchanges in Europe*, 1928, pp. 148, 157, 176.

[27] League of Nations Committee on Intellectual Coöperation, *Bulletin of the International University Information Office*, 1925, Nos. 4-5, pp. 209-210; League of Nations Institute of Intellectual Coöperation, *Handbook of University Exchange in Europe*, 1928, pp. 25, 42, 99, 133, 163, 169, 187.

federation members. As yet, only a small beginning has been made.[28]

At the third session of the International Committee on Intellectual Coöperation members of the Committee urged the importance of post-graduate international scholarships. Later sessions continued the discussion. In 1925 Mme. Curie was instructed to prepare a memorandum on the subject.[29] The memorandum, prepared in 1926, advocates greater freedom in awarding post-graduate scholarships. It stresses the importance of establishing international scholarships instead of foundations of national interest, and protests against the frequent restriction of scholarships to scholars who have already achieved distinction in research, often to holders of the doctorate degree. On the latter point it proposes that an international scheme of minor (or probationary) scholarships and major (or research) fellowships should be established. The proposal is based on the conviction that "all candidates anxious to devote themselves for some time to science must be given a chance at developing their talents on the sole condition that they are recommended by their masters or have obtained satisfactory university degrees."[30]

In 1926 the Polish National Committee evolved a plan for coöperating with Mme. Curie's proposal for international awards. At the suggestion of the Polish representative, the meeting of Delegates of National Committees on Intellectual Coöperation recommended that a part of the credits placed at the disposal of the International Institute for mutual

---

[28] International Federation of University Women, *Report of the Council Meeting,* Brussels, July, 1925, pp. 35-36; 1926, p. 109, *Report of the Fifth Conference,* 1929, pp. 38-39, 126-131.

[29] League of Nations International Committee on Intellectual Coöperation, *Minutes of the Fourth Session,* pp. 47-48; *Minutes of the Sixth Session,* p. 44.

[30] *Memorandum by Madame Curie, Member of the Committee, on the Question of International Scholarships for the Advancement of the Sciences and the Development of Laboratories,* 1926.

4

intellectual assistance should be used for the creation of international scholarships. Accordingly it was decided to create certain scholarships to be awarded in the name of the International Institute. Other National Committees have expressed interest.[31] Finally in 1929 the International Committee proposed to convene a committee of experts to consider the possibility of devising an international scheme for the encouragement of international post-graduate research scholarships.[32]

American Junior Year Abroad.—While general opinion favors graduate scholarships and graduate interchange in general as most beneficial to the individual and most favorable to international interests, the American venture of the Junior Year abroad under faculty supervision is apparently gaining favor. In 1923-24, more or less as an experiment, the University of Delaware sent eight students, with a faculty adviser, to study in France. This has been repeated each year with success. Smith College, William and Mary College, and the University of South Carolina have adopted the plan. In 1926 the American Council of Education

---

[31] League of Nations Committee on Intellectual Coöperation, *Bulletin for University Relations,* 1926, Nos. 4-5, p. 350; League of Nations International Committee on Intellectual Coöperation, *Minutes of the Eighth Session,* p. 35; *Minutes of the Tenth Session,* p. 74.

[32] "The Sub-Committee, referring to the resolutions adopted in 1926 and 1927, and noting with satisfaction that the International Institute is now in possession of abundant information on the question of scholarships,

(1) Requests the International Institute, as soon as possible, to convene the Committee of Experts proposed in the conclusions of Mme. Curie's report;

(2) Recommends that, as desired by Mme. Curie, the Committee of Experts should make a general study of the problem of post-university scholarships, national and international. (League of Nations International Committee on Intellectual Coöperation, *Tenth Plenary Session,* 1928, p. 6.)

"The Sub-Committee hopes that it will be possible this year to summon a committee of experts comprising, not only representatives of qualified institutions but also a certain number of directors of laboratories and university institutions, all of whom are concerned with the exact sciences, as well as with social science, and the humanities. (*Eleventh Plenary Session,* 1929, p. 4.)

secured eight scholarships for students of the Junior Year; the number has been recently increased to eleven.

Under the plan of Junior Year abroad the students, after an intensive training course in the French language in the summer at one of the smaller French universities, follow for an academic year at the Sorbonne courses of French literature and civilization which count as a year's study in the American university.[33] According to a recent report of the Institute of International Education, similar courses were to be organized in the fall of 1930 at some German university.[34]

EQUIVALENCE OF STUDIES

In addition to the establishment of scholarships, as described above, attempt has been made to facilitate international student interchange by the investigation of equivalence of university studies and degrees. This question is generally recognized as constituting a serious impediment to free interchange of students. The International Federation of University Women undertook as a phase of its early activity a study of comparative standards of university studies and degrees, with the hope of arriving at an internationally recognized basis of equivalence. After investigations covering several years, it is continuing to compile and study information concerning requirements and standards in the several countries.[35]

Similarly the International Confederation of Students,

[33] *Educational Record,* Vol. 6, No. 1, January, 1925, pp. 849-890; Institute of International Education, *Seventh Annual Report,* 1926, pp. 3-8.

[34] Institute of International Education, *Ninth Annual Report,* 1928, pp. 6-7.

[35] Studies were presented by the Committee on Standards to the 1925 and 1929 Conferences of the Federation pointing out differences in standards existing in universities of member countries of the Federation. (See International Federation of University Women, *Report of the Council Meeting,* Brussels, July, 1925, pp. 41-43; *Report of the Council Meeting,* Vienna, July, 1927, p. 9; *Report of the Fifth Conference,* Geneva, 1929, pp. 116-118.

on entering upon its constructive program, studied the question of equivalence as a point on which free interchange of students depended. Also the Committee of Representatives of International Students' Organizations, the Directors of National University Offices, and the Representatives of Scientific Institutions for the Study of Politics, each in turn in their initial meetings, recognized the importance of the question of equivalence in facilitating international student interchange.[36]

The International Committee on Intellectual Coöperation has from its first session recognized the importance of the question of equivalence of degrees, with the result that the International Institute of Intellectual Coöperation has for several years been studying the possibility of international agreements through central national organizations.

As its first session the International Committee on Intellectual Coöperation mentioned the question of equivalence of degrees and studies as a part of its agenda.[37] At its second session, after a discussion of the subject by the Sub-Committee on Inter-University relations, it adopted the following proposals:

"The Committee on Intellectual Coöperation lays down the principle that the object of any system of the equivalent recognition of the diplomas and degrees of different countries and different universities should be to maintain or to raise the level of higher education. Consequently, no system may be established which will be prejudicial to the universities of countries in which education has already reached the highest level.

[36] League of Nations Committee on Intellectual Coöperation, *Bulletin of the International University Information Office*, 1925, p. 118, report of the International Confederation of Students, Warsaw, 1924, Resolution XII; League of Nations International Committee on Intellectual Coöperation, *Minutes of the Ninth Session*, p. 73, report of the Meeting of the Committee on International Student Organizations; *Minutes of the Eleventh Session*, p. 93. Resolution III; *Minutes of the Tenth Session*, p. 86, III.

[37] League of Nations International Committee on Intellectual Coöperation, *Minutes of the First Session*, p. 26.

"The Committee is of the opinion that the half-year system is of such a nature as to favour inter-university exchanges.

"The Committee decides that an enquiry into the position of the question of the inter-changeability of diplomas and degrees at present recognized as between various universities and various countries should be instituted for the purpose of furnishing a basis for the subsequent investigations of the Committee."[38]

The question was considered more particularly by the Committee in response to the proposals submitted by the Spanish Government to the Fourth Assembly of the League. General recommendations were adopted to the effect that the practice of allowing students to carry on preliminary studies abroad should be more widely followed, that equivalent examinations for matriculation at universities should be as wide as possible, that certificates of study should be given where university examinations proper do not exist, and that States and universities should publish regularly lists of equivalent values of courses and examinations.[39]

At the meeting in 1926, the Directors of National University Offices requested the International Committee to facilitate the drafting of a general list of equivalent recognition of foreign studies and diplomas in the various countries.[40] Accordingly at its ninth session, in 1927, the Committee requested the International Institute to consult with delegates of student organizations, "which have begun to collect copious documentation of the subject," and with representatives of University Offices, for the purpose of drawing up a detailed scheme of study with a view to publication.[41]

---

[38] League of Nations Committee on Intellectual Coöperation, *Minutes of the Second Session*, pp. 32-33.

[39] League of Nations Committee on Intellectual Coöperation, *Minutes of the Fourth Session*, p. 40.

[40] *Minutes of the Eighth Session*, pp. 83-84.

[41] *Minutes of the Ninth Session*, p. 69.

Finally, in 1929, the Meeting of Directors of National University Offices, recognizing the interest of the International Committee on Intellectual Coöperation, requested the German and French Offices, and other Offices that might choose to do so, to forward to the International Institute "a complete account of the system adopted in each of their countries in regard to equivalence."[42]

Already a number of international official and unofficial agreements concerning equivalence exist with more or less binding force. For the most part, however, these regulate admittance for study towards advanced degrees.[43] The ques-

---

[42] *Minutes of the Eleventh Session*, p. 93.

[43] For example, the Committee on International Education Relations of the American Council on Education recommends that bachelor degrees of universities of Canada, Great Britain and Ireland entitle the candidate to entrance into universities of the United States for graduate study; that the French "licence" be accepted as the equivalent of the American M.A. degree; that a holder of the French Baccalaureate who produces evidence of having done one year of graduate study in a French university be admitted for graduate study in the United States; that without such evidence the holder of a Baccalaureate be admitted for one year as "unclassified student," or until he has proved his fitness. (League of Nations Committee on Intellectual Coöperation, *Bulletin of the International University Information Office*, 1924, No. 3, pp. 130-132, text of the agreement.)

A French Ordinance of January, 1922, lists universities of Great Britain, Ireland, Belgium, Bulgaria, Denmark, the United States, Finland, Greece, Holland, Italy, Poland, Roumania, Sweden, Switzerland, Czechoslovakia, and the Kingdom of the Serbs, Croats, and Slovenes, whose graduates may proceed as candidates for the French degrees of Doctor in Law, Doctor in Science, and Doctor of Letters without the French "license." (*Ibid.*, 1924, Nos. 1 and 2, p. 41.) In 1924 the agreement was extended to holders of certain degrees from certain Canadian universities. (*Ibid.*, 1925, pp. 272-274.) A special treaty concluded with Norway in 1927 also extended the agreement to Norway and provided reciprocally that French baccalaureates could matriculate as students in Norwegian universities. (*Bulletin for University Relations,* 1928, No. 2, pp. 113-114.) A convention of 1928 provides that students holding a diploma of secondary studies from the College Amanyeh of Afghanistan shall be allowed to enter French universities. (*Ibid.,* pp. 114-115.)

Italian Royal Decrees of 1923 and 1924 admit foreign students for doctorate study in Italian universities without special examination. (*Bulletin of the International University Information Office,* 1926, pp. 212, ff.) A Spanish decree permits foreign students with a degree equivalent to the "licence" in Spain to be presented with a doctorate at the University of

tion of equivalence of studies, not attested by diplomas is a more difficult problem. Hence a series of binational treaties concluded by France and Belgium with certain other European countries since 1919 is significant of effort to solve a complicated and comparatively unsettled question in the field of international university relations. These provide that a special Committee of each of the two contracting countries shall meet once a year and shall have among its functions the duty of determining the equivalence of studies in the two countries.

Between 1919 and 1929 France concluded eight formal treaties dealing with university relations with foreign nations. Six of these (with Italy, Belgium, Poland, Luxembourg, Czechoslovakia, and Norway) are concerned with both student and professorial interchanges between the two nations. Two (with Roumania and Jugoslavia) are concerned only with professorial interchange. In addition to the treaty with France, Belgium has concluded since 1919 treaties concerning professorial and student interchange with Luxembourg, Poland, and Netherlands.[44] In each of the six French treaties concerning interchange of professors

Madrid after having completed a year of studies or having presented a thesis. (*La Coöpération Intellectuelle*, August, 1929, pp. 481-482, statement of the Director General of the Junta para Ampliacion de Estudios.)

Certain Latin American government or university agreements provide for the recognition of secondary certificates or university studies covering the same field in the two countries (Guatemala-Salvador, 1876, counted towards a degree in literature; Paraguay-Uruguay, 1915; Bolivia-Uruguay, 1917, Colombia-Uruguay, 1922; Brazil, 1925, Cuba, 1926), or for the recognition of university degrees (Buenos Aires, 1925, 1928, Chile, 1928, Ecquador, 1929, Honduras, 1928). Two special agreements exist with two universities of the United States,—an agreement for equivalence of studies between the University of Buenos Aires and Notre Dame, and an agreement whereby the University of Texas recognizes work done in the summer school of the University of Mexico under certain conditions. (Pan-American Union, Division of Intellectual Coöperation, *Documentary Information compiled for the Information of the Delegates to the Inter-American Congress of Rectors, Deans and Educators*, 1930, pp. 25, 27, 28, 31, 32, 33, 34, 35.)

[44] For the text of these treaties see League of Nations Committee on Intellectual Coöperation, *Bulletin for University Relations*, 1926, No. 3,

and students, and in the Belgian treaties, it is provided that special committees of each of the two contracting countries shall meet once a year to study questions of international relations of scientific, literary, artistic, and educational nature and to propose to the two governments measures to develop them. In the French treaties with Italy, Belgium, Poland, Luxembourg, and Czechoslovakia it stipulated that study abroad shall count as in the country of origin, and that a specific function of the Mixed Committee representing the two contracting countries is to determine equivalence of studies in the two countries.[45] The Belgian treaties with Poland and Luxembourg make the same provisions.[46]

INTERNATIONAL STUDENT TRAVEL

Further evidence of increasing interest in international student relations is the establishment of certain schools and courses of international aspect. These will be discussed later.[47] Mention should also be made of the interest, particularly on the part of international student organizations, in the encouragement of vacation tours and reciprocal visits of groups of students, international summer camps, international conferences, and other forms of occasional contacts.

In particular, the Travel Commission of the International Federation of Students, acting in coöperation with similar Commissions of the several national federations, has been

---

pp. 137-142; 1928, No. 2, pp. 98-114; No. 3, pp. 213-215. See below, pp. 79-81.

[45] *Ibid.*, 1928, No. 2, pp. 99, 195, 108, 119, 112. In matters of equivalence the treaty with Norway provides merely for recognition of degrees. See *Ibid.*, pp. 113-114 and above, p. 58, note 43. It is provided in the treaty with Italy that regular exchanges of students will be arranged and that vacation courses will be encouraged for instruction of students of the foreign nation in the language, history, geography and contemporary civilization of the other nation. *Ibid.*, p. 100.

[46] *Ibid.*, 1926, No. 3, pp. 138, 141. The Belgian-Netherland treaty does not mention equivalence, but provides for one reciprocal graduate scholarship in each of the contracting countries. *Ibid.*, 1928, No. 3, p. 215.

[47] See below, pp. 83 ff.

DIAGRAM ILLUSTRATING THE PASSPORT AND VISA REGULATIONS BETWEEN THE COUNTRIES OF EUROPE, THE BRITISH EMPIRE AND THE UNITED STATES OF AMERICA

COUNTRY ENTERED \ COUNTRY of ORIGIN	Austria	Belgium	Bulgaria	Czechoslovakia	Denmark	Estonia	Finland	France	Germany	Great Britain	Greece	Holland	Hungary	Italy	Latvia	Lithuania	Luxemburg	Norway	Poland	Portugal	Rumania	Spain	Sweden	Switzerland	Turkey	U.S.A.	Yugoslavia
Austria	\	d	d	d	d	d	n	d	n	n	d	n	d	d	d	d	d	d	d	d	d	d				d	
Belgium		\		n					n			n				n	d	n									
Bulgaria			\							d																	·
Czechoslovakia				\			n	n	o								o										
Denmark	d	n	d	d	\	d	n	n	n	n	d	n	d	d	d	n	n	d	n	d	n	n	n	d	d	d	d
Estonia	o	o	o	o	o		n	o	o	o	o	o	o	n	\	o	o	o	o	o	o	o	o	o	o	o	v
Finland	n	o	o	n	n	v		o	n	o	o	o	o	o	d	v	o	o	o	o	o	o	o	o	o	o	v
France	t		t	n	n	t	t		t	n	t	n	t	n	t	t	\	n	t	t	t	n	n	n	t		
Germany	n			n		n		n			n		n						n	n		v					
Great Britain	n	n	xo	xo	n	xc	xo	n	n	\	xo	n	xc	n	xo	xo	n	n	xo	n	xo	n	n	n	xo	xo	xo
Greece											\																
Holland	n			n			n	n	n			\	n			n		n		n	n	n					
Hungary	v	od	v	v	v	v	v	v	v	od	v	v	\	v	od	od	od	od	od	od	od	od	od	v	v	od	od
Italy	d	n	d	d	n	o	d	n	n	n	d	n	d	\	n	n	n	n	d	d	n	n	n	n	d	d	d
Latvia	o	o	o	o	o		v	o	o	o	o	o	o	n	\	o	o	o	o	o	o	o	o	o	o	o	o
Lithuania																\											
Luxemburg	n		x	x	n	x	x		n	x		x	n	x	x	\	n	x	x	n	n	n	n	n	x	x	x
Norway		n			n			n		n		n			n			\	v	n	n	n					
Poland	d	d	d	d	d	d	d	d	d	d	d	d	d	d	d	d	d	\	d	d	d	d	d	d	d	d	d
Portugal									n	o									\								
Rumania		n											n	v						\							
Spain		n		n			n		n			n			n	n					\			n	n		
Sweden	s	n	s	s	n	s	s	n	n	n	s	n	s	n	s	s	n	n	s	s	s	n	\	n	s	s	s
Switzerland	n	n	x	x	n	x	x	n	n	n		x	n	x	x	n	n	x	x	x	n	n	\	x	n	x	
Turkey																									\		
U.S.A.	d	d	d	d	d		v	d	o										d					d		\	
Yugoslavia									o																		\

A blank square indicates that a passport and visa are required.

A shaded square indicates that no passport or visa are required.

n : no visa required.

o : group visas are available to students.

v : visa required, issued gratis.

d : visa required, issued gratis to students holding the International Student Identity Card.

s : individual applications by students for gratis visas receive favourable consideration.

t : 50 per cent reduction in visa charges to holders of the International Student Identity Card.

x : visa required, not gratis, but issued without further formalities to holders of the International Student Identity Card.

active in facilitating international contacts of this nature.[48] Largely through the efforts of the International Federation of Students, supported by the interest of the International Committee on Intellectual Coöperation, the international student identity card has been devised and given recognition since 1926. It secures reduced traveling rates and simplifies passport and visa regulations.[49] Finally, the establishment of international hostels has contributed to international student contact.

THE INTERNATIONAL HOUSE AND THE UNIVERSITY CITY

In addition to a large number of unpretentious international hostels for student residence, encouraged for a number of years, such as those established by the World Federation of Christian Students and the International Federation of University Women, [50] there is the more important University House, or International House, which has recently appeared in a few university neighborhoods.

The first to appear was International House in the vicinity of Columbia University, New York City. A movement for the House was started in 1910 by Mr. and Mrs. Harry E. Edmonds, who began inviting foreign students to visit in their home. Later Mr. John D. Rockefeller, Jr., donated land and building, which gave concrete expression to the idea. The first year after the building was erected "International House" had a membership of 1,250 students from 70 different countries; and of these 525, representing approximately 60 different nations, lived in the building. The

---

[48] A summary of the activity of the Federation is found in the Yearbooks of 1927-1929: International Confederation of Students, *Yearbook*, 1927-1928, pp. 65-70; 1929, pp. 83-101 (French edition).

[49] See chart facing p. 60, reproduced from the League of Nations Institute of Intellectual Coöperation, *Handbook of University Exchanges in Europe*, 1928, p. 197.

[50] World's Student Christian Federation, *Student Hostels, Foyers, Clubs, and Similar Institutions*, Geneva, 1930, 38 pp.; International Federation of University Women, *Report of the Twelfth Council Meeting, Madrid*, 1928, pp. 13-15, "Clubhouses, Hotels, and Pensions."

purpose of the House is the improvement of social, intellectual, spiritual, and physical conditions of men and women students from any land (without discrimination because of nationality, race, religion, or color) who are studying in the colleges, universities, and professional schools of New York City.[51]

A second example of an international house in the United States is the one at the University of California, made possible also by a recent Rockefeller gift of $1,700,000.[52] A third, also a Rockefeller gift, has recently been completed at Chicago.[53]

An extension of the University House is the University City composed of national hostels. An institution of this nature is the University City of Madrid now in the process of erection. The completion, at an estimated cost of $50,000,-000, is anticipated within four years.[54] In establishing the Inter-American Institute of Intellectual Coöperation, in 1928, the Sixth International Conference of American States gave as one of the immediate aims of the Institute: "to favor the creation of a university town or students' home in the countries of America."[55]

The best example of this movement is the University City of Paris. In 1918 M. André Honorat, former French minister of Education and senator, proposed that France set aside

---

[51] Pamphlets: *International House; The Meaning of International House*, by Mrs. Harry Edmonds; *The Object and Brief History of International House; The Activities of International House; The Work of International House*, by John D. Rockefeller, Jr.; *International House*, by Harry E. Edmonds. These pamphlets may be obtained from "International House," 500 Riverside Drive, New York City.

[52] League of Nations International Institute of Intellectual Coöperation, *Bulletin for University Relations*, Nos. 3 and 4, 1928, pp. 232-233.

[53] "La Maison internationale d'étudiants à Chicago, *La Coöperation Intellectuelle*, February, 1930, p. 74 *University of Chicago Magazine*, July-Aug., 1932.

[54] "Nouvelles cités universitaire," *La Coöperation Intellectuelle*, November, 1929, pp. 692-693.

[55] Pan-American Union, Division of Intellectual Coöperation, *Documentary Information Compiled for the Information of Delegates to the Inter-American Congress of Rectors, Deans, and Educators*, 1930, p. 1.

land on which student hostels of various nationalities might be erected. A law providing the land was passed in 1921. In 1925 the first hostel, containing 350 rooms, was finished; it was the gift of Emile Deutsch de La Meurthe of France. Since this beginning there have been added almost a score of hostels for foreign students; still others are in the process of planning or under construction. Some of the hostels have been established by private gifts, some by governmental subsidies, and others by funds coming from various sources. In a few cases governmental officials participated in the dedicatory services. Some of the hostels admit men only; others admit men and women. Some are restricted to one nationality; others admit students of different nationalities. The accompanying table presents in detail information about the hostels now in operation or under construction.[56]

In conclusion, a few points may be made concerning recent developments in foreign student enrollments. Detailed information concerning the extent and nature of international student interchange over a period of years before and after the war is lacking. In a few instances information of a general character exists for years preceding the war, as a result of occasional compilations. Somewhat detailed statistics of more or less official nature compiled for certain years since the war have been available for Great Britain, Germany, France, and the United States. An examination of this information reveals a few points of interest.

In general one notes a continued increase in international student interchange. Since 1922 the Universities Bureau of the British Empire has tabulated the foreign student en-

---

[56] The information tabulated is taken from League of Nations Committee on Intellectual Coöperation, *Bulletin for University Relations* (International Institute of Intellectual Coöperation), 4th year, Nos. 3-4, 1928, pp. 153-160, "La Cité universitaire de Paris," and *La Coöperation Intellectuelle*, July, 1929, pp. 446-447, "Extension Nouvelle de la Cité Universitaire de Paris." The dates of establishment do not have uniform meaning. Some of them are the dates of the laying of the corner stones, others represent the times of final arrangements for erection of the hostels, while still others represent the time of occupying the building.

UNIVERSITY CITY, PARIS

HOSTELS COMPLETED OR UNDER CONSTRUCTION

Nationality	Date of Establishment	No. of Rooms	No. of Students	Sex of Students	Rooms for Foreign Students	Foundation Private	Foundation State	Miscellaneous	State Participation in Dedication
Argentine	1928	75	..	..	..	Yes	Yes	Yes	..
Armenia	1928	..	50	..	Yes	Yes	..	..	Yes
Belgium	1924	225	..	..	..	Yes	Yes	..	..
Bolivia	1928	..	..	..	..	Yes	..	..	..
Canada	1926	75	50	..	Yes	Yes	..	..	..
Cuba	1929	..	..	..	..	..	..	Yes	..
Czecholovakia	1928	..	..	..	..	..	..	..	..
Denmark	1929	50	..	Men & Women	Yes	Yes	..	..	..
England	1927	..	300	Men & Women	Yes	Yes	..	..	..
France	1923	350	..	Men	Yes Vacations	Yes	..	..	Yes
Greece	1928	60	100	Men & Women	..	Yes	Yes	..	..
Holland	1927	..	100	Women	..	Yes	..	..	..
Indo China	1928	..	..	..	Yes	..	Yes	..	..
Japan	1927	60	..	..	Yes	Yes	..	..	Yes
L'institute Agronomique	1928	..	150	..	..	Yes	..	..	..
Morocco	1928	..	30	..	Yes	..	Yes	..	Yes
Spain	1927	..	150	..	..	..	Yes	..	..
Sweden	1927	..	50	..	..	..	Yes	..	..
Switzerland	1928	..	..	..	..	..	Yes	..	..
United States of America	1928	..	270	Mostly Women	Yes	Yes	..	Yes	Yes
Venezuela	1928	..	..	..	..	..	Yes	Yes	..

rollment in Great Britain. The figures, which include students from the British Dominions, show an increase from 4,131 in 1922 to 5,170 in 1929. Of the latter figure, 1,696, were Indian students.[57]

More decided increase in foreign student enrollment is found in the colleges and universities of the United States. This is attributable in part to the interest created by American scholarships for foreign students. In 1911-1912 the foreign student enrollment in the United States was estimated at 4,856.[58] Figures compiled by the Institute of International Education for the period since 1921 show an increase from 6,488 in 1921-1922 to 9,685 in 1928-1929. The greatest increase, more than 2,000, occurred between 1927 and 1929. The nationalities represented in largest numbers in the colleges and universities of the United States are the Chinese, Canadian, Philippine, and Japanese students, who in 1929, constituted one-third of the foreign student population.[59]

France since the war has had phenomenal increase in foreign student enrollment. This is to be attributed in large measure to the rate of exchange and to the increased activities of the Office Nationale des Universités et Écoles Françaises in promoting interchanges.[60] A statement of the American Institute of International Education places the number of foreign students in French higher institutions of learning at 1,770 in 1900, and 5,560 in 1913. Statistics of the French ministry of education gives the foreign student enrollment in French universities in 1923-1924, including students of French Colonies and Protectorates, at 6,420.[61] Statistics from the same source, compiled in the same man-

[57] Universities Bureau of the British Empire, *Yearbook of the Universities of the Empire,* years 1922-1930.

[58] *United States Commerce Report,* 1912, p. 1059, August 28, 1912.

[59] Institute of International Education, *Tenth Annual Report of the Director,* October, 1929, pp. 16-18.

[60] See above, pp. 14-15, 18-19, and the reports of the Office Nationale des Universités et Écoles Françaises.

[61] Tatiana Beresovski-Chestov, *Statistique Intellectuelle de La France, Année 1923-24,* pp. 58-61. Les Presses Universitaires de France, 1926.

ner, show 14,729 foreign students in French universities in 1926-1927[62] and 14,368 in 1927-1928.[63] The greatest increase in the last two figures was for Polish and Roumanian students, numbering more than 4,000 in each year, about equally divided between the two groups, in comparison with a combined total of some 900 in 1923-1924.

On the other hand, the number of French students in foreign universities is small. This may be attributed both to the traditional preference of French students for the national universities and to the rate of exchange, which has been unfavorable to foreign study on the part of French nationals.[64] Where United States and British students in France have averaged about 500 and 600 students respectively for the three years for which statistics of foreign students in France are available (1923, 1927, 1929), French students in Great Britain have numbered only about fifty and in the United States something more than a hundred each year. A similar situation exists in the case of German-French student interchanges, as the table given later indicates.

Figures compiled by the German national university office, the Akademisches Auskunftsamt of Berlin, show that in 1929 the number of foreign students in Germany had reached that of the period before the war. In 1904, according to statistics presented by the United States Bureau of Education in that year, 8,786 students were enrolled in German universities and Polytechnica, 3,097 of the number in the twenty-one universities.[65] In 1914, according to a statement of the Akademi-

---

[62] League of Nations International Institute of Intellectual Coöperation, *Bulletin for University Relations,* 1928, No. 2, pp. 120-125, statistics communicated by the French Minister of Education.

[63] *La Coöpération Intellectuelle,* October, 1929, pp. 660-665, statistics communicated by the Minister of Education of France.

[64] Assemblée Générale de l'Office des Universités et Écoles Françaises, *Rapport du Directeur sur l'Activité de l'Office des Universités en 1928-1929,* pp. 24-25.

[65] *Annual Report of the Department of Interior 1904, Report of the United States Commissioner of Education,* Vol. II, pp. 2335-2336.

sches Auskunftsamt, the number of foreign students in German universities alone was 4,750.[66] In 1925, the students enrolled in universities and Polytechnica numbered 7,813;[67] in 1928, 9,981.[68]

Finally, the records referred to above indicate progress since 1924 in the renewal of student interchange between Germany and three of the principal allied nations; particularly they show a decided increase in the number of German students in the universities of these countries. The following table indicates the student interchange in recent years between Germany on the one hand and France, Great Britain, and the United States on the other.[69]

No. of Students	1914	1922	1923	1924	1925	1926	1927	1928	1929
French in German Universities	25[70]				6[71]			23[71]	
German in French Universities			18				722	696	
British in German Universities	165[70]				65[71]			60[71]	
German in British Universities		0	0	34	78	93	93	121	157
Americans in German Universities	—[72]				85[71]			216[71]	
German in United States Universities	143 (1912)	49	63	79	121	124	183		360

[66] Akademischer Auskunftsamt, *Die Hochschulen Deutschlands,* 1926, pp. 38-39.

[67] *Ibid.*

[68] *La Coöpération Intellectuelle,* October, 1929, pp. 652-656, statistics from the *Deutsche Hochschulstatistik,* summer semester, 1928.

[69] The numbers are taken from the sources cited above, pp. 64-66.

[70] Not including students in the Polytechnica.

[71] Including students enrolled in German Polytechnica.

[72] The number of North and South American students was 301. In 1925 and 1928 the number of United States students was about half of the total number of American students.

CHAPTER III

INTERNATIONAL INTERCHANGE OF PROFESSORS

RECOMMENDATIONS OF THE INTERNATIONAL COMMITTEE ON INTELLECTUAL COÖPERATION

BECAUSE of its character as an international investigative and advisory organ and also because of its intimate contact in each capacity with states, organizations, universities and specialists, the recommendations of the League of Nations Committee on Intellectual Coöperation are especially significant regarding the fields which they cover. They are based upon an examination of opinions, tendencies, and efforts in many countries. Concerning the international interchange of professors, the recommendations of the Committee have been directed towards the nature and duration of interchanges, the recognition of the rights and dignity of the exchanged professor, and the organization of interchanges. The importance of professorial interchange as a means of strengthening the relations between the countries of Western Europe and those of Eastern and Central Europe, has also been urged, particularly in connection with the institute abroad.

Concerning the nature of the exchange[1] the recommendations adopted at the second session of the Committee on Intellectual Coöperation were to the effect that young teachers and professors in highly specialized branches of study should not be excluded from a system of exchanges, and that except in special circumstances the professor sent

---

[1] The term has been interpreted by the Commission loosely to include professorial visits abroad for the purpose of lecture and teaching.

abroad should possess a sufficient knowledge of one of the languages of the place in which he is to continue his teaching.[2] With reference to the latter point, the recommendations adopted by the Committee in 1928, recognized "the impossibility of adopting a general principle in regard to the language employed by foreign lecturers," but drew attention to "the great desirability of affording them as much opportunity as possible of speaking in their own languages."[3]

Concerning the duration of exchange, the Committee at its second session approved the principle of exchange of visits covering a complete course. The recommendation reads:

"In cases in which the period of such exchanges is not limited to a single lecture or series of lectures, it should be extended so as to cover a complete course."[4]

This principle met the approval of the Directors of National University Offices at the Meeting in 1927. Among suggestions for making more effective the professorial exchanges, or visits paid by professors of one country to another for the purpose of giving lectures or courses of lectures, the Conference of Directors recommended the principles of "seeking the most suitable means of enabling professors to teach systematically abroad for a term, a half-year, or even a whole year."[5]

Concerning the recognition of the rights of the professor sent abroad, the Committee in the resolution adopted at the second session, made the following suggestions:

"We may even at this early stage lay down the following principles, which are in conformity with the dignity and the

---

[2] League of Nations International Committee on Intellectual Coöperation, *Minutes of the Second Session*, p. 30.

[3] *Minutes of the Tenth Session*, p. 75.

[4] *Minutes of the Second Session*, p. 30.

[5] League of Nations International Committee on Intellectual Coöperation, *Minutes of the Ninth Session*, p. 82.

disinterestedness of science and advanced education, but which, nevertheless, do not lose sight of the economic position of professors, which is often precarious:

(1) That those exchanges must not be made with a view to profit;

(2) That the professor exchanged should, in one way or another, be freed from expenditure and compensated for any loss which his change of residence may occasion."[6]

Again, at its fourth session the Committee in the following resolution recommended that universities grant the same recognition to courses offered by foreign professors as to those of the regular faculty:

"The Sub-Committee recommends to States and universities, while fully preserving their autonomy, to grant as far as possible the same value in respect of all benefits accruing therefrom to courses given by foreign professors on the invitation of the universities as to courses given by national professors."[7]

At its second session the Committee considered the financial aspect of providing more widely for the international interchange of professors in such manner as to insure their just compensation in accordance with the dignity of such interchange. In the resolutions adopted the Committee recognized that the moment was not opportune for the proposal of an international scheme and that "states and universities must themselves estimate the financial sacrifices they may be prepared to make, and regulate the allocation of expenses, if occasion arises in accordance with special agreements." It recommended, however, that

"it would be highly desirable for a fund to be set up or a university convention to be concluded, the special object of which would be to meet the financial difficulties which are a bar to the extension of the system of exchanges,"

---

[6] *Minutes of the Second Session,* p. 30.
[7] *Minutes of the Fourth Session,* p. 41.

and added that

"it might be possible to obtain the establishment of such a fund by private initiative, if the League of Nations is unable to provide it."[8]

As for the method of arranging inter-university exchanges, the Committee recognized at its first session the rights of universities themselves to full autonomy in such matters. At its second session the Committee suggested that each country could draw up a list of professors available for exchange and communicate it to other countries; it drew attention to the proposed University Bureau of the Committee[9] as a medium of extending inter-university agreements, the organization of which must of necessity be left to individual countries and individual universities.

In 1928 it approved resolutions of the Sub-Committee on Inter-University Relations, which recommend that authorities concerned in the different countries exert efforts to ensure a more systematic preparation of exchanges without in any way restricting the freedom of the choice of professors. The resolutions read:

"[The Sub-Committee] endorses the general conclusion that it would be impossible to apply to the organization of these interchanges, and to exchanges of professors in general, a rigid system which would in any way restrict the freedom of choice of professors called to lecture abroad;

"Nevertheless considers that, if sufficiently elastic agreements are concluded between the authorities concerned in different countries, they may ensure a more systematic preparation of exchanges, and that organs of liaison, in particular the National Committee on Intellectual Coöperation, can do most valuable work in this field, especially in connection with

[8] League of Nations, International Committee on Intellectual Coöperation, *Minutes of the Second Session*, p. 30.
[9] See above, pp. 4-5.

courses of a certain duration, which are especially desirable from the scientific point of view."[10]

This is in agreement with the resolution of the Meeting of Directors of National University Offices in 1927, referred to above. In recognition of the fact that "the experience of all the Offices shows that these visits contribute most effectively to the establishment of closer intellectual relations," the Meeting of Directors recommended that the custom should be made more general and at the same time more effective, by

"(a) Making systematic preparations for such exchanges by agreements between the universities concerned;

"(b) Selecting for these courses periods at which the foreign professors can count upon a particularly wide hearing;

"(c) Taking advantage, as far as possible, of every journey made by a professor to invite him to give not only single lectures but also courses of lectures, with or without practical experiments;

"(d) Seeking the most suitable means of enabling professors to teach systematically abroad for a term, a half-year, or even a whole year."[11]

A final point of interest in the question of professorial interchange is its place in establishing closer bonds between the countries of Western Europe and those of Central and Eastern Europe. The Committee at its initial session considered the question of professorial interchange, in connection with the question of intellectual interchange in general as a means of relief to the countries of Central and Eastern Europe whose intellectual life was endangered by war. In 1924 at a meeting of the Sub-Committee on Inter-

---

[10] League of Nations International Committee on Intellectual Coöperation, *Minutes of the Tenth Session*, p. 75.

[11] League of Nations, International Committee on Intellectual Coöperation, *Minutes of the Ninth Session*, p. 82.

University Relations the Polish member commented on a report on the intellectual life of the new countries of Central and Eastern Europe, which he had undertaken at the suggestion of the Committee. He drew attention to the fact that absence of intellectual ties with other countries was felt severely in these newly created countries, and suggested as the only remedy for the situation the extension and the development of the international or binational institute.[12]

At its fourth session the Committee, in adopting the following resolutions made in this connection, formally recommended interchange as a remedy for the situation and particularly designated the possibilities of the Institutes à l'étranger (national institutes established abroad) :[13]

"The Sub-Committee on Inter-University Relations recommends the plenary Committee. . . .

"To recommend to the National Committees concerned, the joint extension and development of the Instituts à l'étranger with a view to establishing and drawing closer the intellectual bonds between the countries of Central and Eastern Europe and the Western Countries.

"To encourage special conferences between the National Committees belonging to these two groups of countries with a view not only to realizing the previous recommendation, but generally speaking, the former wishes of the International Committee with regard to inter-university exchanges."[14]

The recommendations of the Committee on Intellectual Coöperation are of advisory rather than executive force. They are based, as was mentioned above, upon a consideration of international experience in the fields which they cover. In the question of professorial interchange, an examination of certain movements for regular interchange show

---

[12] League of Nations Committee on Intellectual Coöperation, *Bulletin of the International University Information Office,* 1924, No. 4, pp. 181-182.

[13] See below, pp. 96-100.

[14] League of Nations International Committee on Intellectual Coöperation, *Minutes of the Fourth Session,* p. 46.

the background, and probably, though to an extent at present undeterminable, the influence, of the action of the Committee.

METHODS OF PROVIDING PROFESSORIAL INTERCHANGE

Interest in the Extension of Regular Professorial Interchange.—The question of regular professorial interchange for a definite teaching period is a point of active interest in international interchange at present. In addition to the very large number of occasional interchanges in recent years, including lecturers, visiting professors, and foreign professors and directors of education on semi-official visits for the purpose of studying, singly or in groups, the cultural life or educational systems of a given country,[15] there is evident

---

[15] A few examples may illustrate the interest. The Junta para Ampliacion de Estudios (according to an article by the Secretary-General of the Association) claims to have initiated the system of interchange of professors between Spain and other countries in 1917, and to have brought to Madrid in the period between 1917 and 1929 as assistants or professors of Spanish 55 professors from France, Germany, America, Italy, Switzerland, and Portugal; and to have sent abroad during that period Spanish professors or assistants to 3 universities in England, 5 in Germany, 3 in France, 8 in the United States, 2 in Italy, 3 in South America, 2 in Japan, 2 in Sweden. ("Relations Internationales dans la Vie Scientifique Espagnole," *La Coöpération Intellectuelle*, pp. 483-5, 485, note, August, 1929.)

During the third year of its existence the Institute of International Education in New York arranged for 12 American professors to be sent on leave to England, France, Spain, China, and Italy to teach in fields of Literature, Science, and Social Studies. (Institute of International Education, *Third Annual Report*, pp. 3, 18.) The report of the Institute for 1928 stated that 20 lecturers had been circuited among American universities from Germany, Scotland, Spain, France, Czechoslovakia, Austria, England, Holland, Russia, and Italy, the number consisting of professors and educational authorities in the fields of Literature, Philosophy, Science, Religion, History, Law, and Education. "The lecturers," the report adds, "form but a very small part of the many visitors from abroad who come for purposes of educational observation and investigation." (*Ninth Annual Report*, pp. 7-10.)

Numerous group visits may be mentioned. The Report of the Institute of International Education in 1920 stated that during its first year the Institute had arranged the itinerary of the most representative and important visiting delegation of educators that China has ever sent abroad.

an increase in interchanges on more regular bases. Besides the foreign professorial contacts occasioned by the establishment of the institutes abroad, discussed later,[16] regular international professorial interchange is provided chiefly by (1) private endowment of lectureships, (2) university agreements for regular interchange, either made independently by a university of one country with a university of governmental authority of another country, or arranged between universities of two countries through university offices or committees; and (3) formal treaties between two governments concerning educational interchanges.

One may cite numerous recent instances of private endowment of chairs or lectureships for foreign professors. Chairs of Italian and Spanish were established at the University of Glasgow in 1924.[17] The Westinghouse Exchange professorship established in 1923 sends each year an American to the University of Rome to lecture on American economics and business problems.[18] A chair of American History and

---

(*First Annual Report*, 1920, p. 6.) In 1925 a party of 150 professors and teachers from all parts of Switzerland made a study tour of Greece for 23 days. (*Bulletin of the International University Information Office*, 1925, No. 3, p. 176.) In 1929, with the aid of the Carnegie Endowment for International Peace, the Pan-American Union, assisted by the Institute of International Education, arranged a visit of 25 Argentine professors and students in the colleges and universities of the United States. (*La Coopération Intellectuelle*, March, 1929, p. 157; *Institute of International Education, Tenth Annual Report*, pp. 5-7.) In 1925 the same Endowment provided the American Historical Society with funds to invite 10 British professors of history to the annual meeting of the Association during the Christmas holidays. Through the intermediary of the Institute visits were arranged to American Universities. (Institute of International Education, *Sixth Annual Report*, p. 30.) In the summer of 1926, the Endowment sent 50 American college professors to Geneva. (International Federation of League of Nations Societies, *Bulletin*, Jan.-Feb. 1927, p. 69.)

[16] See below, pp. 96-100.

[17] "Sir Daniel Stevenson, of Glasgow, has given the sum of £49,000 to that city for the creation of two new chairs, one of Italian and the other of Spanish." (*Gazette de Lausanne*, Jan. 29, 1924. Quoted, League of Nations Committee on Intellectual Coöperation, *Bulletin of the International University Information Office*, 1924, Nos. 1, 2, p. 86.)

[18] *Ibid.*, 1926, No. 4-5, pp. 342-343.

Institutions was created at the Sorbonne in 1927.[19] A chair of Italian civilization was established at the University of California in 1928.[20] The George Eastman Visiting Professorship for American professors at Oxford[21] and the Frederic Yves Carpenter Visiting Chair of English at the University of Chicago[22] were instituted in 1929. The chair of German Civilization at Harvard[23] and the Chair of German language at La Hogskola of Stockholm were established in 1930.[24]

By Formal Agreement.—Among lectureships recently established by formal agreement one may cite the French lectureships at the University of Amsterdam (1923)[25] and at the University of Fribourg (1924).[26] Two lectureships in the History of Roumania and the Near East and in Roumanian Language and Literature were established in 1925 by the Roumanian Government at King's College, London, with the consent of the Senate of London University. These were to continue for a period of three years.[27] A chair of Czech Language was instituted at the University of Trieste in 1921 by arrangement between the University and the Czech Ministry of Education.[28] A chair of Hungarian his-

---

[19] League of Nations Institute of Intellectual Coöperation, *Bulletin for University Relations,* 1928, No. 1, p. 55.

[20] "Establishment of a Chair of Italian Culture," *School and Society,* April 21, 1928, Vol. 27, pp. 470-471.

[21] *La Coöperation Intellectuelle,* August, 1929, p. 526.

[22] *Ibid.,* April, 1929, p. 249.

[23] *Ibid.,* January, 1930, pp. 19-20.

[24] *Ibid.,* p. 20.

[25] *Rapport sur l'Expansion Universitaire Scientifique de la France et l'Activité de l'Office National des Universités en 1923 et 1924,* p. 21. Arranged by the Office National des Universités et Écoles; voted by the Municipal Council of Amsterdam and ratified by the Netherlands Government. The Comité Hollande-France guarantees the payment; the Office National proposes the candidates.

[26] With the consent of the canton of Fribourg an agreement was made whereby three French professors would occupy regular posts in the university, in the faculty of Law, Science, and Letters. *Ibid.,* p. 20.

[27] League of Nations Committee on Intellectual Coöperation, *Bulletin of the International University Information Office,* 1925, No. 3, p. 176.

[28] *Ibid.,* Nos. 4, 5, p. 214.

tory and literature was established at the Royal University of Rome by decree of the Italian Government in 1927.[29]

Other instances of recent arrangements for regular interchange are the agreements for annual exchange of professors existing since 1923 between the English and Swiss universities Bâle and Cambridge,[30] and since 1925 between the University of Vienna and the Medical Faculty of Rosario de Santa Fe (Argentine).[31] A formal convention of exchange was also made between the University of Chile and the University of California in 1919.[32]

Less fixed in nature are arrangements made by the Office National des Universités et Écoles Françaises for interchange on the part of French universities with English and German universities. The former is a coöperative venture in exchanges. In 1924 the Office National des Universités et Écoles Françaises concluded a convention of regular exchange between French and English universities, whereby annually each of seven English Universities receive at their expense for a period of three weeks two French professors who give successively a series of lectures in each of the universities. In return two English professors, chosen by a committee representing the English universities, are sent to seven French universities.[33]

---

[29] League of Nations Institute of Intellectual Coöperation, *Bulletin for University Relations*, 1928, No. 2, p. 117.

[30] League of Nations Committee on Intellectual Coöperation, *Bulletin of the International Univirsity Information Office*, 1924, No. 3, p. 171; League of Nations Institute of Intellectual Coöperation, *Handbook of University Exchanges in Europe*, 1928, p. 190.

[31] League of Nations Institute of Intellectual Coöperation, *Bulletin for University Relations*, 1926, Nos. 4, 5, pp. 269-270.

[32] Pan-American Union, Division of Intellectual Coöperation, *Documentary Information Compiled by the Division of Intellectual Coöperation for the Information of the Delegates to the Inter-American Congress of Rectors, Deans, and Educators*, 1930, p. 33. The exchange in this instance is for the purpose of study from 2 to 4 years.

[33] *Rapport sur l'Expansion Universitaire et Scientifique de la France et l'Activité de l'Office National des Universités en 1923 et 1924*, pp. 14, 15; Assemblée Générale de l'Office National des Universités et Écoles Françaises,

In 1927 the Office National began negotiations with Germany for the exchange of professors. In 1929, as a result of these negotiations a commission was officially designated to draw up a list of German professors who would be invited as exchange professors in French universities (the lists to be made from the requests submitted by the several individual universities), and in turn to examine the lists of French professors asked for by German universities.[34] Also, in 1927, the Office concluded agreements with three Portuguese universities (Coimbra, Lisbon, and Porto) that yearly at least three French professors would be heard in the three universities.[35]

By Arrangement of National Committees on Intellectual Coöperation.—A single instance of attempt on the part of National Committees of Intellectual Coöperation to regulate professorial exchange in general agreement with the recommendations of the League of Nations International Committee on Intellectual Coöperation is found in the Polish-Swiss convention of university exchanges (professors, stu-

---

Rapport sur l'Activité de l'Office des Universités, 1925-1926, pp. 22-24; *Ibid.,* 1928-1929, p. 19.

The agreement grew out of a Franco-British university conference in 1923, on the occasion of the Pasteur centenary. The English universities were at first those of Manchester, Liverpool, Durham, Sheffield, Birmingham, Bristol, and Leeds. The agreement was extended in 1925 to include the University of London. In 1928–1929 the Scotch universities had expressed interest in the arrangement. The list of the professors exchanged up to 1929 specified on the part of the French universities exchange professors from Strasbourg, Poitiers, Paris, Lyon, Bordeaux, Grenoble, Lille, and Rennes.

A similar coöperative experiment was made in 1922-1923 by American universities. In that year seven American institutions appropriated $1,000 each to enable an American professor of applied science or engineering to lecture in French universities in exchange for a French professor to spend one month in each of the seven American universities. (Institute of International Education, *Third Annual Report,* pp. 2-3.)

[34] *Assemblée Générale de l'Office National des Universités et Écoles Françaises, Rapport sur l'Activité de l'Office National,* etc., 1927, p. 22; *Ibid.,* 1928-1929, pp. 30-32.

[35] *Ibid.,* 1927, p. 19.

dents, publications). This was concluded in 1927 after a period of deliberation covering three years.

While the National Committees have no legal powers to enforce the provisions of the convention, the treaty has received the support of the universities of the two countries and of the Polish Government. It provided for exchange of professors beginning in 1927-1928, preferably prolonged and systematic exchanges. As an experiment, at the expense of the Polish Government, a "Polish-Swiss Chair" was established for two Polish and two Swiss professors for a period of two months each.[36] A peculiar feature of the convention is the provision that the visiting professor shall select one or more students of the country in which he teaches as exchange professor, who will pursue studies the following year in some higher institution of learning in the country of the visiting professor.

By Official Treaties of Exchange and Government Decrees. Of particular interest as a recent experiment in regulating international professorial exchanges are the official treaties arranging university exchanges between two countries. Of these the earliest seem to have been inter-American conventions. In 1915 and 1916 Uruguay concluded treaties with Argentine and with Chile providing that the universities of the two nations concerned should exchange annually reports relative to the subjects that their professors teach and the subjects the universities would like treated by foreign professors, dealing with scientific matters or conditions with special reference to the Americas.[37] In 1922 Uruguay con-

---

[36] League of Nations Institute of Intellectual Coöperation, *Bulletin for University Relations*, 1928, No. 1, pp. 14-23. International Committee on Intellectual Coöperation, *Meeting of Representatives of National Committees for Intellectual Coöperation, 1929, first session, second meeting*, p. 16.

[37] Pan-American Union, Division of Intellectual Coöperation, *Documentary Information Compiled by the Division of Intellectual Coöperation of the Pan-American Union for the Information of the Delegates to the Inter-American Congress of Rectors, Deans, and Educators to be held at Havana, Cuba, February, 1930*, pp. 25, 27.

cluded a similar treaty with Colombia specifying as subjects to be presented by the visiting professor "scientific, literary, or artistic matters relative to the Americas and especially to the country of origin."[38]

More formal and detailed in specifications concerning professorial interchange are the treaties concluded since 1919 between governments of European States to establish closer intellectual relations between the two countries.

Between 1919 and 1929 France concluded eight formal treaties concerning university interchanges with other nations. These fall into two groups: first, treaties regulating exchanges of professors and students between the two countries; second, those whereby the French Government places French professors at the disposal of a foreign government. The latter condition applied to the treaties with Roumania (1919)[39] and Jugoslavia (1920);[40] the former to treaties with Italy (1919),[41] Belgium (1921),[42] Poland (1922),[43] Luxembourg (1923),[44] Czechoslovakia (1923),[45] and Norway (1927).[46] Also, in addition to the treaty with France, Belgium has concluded similar treaties with Luxembourg (1923),[47] Poland (1925),[48] and the Netherlands (1927).[49]

In each case the appointment is to be determined by the requests of the universities themselves. In the case of the French treaties with Roumania and Jugoslavia, lists of available French professors are presented to the universities in those two countries. In the case of the other binational treaties, lists are drawn up by universities on each side and

[38] *Ibid.*, p. 28.

[39] League of Nations Institute of Intellectual Coöperation, *Bulletin for University Relations*, 1928, No. 2, pp. 100-102, text of the convention.

[40] *Ibid.*, pp. 102-103.   [41] *Ibid.*, pp. 98-100.   [42] *Ibid.*, pp. 103-106.

[43] *Ibid.*, pp. 106-108.   [44] *Ibid.*, pp. 108-110.   [45] *Ibid.*, pp. 110-112.

[46] *Ibid.*, pp. 112-114.   [47] *Ibid.*, 1926, No. 3, pp. 137-139.

[48] *Ibid.*, pp. 139-142.

[49] *Ibid.*, 1928, No. 3-4, pp. 213-215. In addition Belgium proposed similar conventions of exchange to the United States, England, Italy, Norway, Sweden, Switzerland, Czechoslovakia, and Portugal. The proposals have not been accepted. *Ibid.*, No. 2, p. 85.

are submitted to a Mixed Commission representing the two countries. In the treaties of exchange it is specified that preference will be given to professors who will be in a position to set forth original researches or new methods little or not at all represented in the universities in which they will teach. It is further stated that the choice may be extended to savants not officially connected with universities (to state library officials, in the instance of the treaties with Poland and Norway).

Regulations concerning tenure, salaries, indemnities, and prerogatives are specified in each treaty. In the treaties calling for exchanges between two counties, the time specified is a semester, six months, or a school year, with the possibility of extension over a number of years or of limitation to a series of lectures. In the French treaties with Roumania and Jugoslavia, the period is five years, revokable at the end of the first and the third year. In the treaties of exchange, the professors concerned are to draw their remuneration (including regular salary, indemnities, and traveling expenses) from the country of origin. In the French treaties with Roumania and Jugoslavia, the foreign government bears the expenses of the visiting French professor.[50]

It is stipulated in each instance that except in matters of internal administration and control, the visiting professor will be accorded the privileges, honors, and powers (on examining juries, etc.) that national professors of corres-

---

[50] In each case except Netherlands it is stipulated that the professor is to receive the salary accorded his rank in the country of origin and, in addition, traveling expenses involved (including the traveling expenses of his family), certain indemnities of residence abroad, and whatever special indemnities are accorded the national professors. The Belgian-Netherlands treaty merely provides for the exchange, stipulates that the choice is to be made from lists compiled and submitted as described above, and that the expense of exchange is to be borne by the country of origin according to agreements reached between the two governments.

The French treaties with Jugoslavia and Roumania state that where special contracts are not made the special indemnity shall be of 25 per cent the salary.

ponding rank enjoy; and that in matters of seniority, promotion and honorary distinction, the service abroad will count
in the country of origin as the same period of service at home.
In these treaties officially recognizing the value of professorial interchanges there is official recognition also of the
inherent difficulties of such arrangements and of the necessity
of offering protection and even inducement if the nation is
to receive the most desirable representation abroad.

France as early as 1913 enacted legislation protecting the
French professor and teacher abroad. A law of 1913 removed discrimination against the French professor abroad
in the matter of pension. Later laws, in 1919 and 1923,
removed discrimination in the matter of promotion, even
extending to young teachers serving abroad before having
taught in France.[51] Likewise the Italian Royal Decree of
1926, placing Italian professors at the disposal of the Ministry of Foreign Affairs for teaching positions abroad, provides that service by Italian professors in accordance with
the provisions of the decree, and duly recognized abroad,
shall count as service at home in that which concerns
seniority, periodic promotion, and career.[52] Spain also has
enacted protective legislation, reserving for five years the
posts of professors of public instruction invited to give
courses in foreign universities.[53]

The official binational conventions of interchange cited

---

[51] *Rapport sur l'Expansion Universitaire et Scientifique de la France et
l'Activité de l'Office National des Universités en 1923 et 1924*, pp. 8, 9. A
summary of French legislation protecting the professor in service abroad.

[52] League of Nations Institute of Intellectual Coöperation, *Bulletin for
University Relations*, 1928, No. 1, p. 47. The decree provides that the
Italian Government is to bear the expense of replacing State professors
placed at the disposal of the Ministry of Foreign Affairs, that the Ministry
of Public Instruction is to bear the expense of replacing professors of
free universities, and that the Ministers of Public Instruction, Foreign
Affairs, and Finance are to pay the fees of foreign professors given teaching appointments in State and free (autonomous) institutions.

[53] According to a statement in the report of the Junta para Ampliacion
de Estudios, *La Coöpération Intellectuelle*, August, 1929, p. 485.

above, however, contain provisions of less negative value than this legislation. They propose to a certain extent to make positive provision for the reception and treatment of the exchanged professors. The treaty concluded between France and Roumania, placing French professors at the disposition of the Roumanian government, goes even so far as to regulate hours of service, specifying special compensation for hours in addition to the hours imposed upon French professors of the same rank.[54]

In this chapter it has been pointed out that recent interest has been directed to increasing the number of international professorial contacts and making them regular and of satisfactory duration. Numerous international intellectual contacts of more or less regular nature have been established through private endowment of lectureships, inter-university agreements for professorial exchanges, and formal conventions concluded between two governments arranging the terms of professorial interchange. In a few instances also official decrees recognizing foreign service of national professors have been enacted as a means of encouraging interchange. In addition, as is pointed out in the course of the following chapter, the recent development of institutes of national culture established in foreign countries has afforded increased opportunity for both regular and occasional interchange of professors between nations.

---

[54] League of Nations Institute of Intellectual Coöperation, *Bulletin for University Relations,* 1928, No. 2, p. 101.

CHAPTER IV

INTERNATIONAL SCHOOLS AND STUDIES

THE INCREASING conviction that a satisfactory world civilization can be built only upon mutual appreciation of national civilizations and upon understanding of world problems has given added stimulus to the development of institutions and studies of international aspect. In particular, interest has been manifested in the international school or institute, the study of modern civilizations and international affairs in national centers of learning, national schools and courses for foreign students, and the institute of national culture abroad.

THE PROJECT OF AN INTERNATIONAL UNIVERSITY

The idea of a great international university was natural in the movement for international reconciliation following the World War. At any rate, the proposal for the creation of an international university proceeded almost simultaneously from numerous quarters at the close of the war. In 1920 the Union of International Associations organized and founded at Brussels the International University, a modest beginning of what it was hoped would develop into a great world center of learning.[1]

Two years later the International Committee on Intellectual Coöperation held its first session. Among some forty-eight proposals or schemes, from various organizations and persons, which the secretariat of the League of Nations sub-

---

[1] League of Nations *Handbook of International Organizations*, 1929, p. 24. Provisionally established in buildings belonging to the Brussels Palais Mondial. It has conducted only summer courses. For a statement of its resources and aspirations in 1925, see the statement of Professor Paul Otlet, *Proceedings of the First Biennial Conference of the World Federation of Education Associations, Edinburgh*, 1925, Vol. 1, pp. 413 ff.

mitted for consideration, three were concerned with the establishment of an international university.[2] In addition to these, the question of an international university was also brought forward at the first session by the Belgian member, M. Destrée, who, while expressing the belief that the realization of the proposal was at the moment impossible, asked that "for the benefit of posterity, note should be taken of the fact that in 1922 someone had had the idea of an International University."[3] No resolution was taken on the subject, however, because of the Committee's conviction that its work should not consist of "the formulation of platonic resolutions."[4]

The question was again proposed for consideration by the Committee at its second meeting, July-August, 1923, by the member from India, Professor Bannerjea, Professor of Political Economy at the University of Calcutta.[5] Still other expressions of interest in the subject might be cited as evidence of rather widespread concern.[6]

---

[2] League of Nations International Committee on Intellectual Coöperation, *Minutes of the First Session*, pp. 43-44.

"11. October 13, 1920, Mr. H. C. Anderson transmits a scheme for establishing a 'University of the Nations,' together with an association for its development."

"12. Paris, March 30, 1921. The French League of Nations Department transmits a Memorandum from M. Gustave Hubbard, a former deputy, addressed to the Council of the League of Nations, on behalf of the 'Independence et Concours' Committee, requesting it to undertake a preliminary enquiry with regard to the foundation of a 'super-national' university."

"32. Meilen (Switzerland), September, 1921. Dr. Rudolph Laemmel forwards to the President of the Assembly of the League of Nations his pamphlet containing an account of the scheme for the foundation of an International School (Volkerschule)."

[3] League of Nations International Committee on Intellectual Coöperation, *Minutes of the First Session*, p. 29.

[4] *Minutes of the First Session*, p. 29, a statement of Professor Bergson, Chairman, in response to M. Destrée's proposal.

[5] *Minutes of the Second Session*, pp. 35, 69-71.

[6] For example, the Greek and Roumanian National Committees in communications to the third session of the International Committee on Intellectual Coöperation called attention to the desirability of the undertaking. The Roumanian Committee expressed the opinion that, though the under-

At length at its third session, December, 1923, the Committee was asked by the Fourth Assembly of the League to consider the Spanish Government's proposals concerning inter-university relations, including the question of an international university.[7] Concerning the proposal of the Spanish Government with reference to this phase of international education, the Committee at its fourth session returned the opinion "that obstacles, at the moment insurmountable, stand in the way of the immediate creation of an official international university."[8]

In arriving at this decision, the Committee had accepted the reports of M. Castillejo, Secretary-General of the Junta para Ampliacion de Estudios, of Madrid. In analyzing the

---

taking was desirable as a step in international coöperation, "the realization of the idea seems difficult if not impossible." The Greek Committee, offering a series of proposals regulating such a university, held that it could not too strongly recommend the establishment of the university, which it considered as "the best means of organizing mutual intellectual assistance." (*Minutes of the Third Session*, pp. 42-43, 46.) The creation of an international university was also approved by the Third International Sociological Congress at Rome, April, 1924. One of its recommendations was "that the foundation of an international university should be energetically undertaken with the help of adequate funds and with the assistance of the different states." (*Bulletin of the International University Information Office*, 1924, p. 233, report of the Congress.) Also, the Chairman of the International Committee on Intellectual Coöperation at its fourth session "recalled the fact that M. Doktorwicz, of Warsaw, had written to ask for the approval and support of the Committee in regard to the establishment of an International university on the territory of the Free City of Danzig." (*Minutes of the Fourth Session*, p. 41.)

[7] League of Nations International Committee on Intellectual Coöperation, *Minutes of the Third Session*, p. 29.

[8] *Minutes of the Fourth Session*, pp. 40-41.
"The Sub-Committee has examined with the greatest attention the proposals of the Spanish Government. It is of the opinion that they show the present importance of doing everything possible to combat in universities the tendency to isolation and the fostering of a spirit of nationalism, which are contrary to good understanding between the nations since they may prove harmful to the preservation of peace among mankind.

"After having taken note of the reports presented by M. de Halecki and M. Castillejo on the questions raised by the Spanish Government, the Sub-Committee agrees, with them, that obstacles, at the moment insurmountable, stand in the way of the immediate creation of an official international university."

proposal of his government with reference to an international university M. Castillejo expressed the opinion that the chief obstacles in the way of its present realization were these: "(1) the system of protection in vogue in many countries regarding professional titles; (2) the question of the conferring of titles and of the difficulty of making sure that the different nations would send their best professors to the new university; (3) the difficulty of creating a corporate life and finding a suitable 'milieu,' two conditions essential to the success of the university; (4) the problem of the maintenance of the neutrality of an international university; (5) the dangers of a 'super-university.' "[9]

In general the idea at the basis of most of the proposals for an international university was that of a university under the protection and control of the League of Nations, internationally staffed with eminent professors, and drawing to it as a student body the superior intellects of all nations. It would differ from national universities chiefly in that its personnel would be thoroughly international, its curriculum would be entirely lacking in nationalistic spirit, and its degree would be internationally recognized.

In 1925 the idea was again brought to the consideration of the Committee in the form of a proposal for an international university for political studies—"a scheme for the Establishment of an International University for the Education of Statesmen, Diplomats, Politicians, Political Writers, Professors of Political Science in High Schools, etc."[10] The consideration of this proposal, as will be pointed out below,[11] resulted in steps to coördinate higher political studies within the national sphere and to encourage international collaboration and exchange between institutions dealing with them.

[9] League of Nations Committee on Intellectual Coöperation, *Bulletin of the International University Office*, 1924, pp. 101-102.

[10] League of Nations International Committee on Intellectual Coöperation, *Minutes of the Sixth Session*, pp. 9, 26, ff.

[11] See below, pp. 89-93.

The international school of the last decade is confined to certain independent international institutions of limited scope, established particularly for instruction or research in the field of international problems, such as, for example, the Brussels institution mentioned above, the International People's College of Elsinore, Denmark, (1921),[12] and the more important Geneva School of International Studies (1924)[13] and Institute of Pacific Relations, Honolulu (1925).[14]

COÖRDINATION OF INSTITUTIONS FOR INTERNATIONAL STUDIES

Increasing interest has been manifested in the encouragement of the scientific study of international questions in national institutions, with the result that within the last decade numerous schools or institutes for the scientific study of international problems have been founded in the several nations. Very recently a movement has been initiated to coordinate national institutes of this nature and to promote international collaboration among them. The interest of the League of Nations Committee on Intellectual Coöperation in the development of the study of international problems has been largely instrumental in effecting this movement of international coördination.

The International Committee on Intellectual Coöperation considered at its second session the problems of inter-

---

[12] The International People's College was established with the support of Danish, English, and American contributions. It numbered in 1925 sixty-five students. (League of Nations *Handbook on International Organizations,* 1929, p. 86; World Federation of Education Associations, *Proceedings of the First Biennial Conference,* Edinburgh, 1925, Vol. II, p. 733.)

[13] See below, p. 95.

[14] The Institute of Pacific Relations, which is international in a regional sense, defines itself as a "research and conference body, international and inter-racial in composition, its interests centered in the Pacific area." It was founded in 1925 as an independent organization representing no class interest, creed or political unity. (League of Nations International Committee on Intellectual Coöperation, *Handbook of Institutions for the Scientific Study of International Relations,* p. 20.)

university relations as a means of promoting international understanding. Recognizing the interest already manifested in the several countries, it passed the following resolution in favor of courses dealing with modern civilization:

"In order to diminish the sources of misunderstanding and the lack of sympathy between nations, the universities are invited to organize courses on the nations of today according to the facilities at their disposal.

"It would be the aim of these courses to familiarize the students with the political, economic, and moral conditions.

"The programs of these courses would be communicated to the International Bureau of University Information whose creation has been recommended by the Committee."[15]

This resolution was followed at the third session by more specific recommendations, referring to particular institutions for the higher study of international affairs, rather than the international courses in universities of general culture. The resolution reads:

"The Sub-Committee, with reference to a proposal concerning the course of lectures on modern nations, and desiring to draw attention once more to the exceptional importance of this proposal, recommends that schools, institutes, or permanent educational organizations should be formed with the object of carrying out a methodical study of the great international problems of the moment and of problems connected with the economic, political, and moral life of modern nations. It recalls the fact that a beginning has already been made—for example, in the international courses delivered at the Universities of Geneva and Vienna, at the International University of Brussels, at the Academy of International Law at the Hague, international courses at the University of Chicago and at Williams College, the courses at the University of London and at the University of Aberyswyth, etc.

---

[15] League of Nations International Committee on Intellectual Coöperation, *Minutes of the Second Session*, p. 34.

"The Sub-Committee proposes that these schools, institutes, and organizations should maintain more regular relations with each other and with the Sub-Committee in order to assure a certain unity in the general conduct of the instruction, which is of such great value in bringing about an understanding between various schools of thought, in accordance with the principles of the League of Nations. It also approves the suggestion of M. Castillejo that an organization for instruction in the international problems raised by the new legal, social and economic state of affairs, as represented principally by the League of Nations should be established to work in connection with the League."[16]

A recommendation of similar effect was contained in the report submitted in 1926 by the special sub-committee to consider the instruction of children and youth in the League of Nations.[17] Among the methods of promoting indirect international contacts, the Sub-Committee of Experts suggested "studies of different civilizations and the scientific. and comparative study of present-day events."[18] Finally, at its eighth and ninth sessions, in 1926 and 1927, the Committee, as a result of its consideration of Professor Barany's proposal for an International University of political studies, referred to above, again emphasized the importance of international studies, with the definite result that steps were initiated for international coördination of these studies.

In 1925 the Committee on Intellectual Coöperation referred to its Sub-Committee on Inter-University Relations the scheme of Professor Barany for the establishment of an

[16] League of Nations International Committee on Intellectual Coöperation, *Minutes of the Fourth Session*, p. 41. The recommendations resulted from a discussion of the proposals of the Spanish Government, *Minutes of the Fourth Session*, p. 34.

[17] See below, pp. 136 ff.

[18] League of Nations Committee on International Intellectual Coöperation, *Recommendations of the Sub-Committee of Experts*, 1927, p. 7, recommendation No. 15, g.

"International University for the Education of Statesmen, Diplomats, Politicians, Political Writers, Professors of Political Science in High Schools, etc."[19] The Sub-Committee, after discussing the scheme, expressed itself in favor of the coördination of national institutions where international studies are carried on, and the international collaboration of these national institutions, rather than the establishment of a world university of such studies. Consequently it returned the following resolution:

"The Sub-Committee, after having heard the statement of M. Barany concerning the creation of an international university and recalling the previous resolution of the Committee on Intellectual Coöperation on this subject, considers it extremely desirable that an international school for higher political studies should be instituted.

"It instructs the International Institute for Intellectual Coöperation to examine the possibilities of putting the scheme into practice and of discovering what results could be achieved by coördinating the national and international organizations already in existence, in conformity with the steps taken in this direction in the various countries."[20]

---

[19] League of Nations International Committee on Intellectual Coöperation, *Minutes of the Sixth Session*, pp. 7, 26-29.

[20] *Minutes of the Eighth Session*, p. 64. See also pages 30 ff. The same conclusion was arrived at by the International Federation of League of Nations Societies in 1925 on hearing the same proposal. In 1925 it adopted the following resolution:

"IV. International University Studies.

Having taken sympathetic note of the guiding principles in the memorandum of the Swedish Society relative to the creation of an international University for the purpose of training Statesmen, Diplomats, Politicians, Teachers of Political Science in the High Schools and Editors of Political Journals;

In view of the fact that there already exist important organizations aiming at realizing that object, such as the Paris Institute for the Study of International Affairs (terms of eight months for two years), the Academy of International Law at The Hague (two months in the summer), etc.; that in addition special courses are organized every year at Geneva by the International Students Federation for the League of Nations, etc.;

In 1927, after hearing the report of the Director of the International Institute concerning preliminary and official negotiation with different schools of international studies, the Sub-Committee authorized the Institute to convene a committee of experts in the course of the year, when negotiations seemed sufficiently advanced. "This Committee," it advised, "would consider the best means of permitting students to carry on international studies successively in various countries."[21] As for the purely international institution the Sub-Committee expressed itself in favor of international vacation courses.[22]

As a result of the negotiations of the Director of the Institute, the meeting of experts and of representatives of various types of scientific institutes for the study of politics was held in Berlin in March, 1928.[23] This meeting was fol-

---

Invites the members of the Federation to make those and other similar Institutions known and to give them their support;

And finally to second the efforts at Coördination of the Committee on Intellectual Coöperation." (International Federation of the League of Nations Societies, *Ninth Assembly, Plenary Sessions*, 1925, pp. 31-32.)

Among the resolutions adopted by the XIIIth plenary Congress of the International Federation of League of Nations Societies is the following concerning the promotion of mutual understanding between nations:

"I. In conformity with the previous decisions of the International Federation of League of Nations Societies and in conformity with the recommendations of the League's Sub-Committee of Experts,

The XIIIth Plenary Congress recommends to constituent Societies . . . to encourage the development and coördination of University departments, or specialized institutions for the advanced study of international affairs." (*XIIIth Plenary Congress, Proceedings and Resolutions*, 1929, p. 104.)

[21] League of Nations International Committee on Intellectual Coöperation, *Minutes of the Ninth Session*, p. 67.

[22] *Ibid.*

[23] *Minutes of the Tenth Session*, pp. 71-73, 83-88. An analysis of the kinds of institutions represented, made at this meeting, showed that the institutions could be classified as (1) centers of study and discussion, such as the Royal Institute of International Affairs, which does no teaching work; (2) special and supplementary courses, such as the Academy of International Law at The Hague, the Geneva School of International Studies, the Williamstown Institute of Politics and the Royal Italian University for Foreigners at Perugia; (3) teaching institutions outside the university proper, such as the Deutsche Hochschule fur Politik at Berlin, the École libre des Sciences politiques in Paris, the University Institute for Higher

lowed by a second meeting in London in March, 1929.[24] At the two meetings of representatives, plans were laid for international coöperation among institutes of this type in research, bibliography, exchange of professors and students, and other points. At the first meeting there existed national coördinating committees, of recent formation in three countries,—in Berlin, Paris, and Rome;[25] in 1929 committees had been formed also for Great Britain, Poland, and the United States.[26]

An important result of the two meetings was the proposal of a conference of teachers concerned with international studies, "for the purpose of discussing among other matters, methods of teaching, relations and arrangement of subjects, relations of academic teaching and practical experience."[27]

Of the thirty-nine institutions of twelve nations participating in this plan of coöperation in 1929,[28] twenty-one have been established since 1919;[29] two others were estab-

---

International Studies at Geneva, and the Consular Academy at Vienna; (4) university faculties, such as the London School of Economics and Political Science (University of London), the Faculty of Law and the Faculty of Letters of the University of Paris, and the Faculties of Political Science at the Universities of Rome, Padua, Pavia, and Perugia. In these divisions there is considerable overlapping. (*Ibid.*, p. 84.)

[24] *Minutes of the Eleventh Session*, pp. 88-93.

[25] *Minutes of the Tenth Session*, pp. 83, note; 84.

[26] League of Nations *Handbook of Institutions for the Scientific Study of International Relations*, 1929, pp. 35, 42, 63, 71, 80.

[27] League of Nations International Committee on Intellectual Coöperation, *Minutes of the Eleventh Session*, p. 93.

[28] Three of these are international organizations.

[29] Geneva School of International Studies (1924); Institute of Pacific Relations (1925); Canadian Institute of International Affairs (1927); School of Political Science of Prague (Svobodna Skola Politickych Nauk V Praze, 1928); Institute of Economics and History of Copenhagen (Institutet for Historie og Samfundsökonomi, 1927; Institut des Hautes Études Internationales of Paris (1921); Deutsche Hochschule für Politik, Berlin (1920); Deutsches Institut für Zeitungskunde an der Universitat Berlin (1924); Institut für Auswärtige Politik, Hamburg (1923); Institut für Sozial-und Staatswissenschaft an der Universität Heidelberg (1924); Institut für Zeitungswesen an der Universität Heidelberg (1927); Royal Institute of International Affairs, London (1920); Scuola di Scienze Politiche, Economiche e Sociali Universita Cattolica del Sacro Cuore,

lished in 1918;[30] and three in 1914 and 1915.[31] These numbers are only suggestive of the recent increase of interest in the study of international affairs. Other recently founded institutions and organizations dealing with international studies in scientific or popular manner, not represented in the plan of coördination mentioned above, might be added as evidence of recent development of interest in the study of international affairs.

The numbers mentioned above do not include, for example, among American institutions, the Norman Wait Harris Memorial Foundation for the Study of International Relations (1924),[32] the Walter Hines Page School on International Relations, Johns Hopkins (1925),[33] the graduate school of international affairs at Washington, provided for by the Parker Endowment (1929),[34] and the

Milan (1920); Scuola di Scienze Politiche e Sociali; Facoltà di Scienze Politiche, Pavia (1926; Facoltà di Scienze Politiche, Rome (1925); Institute of Constitutional and International Law (Instytut Prawa Polityscnego I Prawa Narodow) Lemberg, 1923; Association for the Study of International Relations (Towarzystwo Badania Zagadnien Miedzynarodowych), Warsaw, 1926; Institutul Social Roman, Bucharest (1921); Institut Universitaire des Hautes Études Internationales, Geneva (1927); Council on Foreign Relations, New York (1920). (League of Nations, *Handbook of Institutions for the Scientific Study of International Relations*, 1929.)

[30] Institut für Wirtschaftswissenschaft an der Universität Frankfurt (1918); Foreign Policy Association, Inc., New York (1918). (League of Nations, *Handbook of Institutions for the Scientific Study of International Relations.*)

[31] Academy of International Law, The Hague (1914); Institut für Weltwirtschaft und Seeverkehr an der Universität Kiel (1914); Szkola Nauk Politycznych, Warsaw. (*Ibid.*)

[32] League of Nations Committee on Intellectual Coöperation, *Bulletin of the International University Information Office*, 1924, p. 214; League of Nations Institute of Intellectual Coöperation, *Bulletin for University Relations*, 1926, p. 243.

[33] League of Nations Committee on Intellectual Coöperation, *Bulletin of the International University Information Office*, 1925, pp. 36-37.

[34] *Bulletin of the American Association of University Women*, January, 1930, p. 102. Of interest also as a recent development in the field of international studies is the program of the School of Law at Harvard University. A recent gift to Harvard University provides for the creation of sixty scholarships to enable sixty students from sixty nations to attend

school of public and international affairs established at Princeton University in 1930;[35] and, among European institutions, the Diplomatic School of the Hungarian Association for Foreign Affairs and for the League of Nations (1927),[36] and a number of vacation courses for the study of the League of Nations and international affairs, such as the League of Nations summer schools, the international courses at the University of Vienna, at Davos (Switzerland), and others.[37]

THE LEAGUE OF NATIONS IN THE HIGHER SCHOOLS

A specific interest in international studies, particularly in States Members of the League, is the study of the League of Nations. The most common method of stimulating interest in the study of the League is the encouragement of occasional lectures on the League, organized in particular by League of Nations Societies. The reports of League of Nations Societies and the replies of governments to the investigations of the International Committee on Intellectual Coöperation indicate that occasional lectures on the League are organized annually in universities in practically all States Members of the League.[38] Regular courses form naturally a part of the university curriculum in many instances. At the University of Bulgaria the League of Nations Society has brought about the establishment of a Carnegie

---

Harvard annually for the purpose of studying International Law. (*La Coöpération Intellectuelle*, January, 1929, pp. 29-30).

[35] *La Coöpération Intellectuelle*, April, 1930, p. 167.

[36] International Federation of League of Nations Societies, *Bulletin*, May-June, 1929, No. III, p. 54.

[37] League of Nations International Committee on Intellectual Coöperation, *Holiday Courses in Europe*, 1930.

[38] See, for example, the reports of the national societies in the *Bulletin* of the International Federation of the League of Nations Societies; the reports made by State Members of the League on the progress of instruction in the League of Nations (see below, pp. 135-139); *How to Make the League of Nations Known* (League of Nations Publication); and the League of Nations, *Educational Survey*, Vol. I, Nos. 1 and 2.

Chair for teaching subjects dealing with Peace and the League of Nations.[39] Further, interest is stimulated by prize essay competitions and Model Assemblies in the higher as well as in the lower schools.[40]

Finally, the International summer schools on the League held at Geneva offer students opportunity for more intimate study of the League. The courses of the Geneva School of International Studies include in large measure the study of the League of Nations. The school is an international institution established in 1924 for the study of contemporary problems. Its session begins eight weeks before the League of Nations Assembly and continues to its close. In 1928 its 316 students represented thirty nations. In that year nine governments granted twenty-four scholarships. In addition, eighteen scholarships were granted by individuals and organizations of several nations. Besides these, scholarships are granted annually by the school; in 1929 eighty such scholarships were to be awarded.[41]

Two other international summer schools on the League have been regularly conducted for a number of years. The British League of Nations Society organized a summer school at Geneva immediately after the Secretariat came to Geneva. After 1923, with the participation of the American group, it was merged with the Geneva Institute of International Relations, the course being designed chiefly for

[39] International Federation of League of Nations Societies, *Bulletin,* 1927, No. 1, p. 50.

[40] *Ibid.,* 1924, No. 4, p. 37; 1928, No. 3, p. 35 (Report of the British League of Nations Union for 1927); 1928, XIIth Plenary Congress, p. 22; 1929, *Bulletin* No. 3, p. 33; League of Nations Associations of the United States, "League of Nations News," Vol. VI, No. 85, p. 4; *Ibid.,* No. 90, p. 11; League of Nations, *Educational Survey,* 1929, Vol. I, No. 1, "Education for the League of Nations in the United States of America," pp. 140-146.

[41] League of Nations Committee on Intellectual Coöperation, *Handbook of Institutions for the Scientific Study of International Relations,* pp. 17-20; *Bulletin for University Relations,* 1926, pp. 144-145; 1928, pp. 39 ff.; 216-217.

the Anglo-Saxon public.[42] Also since 1926 the International Federation of League of Nations Societies has organized lectures at Geneva. These courses, discussed later,[43] are designed particularly for teachers and teachers in training.

The international education relations discussed above chiefly concern international studies pursued by students in their respective national universities and in international institutions. Further aspects of interest in developing international relationships through studies in universities and other higher schools are found in the chair of foreign culture, the institute abroad, and the international school or course which a nation establishes for foreign students.

THE INSTITUTE ABROAD

The institute abroad is a relatively recent extension of the chair of foreign culture. Since it has been developed in the last decade or so, it differs in purpose from a type of institute abroad commonly known before the twentieth century. The latter is chiefly the foreign school of archaeology, classical studies, art, or religion. Examples are found in the British, French, German, and American schools of classical studies in Athens,[44] similar schools of classical studies and history in Rome,[45] the French Biblical and Theological School in Jerusalem,[46] and others. These present instances of a national school established in a foreign country for the purpose of studying a particular aspect of the past civilization of the foreign country, under the direction

[42] League of Nations Institute on Intellectual Coöperation, *Bulletin for University Relations*, 1926, pp. 9-10, 170; International Federation of League of Nations Societies, *Bulletin*, May-June, 1928, No. III, p. 33; 1926, Jan.-March, No. 1, pp. 67, 82.

[43] See below, pp. 169-172.

[44] League of Nations Institute of Intellectual Coöperation, *Handbook of University Exchanges in Europe*, 1928, p. 140.

[45] *Ibid*, pp. 146-153.

[46] League of Nations Institute of Intellectual Coöperation, *Bulletin for University Relations*, 1926, No. 2, pp. 70-71.

of a small professorial staff whose services are practically limited to the group concerned. In addition, a different type of national school abroad has been the product largely of very recent development.

The purpose of the institute abroad of recent development is in general twofold: to facilitate research in a foreign country by graduates or young professors of the country of origin, and also to promote in the foreign country knowledge and appreciation of the culture of the country of origin. It is often attached to a university of the country in which it is established. Its functions are usually to direct courses in language, literature, and general culture both for students of the country establishing it and for students of the country in which it is established; to organize vacation courses; and to arrange interchange of professors and savants between the two countries for public lectures. Hence it functions as a medium of professorial and student interchange for the purpose of making the civilization of one country known to another through personal contact and instruction.

Earlier examples are the French Institutes in Madrid[47] and London,[48] founded in 1908 and 1910, respectively, and the Institute of Spanish Studies in Paris, founded in 1913.[49] Since 1919 there has been manifested an increasing interest in foundations of this nature. France has been particularly active in establishing institutes abroad, with the result that France now has intellectual ties of this kind with South America, Japan, and most countries of Europe. These range in size from the institute represented by one profes-

[47] League of Nations Institute of Intellectual Coöperation, *Bulletin for University Relations,* 1926, pp. 152-153.

[48] *Rapport sur l'Expansion Universitaire et Scientifique de la France et l'Activité de l'Office National des Universités en 1923 et 1924,* pp. 13-14.

[49] League of Nations Institute of Intellectual Coöperation, *Bulletin for University Relations,* 1926, p. 154; *La Coöpération Intellectuelle,* June, 1929, p. 357; League of Nations Institute of Intellectual Coöperation, *Handbook of University Exchanges in Europe,* 1928, pp. 65-66.

sor[50] to the rather substantial institute in London, which in 1923 counted some 388 students in the faculty of letters, 438 in the reading circle, and 198 in the two lycées attached.[51]

Institutes abroad established since 1919 include the French institutes in Naples,[52] Lisbon,[53] Kioto,[54] and Caracas (Venezuela),[55] and in the cities of Eastern Europe mentioned below; the British Institutes at Florence[56] and Paris;[57] the Spanish Institute in Buenos Aires,[58] the Institute of Italian Culture in Argentine and the reciprocal institute of Argentine Culture in Genoa,[59] the Institute of Latin American culture at Berlin and the German institutes in Buenos Aires, Rio de Janeiro, and Madrid.[60]

Attention was called above to the resolution of the Committee on Intellectual Coöperation which recommended the institute of foreign culture as a means of establishing intellectual contacts between Eastern and Western Europe. A number of recently established institutes abroad constitute such bonds. Between 1920 and 1925 France established in-

---

[50] This is the situation at Zagreb, for example. See below, p. 99, note 64.

[51] See above, p 97, note 48.

[52] League of Nations Institute of Intellectual Coöperation, *Handbook of University Exchanges in Europe*, 1928, pp. 149-150.

[53] League of Nations Institute of Intellectual Coöperation, *Bulletin for University Relations*, 1928, pp. 48-49; *Handbook of University Exchanges in Europe*, 1928, p. 175.

[54] *Bulletin for University Relations*, 1928, p. 47. [55] *Ibid.*, 1928, p. 230.

[56] League of Nations Committee on Intellectual Coöperation, *Bulletin of the International University Information Office*, 1924, p. 224; League of Nations Institute of Intellectual Coöperation, *Bulletin for University Relations*, 1926, p. 360. Britain established as many as twelve during the war but only this one, privately financed, remained in 1925.

[57] Royal Institute of International Affairs, *Directory of Societies and Organizations in Great Britain dealing with International Affairs*, p. 58; Office National des Universités et Écoles Françaises, *Rapport du Directeur sur l'Activité de l'Office des Universités en 1926*, pp. 17-21; *London Times, Educational Supplement*, February 8, 1930, p. 58.

[58] League of Nations Institute of Intellectual Coöperation, *Bulletin for University Relations*, 1926, pp. 33-34.

[59] *Ibid.*, 1926, p. 136.

[60] *La Coöpération Intellectuelle*, February 1929, pp. 98-99.

stitutes in Prague (1920);[61] Tartu (Estonia, 1922);[62] Sofia (1922);[63] Zagreb and Ljubliana (1923-1924);[64] Warsaw (1925),[65] and Bucharest (1924).[66] An Institute of Italian culture was established in Bucharest in 1924,[67] and an English College in Budapest in 1925.[68] Likewise the Roumanian Institutes established by the Roumanian Government in Rome and Paris in 1921,[69] and the Hungarian colleges established by the Hungarian State in Berlin (1923),[70] Vienna (1924),[71] and Rome (1928)[72] serve as similar bonds of intellectual relations. The Roumanian institutes, however, are practically limited to research centers, and the Hungarian Colleges were established chiefly as hostels and advisory agencies for Hungarian students.

In 1926, the Italian Government officially recognized the importance of the institute abroad as a means of diffusing knowledge of Italian culture and developing intellectual relations with other nations. Anticipating the establishment of such institutions, it passed a special decree, December, 1926, encouraging and subsidizing institutes abroad which would be established in accordance with the regulations set

---

[61] League of Nations Committee on Intellectual Coöperation, *Bulletin of the International University Information Office*, 1925, pp. 165-166.

[62] League of Nations Institute of Intellectual Coöperation, *Bulletin for University Relations*, 1928, pp. 130-131.

[63] *Ibid.*, 1926, pp. 13-15.

[64] *Rapport sur l'Expansion Universitaire et Scientifique de la France et l'Activité de l'Office National des Universités en 1923 et 1924*, pp. 22-24.

[65] League of Nations Committee on Intellectual Coöperation, *Bulletin of the International University Information Office*, 1925, pp. 126, 308-310.

[66] *Ibid.*, 1924, p. 135.

[67] League of Nations Committee on Intellectual Coöperation, *Bulletin of the International University Information Office*, 1924, p. 135.

[68] *London Times, Educational Supplement*, September 12, 1925. Quoted, League of Nations Committee on Intellectual Coöperation, *Bulletin of the International University Information Office*, 1925, No. 6, pp. 312-313.

[69] League of Nations Institute of Intellectual Coöperation, *Bulletin for University Relations*, 1926, pp. 15-16; *Handbook of University Exchanges in Europe*, 1928, p. 82.

[70] *Bulletin for University Relations*, 1928, p. 208.

[71] *Ibid.*, p. 208.

[72] *Ibid.*, 1928, pp. 58, 208.

forth in the decree. These provisions were in particular these: (1) that the Institutes should be organized by the Ministry of Foreign Affairs in agreement with the Ministry of Finance; (2) that they should, preferably, be affiliated with the universities of the Italian Kingdom and form an integral part of them, in which case the Minister of Public Instruction or other competent person should be equally responsible for their organization; (3) that they should be staffed by eminent savants, preferably university professors, and should acquire suitable location and library facilities; (4) that, in addition to concerning themselves with the culture of the country of residence, they should also diffuse Italian culture abroad by means of instruction, public lectures, publications and translations, and intellectual interchanges; and (5) that they should be at the service of the Italian government to consider questions of cultural interest which it might submit, including exhibition of diverse forms of Italian art and regulation of Italian scholarships for foreign students.[73]

VACATION COURSES FOR FOREIGN STUDENTS

Especially in recent years vacation courses for foreigners have been encouraged by universities interested in attracting foreign students and by other organizations and institutions interested in the promotion of international contacts. The establishment of vacation schools for foreigners has been urged by the International Committee on Intellectual Cooperation, the Sub-Committee of Experts for the Instruction of Youth in the Existence and Aims of the League of Nations, the Meetings of the Directors of National University Offices, and the International Students Organizations.[74] Bulletins intended for international distribution have

---

[73] League of Nations Institute of Intellectual Coöperation, *Bulletin for University Relations*, 1928, No. 1, pp. 45-46.

[74] League of Nations International Committee on Intellectual Coöperation, *Minutes of the Second Session*, p. 34; *Recommendations of the Sub-*

published descriptions of such courses for the purpose of making them better known. In particular, the *Bulletin* of the League of Nations International University Office and the pamphlets published by the Central Office of the International Confederation of Students have performed this function.[75] Recently these publications have been superseded by the annual List of Holiday Courses in Europe (1928, 1929, 1930) compiled by the League of Nations Institute of Intellectual Coöperation.

European vacation schools organized for foreign students had their origin apparently in the last decade of the nineteenth century. In a communication to the International university Information Office of the Committee on Intellectual Coöperation in 1925, the University of Geneva claims to have initiated the European summer courses for foreign students when in 1892 a professor of its Faculty of Arts conducted during the summer a continuation of the practical course,"Seminaire de français moderne," founded during the previous year. This venture served as the model for the summer courses established within the next few years at the Universities of Lausanne, Neuchatel, and, later, Grenoble.[76] In the first few years of the existence of the summer school at Geneva, small notices were sent by the director to universities in Germany, Austria, Russia, and England, attracting annually some two hundred students.[77] The summer course in French language at the University of

Committee of Experts for the Instruction of Children and Youth in the Existence and Aims of the League of Nations, 1927, pp. 6, 8, recommendations 16, 17; *Minutes of the Eighth Session*, p. 84 (report of the Meeting of Directors of National University Offices, Recommendation V); International Confederation of Students, *Yearbook*, 1927-1928, pp. 59, 64.

[75] League of Nations Committee on Intellectual Coöperation, *Bulletin of the International University Information Office*, 1924, 1925; League of Nations Institute of Intellectual Coöperation, *Bulletin for University Relations*, 1926, 1928; International Confederation of Students, *Yearbook*, 1927-1928, pp. 19, 117, etc.; 1929, pp. 8, 9, 14, 81, 82.

[76] League of Nations Committee on Intellectual Coöperation, *Bulletin of the International University Information Office*, 1925, No. 6, pp. 290, 291.

[77] *Ibid.*, p. 290.

Lausanne began three years after the Geneva course was initiated and has been held regularly since.[78]

In 1897 the first annual summer courses for foreigners in France were initiated by the Alliance Française, in Paris,[79] and by the University of Grenoble.[80] The first summer school for foreigners in Spain was probably the course at Madrid, beginning in 1912, and organized annually since by the Junta para Ampliacion de Estudios.[81] In Italy probably the beginning was in the literature courses for foreigners at the Royal University of Florence in 1907.[82] Summer schools for foreigners in England were begun in 1904 at the University of London.[83] A few years later Oxford initiated biennial vacation courses,[84] and in 1925 the University of Cambridge conducted its first summer courses for foreigners.[85]

The rapid increase in popularity of the European summer school for foreigners is attested by the fact that the list published in *Holiday Courses in Europe* in 1930 names 118 summer courses expressly organized for foreign students or accessible to them. These are distributed in fourteen Euro-

[78] League of Nations Institute of Intellectual Coöperation, *Bulletin for University Relations*, 1926, p. 233.

[79] University of Paris, *Livret de l'Etudiant*, 1929-1930, p. 223.

[80] University of Grenoble, *Summer Vacation Courses*, 1930, p. 1.

[81] *La Coöpération Intellectuelle*, August, 1929, p. 483.

[82] In the list of Italian summer schools communicated to the International University Office of the League of Nations Committee on Intellectual Co-operation by the Italian University Office in 1925, the following are described and their dates of origin indicated: Florence, 1907; Siena, 1917; Naples, 1921; Perugia, 1921, Venice, 1923. (See *Bulletin of the International University Information Office*, 1925, No. 4-5, pp. 198-200.) A report of the Director of the Institute of International Education, New York, to the League of Nations Committee on Intellectual Coöperation, states that the first summer session of an Italian university in Rome was held in the summer of 1923 as a result of the coöperation of the Director of the Institute. (*Bulletin of the International University Information Office*, 1924, p. 129.)

[83] Universities Bureau of the British Empire, *Yearbook of the Universities of the Empire*, 1925, p. 109.

[84] *Ibid.*, p. 212.

[85] *Ibid.*, 1926, p. 64.

pean countries: Austria (6), Belgium (2), Denmark (3), France (23), Germany (25), Great Britain (21), Holland (3), Hungary (1), Italy (11), Jugoslavia (2), Portugal (1), Spain (10), Switzerland (10). A large number of them are of very brief duration, lasting less than one month; several are "semaines" of study, lasting only a few days or a week. Half of them, however, are from one to three months in duration, a few even longer.

Fourteen are particularly concerned with the study of international relations; eight are concerned with scientific studies, including three in the science of education. The others are courses of general culture, particularly courses in fine arts and literature and language designed to give foreign students, especially secondary teachers, a knowledge of the language and culture of the nation organizing the course.[86]

In America also interest has been manifested in the summer school for foreign students. In 1910 McGill University instituted courses in the French language for Canadian and United States students.[87] The first summer session of the University of Mexico was held in the summer of 1923, offering courses for foreign teachers and students of Spanish.[88] In Rio de Janeiro the first series of vacation courses were organized in 1929, chiefly for North Americans.[89]

The increasing sense of the importance of international university relations in advancing the interests of science and learning and in promoting international understanding is evident in the growth of private and organized interest in its favor within the last decade. The period since 1919 is marked by a phenomenal increase of private resources

[86] See League of Nations Institute of Intellectual Coöperation, *Holiday Courses in Europe*, 1930, pp. 4-47.

[87] League of Nations Committee on Intellectual Coöperation, *Bulletin of the International University Information Office*, 1925, No. 2, p. 9. These lapsed for eight years, because of the war, and reopened in 1922.

[88] *Ibid.*, 1924, p. 129.

[89] *La Coöpération Intellectuelle*, June, 1929, p. 359.

devoted to the encouragement of international university contacts or international studies; by the foundation of numerous societies and organizations to initiate or develop academic relations between two or many nations; by the growth of government interest in international university relations; and by the strengthening of national and international organizations for inter-university relations.

International student organization for constructive activity in the field of international student interests had only begun at the outbreak of the war. It has developed during the past decade into an organism for effective international coöperation in student interests. Similarly, national university offices to facilitate university contacts existed in few instances in the first decade of the twentieth century. Since 1919 the number has multiplied, and an organism for international coöperation among the several national offices has been effected. Also, very recently, effective organization for national and international coördination of international studies has been initiated.

As a result of official and voluntary interest in breaking down national intellectual isolation, definite accomplishment has been made in facilitating international interchange of students, establishing regular international interchange of professors, and developing opportunities for the study of national civilizations and international problems. Much of this activity has been based upon the conviction that international contacts which have something to offer for the advancement of science and learning are the most effective contacts for international conciliation, since they tend to foster mutual respect of nations, to encourage the sense of world unity, and to advance civilization. This conviction is particularly evident in the increase of research scholarships and professorial interchanges.

Much of the activity discussed above is based also upon the realization that world civilization is the sum of national cultures, and that the basis of international conciliation is not a supra-national culture but a mutual appreciation among nations of the several national civilizations, and an understanding of the international problems arising from the differences in these several civilizations. This conception explains the preference expressed for the coördination of national institutes of international relations rather than the "supra-national" international university. It also explains the increase in institutions, for promoting cultural relations between individual nations. While courses and chairs of foreign culture and institutes of national culture established in a foreign nation have undoubtedly in some instances propagandist significance and suggest political motives, the development of interest in such institutions has also at its basis genuine interest in the enrichment of national culture and the furthering of international conciliation. Properly conducted, these institutions constitute a practical means of cultural expansion and international *rapprochement.*

PART II

EFFORTS TO PROMOTE INTERNATIONAL UNDERSTANDING THROUGH THE LOWER SCHOOLS

CHAPTER V

ORGANIZATIONS PROMOTING INTERNATIONAL UNDERSTANDING THROUGH THE LOWER SCHOOLS

BEFORE THE World War the work of fostering an attitude of international friendship through the public schools had been undertaken chiefly through the activity of peace organizations. These enlisted the sympathy of teachers and educational organizations, in some instances developing special school organizations to encourage international friendships. In the period since the war attention of social and educational forces, both voluntary and official, has been directed with increased emphasis to programs of international conciliation in schools of all types.

EDUCATIONAL PROVISIONS WITH REFERENCE TO ETHNIC MINORITIES

A development in the period immediately following the war gave support to the principle of encouraging conciliation through the schools. This was the recognition of the educational rights of ethnic minorities. Germany made such provision in the Constitution of August 14, 1919. Article 148 of the Constitution reads:

"All schools shall inculcate moral education, civic sentiment, and personal and vocational efficiency in the spirit of German national culture and of international conciliation.

"In the instruction in public schools care shall be taken not to hurt the feelings of those of different opinion."[1]

---

[1] René Brunet, *The New German Constitution*, 1922, translated from the French by Joseph Gollomb, Article 148.

This unique article, coming from the German people so soon after the war, is especially significant in that it places in the constituent law of a great republic the idealism of the immediate post-war period.

Because of the creation of new countries after the World War and the consequent establishing of new international boundaries, there were scattered over the world many people who constituted ethnic minorities. These minorities have been protected to some extent in their desire for self-determination by treaties or declarations enforced by the Allied and Associated Powers, required by the League of Nations as a condition of membership in the League, or executed by two nations as a reciprocal measure.

This study is interested only in those parts of the minority treaties that deal with educational rights of the ethnic minorities. The treaty regarding minorities between the Allied and Associated Powers and Poland is typical of these treaties. The following articles of the treaty, dealing with education, may be cited as typical of the various treaty provisions for education:

"Article 8.—Polish nationals who belong to racial, religious, or linguistic minorities shall enjoy the same treatment and security in law and in fact as the other Polish nationals. In particular they shall have an equal right to establish, manage, and control at their own expense charitable, religious and social institutions, schools, and other educational establishments, with the right to use their own language and to exercise their religion freely therein.

"Article 9.—Poland will provide in the public educational system in towns and districts in which a considerable proportion of Polish nationals of other than Polish speech are residents adequate facilities for insuring that in the primary schools the instruction shall be given to the children of such Polish nationals through the medium of their own language. This provision shall not prevent the Polish Government from making the teaching of the Polish Language obligatory in the said schools.

In towns and districts where there is a considerable proportion of Polish nationals belonging to racial, and religious, and linguistic minorities, these minorities shall be assured an equitable share in the employment and application of the sums which may be provided out of public funds under the state, municipal, or other budget for educational, religious, or charitable purposes.

The provisions of this article shall apply to Polish citizens of German speech only in that part of Poland which was German territory on August 1, 1914.

"Article 10.—Educational committees appointed locally by the Jewish communities of Poland will, subject to the general control of the State, provide for the distribution of the proportional share of public funds allocated to Jewish schools in accordance with Article 9, and for the organization and management of these schools.

The provision of Article 9 concerning the use of language in schools shall apply to these schools.

"Article 12.—Poland agrees that the stipulations in the foregoing articles, as far as they affect persons belonging to racial, religious, or linguistic minorities, constitute obligations of international concern and shall be placed under the guarantee of the League of Nations. They shall not be modified without the assent of a majority of the Council of the League of Nations. The United States, the British Empire, France, Italy, and Japan hereby agree not to withhold their assent from any modification in these articles which is in due form assented to by a majority of the Council of the League of Nations.

Poland agrees that any member of the Council of the League of Nations shall have the right to bring to the attention of the Council any information, or any danger of infraction, of any of these obligations, and that the Council may thereupon take such action and give such direction as it may deem proper and effective in the circumstances.

Poland further agrees that any difference of opinion as to questions of law or fact arising out of these articles between the Polish Government and any one of the principal Allied and Associated Powers or any other Power, a member of the Council of the League of Nations, shall be held to be a dispute of an international character under Article 14 of the Covenant of the League of Nations. The Polish Government hereby consents that any such dispute shall, if the other party thereto demands, be referred to the Permanent Court of International Justice. The decision of the Permanent Court shall be final and shall have the same force and effect as an award under Article 13 of the Covenant."[2]

The second type of treaty mentioned above, usually referred to as a "Declaration," has been made by a number of nations as a condition of their entry into the League of Nations.[3] The League of Nations has made certain requirements regarding the status of ethnic groups in countries asking for admission to the League. This practice has further extended the protection of the League of Nations to minority groups. The Albanian agreement with the League of Nations is typical of this type of treaty or "Declaration." Its provisions for education are practically the same as those of the Polish treaty quoted above; the chief difference is that in the latter the phrase "the League of Nations" replaces the expression "Allied and Associated Powers" in the former.[4]

The third type of treaty mentioned above, a treaty between two nations, regarding minority ethnic groups, may be illustrated by the treaty between the Austrian Republic and the Czecho-Slovak Republic. This treaty, which is too long and involved to be quoted, permits the Austrian and the Czecholovakian ethnic minorities in the respective coun-

---

[2] *Publications de la Société des Nations, I. B. Minorités,* 1927, I. B. 2.
[3] *League of Nations Treaty Series,* Vol, IX, pp. 175-179; Vol. XXII, pp. 395-399.
[4] *League of Nations Treaty Series,* Vol. IX, pp. 175-179.

tries to maintain private schools, to use their native language, and to share, under certain conditions, state money.[5]

The significance of these treaties and "Declarations" is evident when the machinery of the League of Nations regarding the minority peoples is considered. Any state member of the League of Nations may suggest any subject for the consideration of the Council of the League,[6] and the minority group themselves have the right to submit petitions to the Council of the League of Nations. Through this machinery for registering complaints, the minorities have been able to secure and maintain protective measures concerning their educational interests in the lower schools.[7]

The significance of these treaties in international educational relations is fundamental. Each State, in living up to its treaty, must make educational laws compatible with its international engagements. These state laws accustom the citizens to respect the desires of people of different ethnic types. This in principle is a problem involved in international educational relations.

Up to 1927 seventeen countries and sections of countries had assumed educational obligations, similar to the ones pointed out above, towards ethnic minorities in their midst. These countries and sections of countries were Albania, Austria, Bulgaria, Czechoslovakia, Estonia, Finland, Germany, Greece, Hungary, Latvia, Lithuania, Memel, Poland, Roumania, Kingdom of the Serbs, Croats and Slovenes, Silesia, and Turkey.[8]

While the European world was adjusting itself by means

---

[5] *Ibid.*, Vol. III, pp. 216-219.

[6] See *Covenant of the League of Nations; Offial Journal of the League of Nations*, Vol. IV, p. 1293; Vol. VI, p. 876; Vol. IX, p. 1493.

[7] League of Nations, *Minutes of the Fiftieth Session of the Council*, 1928, pp. 854, 881, 882, 922, 924, 945, 946, 949, 950, 951. The International Association of League of Nations Societies has been very active in representing the cause of the minority peoples. See the *Bulletin* of this organization.

[8] *Publications de la Société des Nations*, I. B. 1927, I. B. 2.

of treaties during the immediate post-war period, pre-war voluntary efforts to teach international coöperation were revived and were augmented by post-war official and unofficial activity.

Of particular significance in the field of educational thought and activity during the past decade has been the accumulation of interest around the lower schools as a force in establishing a safe world order. This growth of interest has resulted naturally in international organization for evolving and directing among the several nations common programs of endeavor.

The forces that have been actively instrumental in placing increasing amounts of international instruction in the lower schools are similar to, or in many cases, identical with, those that operate in a similar capacity among higher schools and universities. The greatest difference between the activities in the two fields is due to the difference in supervision and control exercised over the higher and lower schools. While the higher schools and universities have a relatively free hand in content and method in teaching, the lower schools are generally more or less closely supervised. For this reason, development in international understanding in the lower schools has had to come largely by way of national or local governments and concerted action of teachers and school administrators. The governments have assumed one of two attitudes: sympathetic support, and even leadership, or a *laissez-faire* policy.

As most of the states of the world are more or less democratic politically, public opinion finds its way with public officials. A few international organizations and committees which have evolved from public opinion, and which in turn have served as coördinating or directing forces to influence public opinion, are especially significant in the field of international educational relations in the lower schools. These are the international federations of teachers, the League of

Nations, and certain organizations and committees established to extend through the public schools the influence of the League of Nations.

INTERNATIONAL FEDERATIONS OF TEACHERS AND OTHER EDUCATIONAL ORGANIZATIONS

International organization of teachers is to be found in the periodic educational congresses of general or special nature in the latter part of the nineteenth century and the first decade of the twentieth century. Before 1919 there existed two international federations of national associations of public school teachers. Of these one survived the period of the war. Since 1919, chiefly as a result of a growing sense of the importance to be attached to the public schools in preventing a future international catastrophe, more extensive federation of national associations of teachers of the several countries has taken place for the purpose of mutual coöperation in the improvement of teaching and in international conciliation.

International Bureau of National Associations of Secondary Teachers.—The International Bureau of National Associations of Secondary Teachers (Bureau International des Fédérations Nationales du Personnel de l'Enseignement Secondaire Public) had held one meeting before the World War. Its organization grew out of the International Education Congress held in Brussels in 1901, on the fiftieth anniversary of the initiation of the Belgian law on secondary education. At the Congress the formation of a permanent international organization of teachers was proposed.

The proposal, which at the time resulted only in an unanimous resolution in its favor, was again considered in the international congress of education held at Brussels in 1910 on the occasion of the International Exposition. At this time the Congress adopted the idea of an International Bureau and authorized a committee to act on suggestions concerning the Bureau set forth during the Congress. The result was that the International Bureau of National Associations of Secondary Teachers was established May 26, 1912, at Brussels, and held its first session August, 1913. In 1929 the organization was composed of sixteen affiliated national federations uniting 40,000 secondary teachers, five national societies, and seven associated international groups counting several millions of adherents.[9]

On January 20, 1927, the International Bureau was officially installed in the Palais-Royal, the seat of the League of Nations Institute of Intellectual Coöperation. This signified in a material and tangible way that the Organization had been accepted as a support by the League of Nations.[10] It also served to place the International Bureau in constant touch with the Liaison Committee of the Major International Associations ("Comité d'Entente"), which the International Bureau had joined in 1926,[11] and which was also established in the Palais-Royal under the auspices of the Institute of Intellectual Coöperation. Membership in the "Comité d'Entente" greatly extended the liaison activities of the International Bureau by facilitating personal and corporate collaboration.[12]

In a review of its work during the decade following the war, the International Bureau of National Associations of Secondary Teachers points out that its activities have covered four points: (1) the investigation of conditions and regulations governing secondary teachers in the several countries, conducted with a view to advancing the position of secondary teachers; (2) the improvement of secondary teaching in all its branches; (3) propaganda on behalf of the League of Nations in the schools; (4) the encouragement

---

[9] Bureau International des Fédérations Nationales du Personnel de l'Enseignement Secondaire Public, *Bulletin International,* June, 1929, No. 25, p. 19.

[10] *Ibid.,* p. 23.   [11] *Ibid.,* p. 19.   [12] See below, pp. 123-127.

of international school correspondence and exchange.[13]

In connection with the second point the Bureau has adopted the principle that the war and post-war conditions have demonstrated the necessity of creating a new attitude; and it has urged that the teaching of history and geography and the reform of school-books are of particular importance in creating an attitude conducive to world harmony. Similarly, its interest in international correspondence and exchange and in the League of Nations has been based upon the need of developing the spirit of international conciliation through the schools.

Since its foundation in 1912 the Bureau has stated as one of its aims the international interchange of young people. Since the war it has coöperated with the work of the Junior Red Cross to extend international correspondence among school children.[14] In its support of the League of Nations it has worked to familiarize teachers and pupils with the aims and activity of the League. In this connection in 1926 it assisted in conducting an international essay contest among secondary teachers on the subject of the League. The following year it published extracts from the prize essays in a pamphlet designed to acquaint teachers and pupils with the origin, aims, and work of the League.[15]

International Federation of Teachers' Associations.—A second international federation of teachers associations has been especially active in efforts to promote international good-will through the lower schools. This is the Inter-

---

[13] Bureau International des Fédérations Nationales du Personnel de l'Enseignement Secondaire Public, *Bulletin International*, June, 1929, No. 25, pp. 17-34, "Dix Années de Vie Internationale (1919-1920)."

[14] Bureau International des Fédérations Nationales du Personnel de l'Enseignement Secondaire Public, *Bulletin International*, June, 1929, No. 25, "Dix Années de Vie Internationale (1919-1929)," pp. 24-25; November, 1929, No. 26, pp. 124-132.

[15] Bureau International des Fédérations d'Enseignement Secondaire, Fascicule No. 2, *Les Origines, Le But, l'Oeuvre de la Société des Nations, 1927*; *Bulletin International*, November, 1929, pp. 110-111.

national Federation of Teachers' Associations (Fédération Internationale des Associations d'Instituteurs). This federation had its origin in a protest against school textbooks likely to develop or perpetuate international ill-will. In 1926 the Syndicat National of France was engaged in an active campaign against school books containing passages opposed to the spirit of international conciliation.[16] As a result of its interest in the schools as a medium for promoting peace, it invited the General Association of German Teachers (Deutsche Lehrerverein) to work in common with it for international *rapprochement*. The two organizations were joined by the Association of Teachers of The Netherlands (Bond Van Nederlandsche Onderwijzers). Representatives of the three teachers' organizations met in Danzig, June 25, 1926, and by agreement instituted the International Federation of Teachers' Associations.[17]

In 1929, the International Federation of Teachers' Associations comprised twenty-one national organizations of teachers representing seventeen countries and over 550,000 individual members.[18] This Federation, like the International Bureau of National Associations of Secondary Teachers, has its secretariat at the International Institute of Intellectual Coöperation in Paris, and is thus in touch with the Institute. The Federation is also represented on the "Comité d'Entente" and thus collaborates with the major international associations that deal with international intellectual coöperation.[19]

The statutes of the Federation state as the program of the organization (1) education of children for lasting peace between nations and (2) the raising of the level of the

---

[16] See below, pp. 195-197.

[17] Fédération Internationale des Associations d'Instituteurs, *Bulletin* No. 1, July, 1927, p. 2; No. 3, March, 1928, p. 16.

[18] *Ibid.*, No. 7, June, 1927, pp. 3-4.

[19] *Ibid.*, No. 1, July, 1927, pp. 6, 12.

teaching profession and popular education. In executing the former aim the Federation has encouraged (1) the study of textbooks for the purpose of eliminating errors and unjust interpretations of foreign peoples, (2) the teaching of history and kindred subjects in a spirit conducive to international understanding, (3) the international interchange of teachers and pupils, and (4) the instruction of pupils in the aims and organization of the League of Nations.[20]

The corporate members of the Federation have been active in applying the principles of the international organization in their respective countries.[21] The English National Union of Teachers with its membership of 125,000 teachers, the Deutscher Lehrerverein of Germany with a membership of 154,000 teachers, and the Syndicat National des Institutrices et Instituteurs de France et des Colonies with 78,000 members,[22] because of the former political relationships of their countries, occupy a key position relative to international *rapprochement* through the lower schools. Active cooperation between teachers of these nations, which have been traditional political and economic antagonists, is evidence of a genuine belief in the objects of the organization.

World Federation of Education Associations.—A third international federation of education associations is the World Federation of Education Associations. In 1921 the president of Czechoslovakia sent a request to the National Education Association of the United States at its meeting in Des Moines, asking the Association to invite the nations of the world to a conference. The Association referred the request to its permanent Foreign Relations Committee, in-

---

[20] Fédération Internationale des Associations d'Instituteurs, *Bulletin* No. 1, 1927, pp. 9, 11; No. 2, 1927, pp. 3-4; No. 4, 1928, pp. 8-11; No. 5, 1928, pp. 2-13, 40; No. 6, 1929, pp. 42-50; No. 7, 1929, pp. 19-23; No. 8, 1929, pp. 1-11, 28.

[21] See the reports of the national Associations, *Bulletin,* Nos. 1-9.

[22] Fédération Internationale des Associations d'Instituteurs, *Bulletin* No. 7, 1929, p. 3.

structing it to prepare for such a conference in 1923.[23]

Accordingly, the chairman of the committee sent invitations to ministers of education of all foreign countries, to prominent educators, and to all educational associations whose names could be secured. The purpose of the conference was "to afford opportunity for educators of the various nations to agree upon principles and plans for the promotion of good-will and mutual understanding which are universal in their application and which can be adopted as a definite program to be carried out in the schools throughout the world."[24] In response, there assembled at San Francisco on June 28, 1923, groups representing various governments, more than thirty distinct racial groups, and over fifty national divisions, as well as teachers associations and other educational organizations.[25]

Article II of the Constitution stated the objects of the Federation thus: "The objects of this Federation shall be to secure international coöperation in educational enterprises, to foster the dissemination of information concerning education in all its forms among the nations and peoples, to cultivate international good-will, and promote the interests of peace throughout the world."[26]

In 1929 the World Federation of Education Associations was composed of twenty-two national organizations of teachers as full members and twenty-nine organizations as associated members, both representing about twenty different countries.[27] The Federation maintains offices in Europe and

---

[23] *World Conference on Education, June 28 to July 6, 1923,* p. 3, published by the National Education Association; *N. E. A. Addresses and Proceedings,* 1922, "Report of Resolutions Committee," Vol. 60, p. 46.

[24] *World Conference on Education, June 28 to July 6, 1923,* p. 3.

[25] See the secretary's report of the conference, *World Conference on Education,* p. 3.

[26] *World Conference on Education,* p. 16.

[27] World Federation of Education Associations, *Proceedings of the Second Biennial Conference,* 1927, pp. 807-809; Fédération Internationale des Associations d'Instituteurs, *Bulletin* No. 8, 1929, pp. 30-31.

America and employs a field representative.[28] It is also a member of the "Comité d'Entente."[29]

The program of the World Federation of Education Associations is extensive, including specific points in the several departments of education from the pre-school to university departments, and in addition a number of points of general interest, such as moral education, health, thrift, illiteracy, etc.[30] Its program of international education relations centers largely about the Herman-Jordan Peace Plan, five points of which the Federation adopted as a working basis at its first biennial congress.[31] These points are (1) education for peace; (2) the teaching of history (including investigation of textbooks); (3) international relations of youth (including the consideration of international sports, international school correspondence, international exchange of students and teachers, international scholarships and exchange professorships, international essay contests, etc.); (4) a study of the question of military preparedness; (5) a study of methods and instruments used to settle international disputes by peaceful means (including The Hague Court of arbitration and the League of Nations).[32]

Proposals for definite coöperation among these three international educational associations culminated in a plan advanced at the Geneva meeting of the World Federation of Education Associations. Representatives of the World Federation of Education Associations, the International Federation of Teachers' Associations, and the International Bureau of National Associations of Secondary Teachers reduced to writing principles of a union of the three fed-

[28] *Ibid.*, pp. 809-810.
[29] Comité d'Entente des Grandes Associations Internationales, *Liste des Membres*, C. E./12(2)/1929.
[30] See the *Proceedings* of the first and second biennial conferences, 1925, 1927.
[31] World Federation of Education Associations, *Proceedings of the Second Biennial Conference*, 1927, pp. 194-201.
[32] *Ibid.*, pp. 201-295.

erations, to be submitted for ratification to the executive committees of the three organizations.[33]

The International Bureau of Education.—A fourth international organization important in the field of international education relations is the International Bureau of Education. It differs from the three organizations discussed above in that its membership does not consist primarily of teachers' organizations and is not so internationally representative. The Bureau was established in 1925, at Geneva, and has as members the Republic and Canton of Geneva, the States of Ecuador and Spain, the Polish Ministry of Public Education and Worship, and the University Institute of Educational Science of Geneva, each of which makes a minimum annual contribution of 10,000 Swiss francs. Subject to the approval of the Council of the Bureau, any government, public or private institution, or international organization may become a member by contributing a like sum each year.[34]

The activities of the Bureau are set forth in Article II of its statutes:

"The object of the International Bureau of Education is to act as an information center for all matters relating to education.

"The Bureau, which aims to promote international coöperation, maintains a completely neutral position with regard to national, political and religious questions. As an organ of information and investigation, its work is carried on in a strictly scientific and objective spirit. Its activities are of two kinds: (1) the collection of information relating to public and private education; (2) the initiation of scientific investigations within its spheres and the undertaking of statistical enquiries or those

---

[33] Bureau International des Fédérations Nationales du Personnel de l'Enseignement Secondaire Public, *Bulletin International*, No. 26, 1929, pp. 171-177.

[34] International Bureau of Education, *Bulletin*, year IV, No. 1, January, 1930, second page of cover.

relating to experimental projects. The results of these efforts are made available to educators."[85]

In addition to making known internationally the educational movements in the various countries the Bureau conducts investigations and sponsors projects designed to foster international good-will through the schools. Recently its bulletin has devoted a special section ("Education for Peace and International Collaboration") to information about peace education in the several nations. Since 1925 the Bureau has been engaged in the compilation of information about children's literature contributing to international good-will.[36] In 1927 it sponsored an international Congress devoted to Peace through the Schools.[37] Since 1928 it has conducted a special international summer course for teachers on the subject "How to Make the League of Nations Known and to Develop the Spirit of International Coöperation."[38]

THE LEAGUE OF NATIONS AND THE COMITÉ D'ENTENTE

In 1932 the League of Nations assumed an active interest in teaching children and youth the ideals and work of the League of Nations and in developing in them the spirit of international coöperation. This movement on the part of the League of Nations and its committees will be discussed below.[39] An indirect result of the movement was the organization of the "Comité d'Entente," which has as its *raison d'être* the teaching of children and youth to

---

[85] International Bureau of Education, *Bulletin*, year IV, No. 1, January, 1930, second page of cover.

[36] International Bureau of Education, *Children's Books and International Good-Will, Report and Book List*, 1929, 80 pp.

[37] The Congress, designated "La Paix par l'École," was held at Prague April 16-20, 1927. See the report of the proceedings edited by Pierre Bovet: *La Paix par l'École, travaux de la Conférence Internationale tenue à Prague du 16 au 20 avril 192.* Published by International Bureau of Education, 1927, 150 pp.

[38] International Bureau of Education, *Bulletin*, Year IV, No. 1, January, 1930, p. 7.

[39] See below, pp. 133 ff.

regard international coöperation as the normal method of conducting world affairs.[40]

As a result of the inquiry made by the Secretariat of the League of Nations relative to what was being done to teach children and youth that international coöperation is the normal way of conducting world affairs, many unofficial organizations responded, including the International Bureau of National Associations of Secondary Teachers, the World Federation of Education Associations, and two international organizations mentioned in Chapter III which have been active in international education relations in both lower and higher schools: the International Federation of League of Nations Societies and the International Federation of University Women.[41]

At the International Institute of Intellectual Coöperation (the League of Nations institution that deals primarily with unofficial organizations) there developed a feeling that something should be done to coördinate the work of these organizations which have the instruction of youth in international understanding as a part of their interest. As a result of informal discussions at the Institute among representatives of the interested organizations and the Director of the Institute, a meeting of the representatives of sixteen international association[42] formed on December 15, 1925, the Comité

[40] League of Nations International Institute of Intellectual Coöperation, *Neuvième Réunion des Délégués des États auprès de l'Institut International de Coöpération Intellectuelle, March 20, 1929, Annexe No. 1, au procès-verbal,* "Comité d'Entente des Grandes Associations Internationales," pp. 4-5.

[41] See League of Nations Document, A. 10, 1925, XII; Document, A. 10(a), 1925, XII.

[42] League of Nations International Institute of Intellectual Coöperation, *Neuvième Réunion des Délégués des États, Annexe No. 1 au procès-verbal,* "Comité d'Entente des Grandes Associations Internationales," p. 2. The Associations represented were World Alliance of Young Women's Christian Associations; World Alliance of Young Men's Christian Associations; International Catholic Girls' Society; International Board of Boy Scouts; International Board of National Associations of Secondary School Teachers; International Confederation of Students; International Council

d'Entente des Grandes Associations Internationales (Coordinating Committee of Major International Associations for teaching peace in the schools).[43]

In 1929 the "Comité d'Entente" included twenty-four organizations as full members and four as correspondent members. The Institute provides the secretariat of the Committee, and a member of the Institute serves as its president.[44]

Immediately after its formation the "Comité d'Entente," in keeping with the spirit that created it, set about its work of coördination. On March 18, 1926, it issued a Declaration, or set of principles, which has been so generally adopted by great international organizations that its repetition here seems desirable. It reads:

"To enable the child to strike roots in its natural setting of family and homeland remains today, as in the past, the first principle of all sound education.

". . . It is indeed a permanent necessity but perhaps more urgent on the morrow of the calamity which has shaken the whole of mankind, broken down so many established social settings, and left so many sources of disturbance in men's spirits as well as in the material order.

"Alike for its own balance and for the general well-being, the child, who is the citizen of tomorrow, should be brought up to the idea of duty and should learn that it will have to fulfill actively all its obligations to its family, to its companions, to its village, town or city and to its country. At the same time the instruction given to children should not stop there. They should be taught that this essential solidarity neither can nor

---

of Women; International Council of Girl Guides; Carnegie Foundation for International Peace; Junior Red Cross; International Federation of University Women; World Federation of Educational Associations; International University Federation for the League of Nations; Catholic Union of International Studies; International Union of Associations for the League of Nations; Conference Universelle du Christianisme Pratique; World Federation of Christian Students.

[43] International Association of League of Nations Societies, *Bulletin* No. 4, 1926, pp. 45-46.

[44] Comité d'Entente, *Liste des Membres*, C. E./16(2)/1929, pp. 1, 2.

should be confined within the national boundaries; for there exists between peoples as between the various members of any one society a community of rights and duties as well as an actual and ever-increasing interdependence.

"Children should learn especially that civilization is the common work of all peoples—including those who, in the course of centuries have been the most bitter enemies; and that, notwithstanding inevitable differences, it is out of the feeling for this common heritage and this desire to preserve and to develop it, that the League of Nations was born.

"Therefore in the home, and from the earliest days in which they receive their education together, alike in the school and in the other groups in which the work of the school is continued, children should be taught courtesy to strangers and inspired with curiosity to know their habits and to understand their thoughts.

"To illustrate, in this spirit, the teachings of geography and history, of literature, of science and the arts, the teacher should be able to find invaluable help in books, pictures.

"Ways and means should be studied to secure the utmost effect from these several instruments of instruction and to adapt them to the changing needs of primary and secondary education.

"Similarly, travel and periods of study in foreign lands, athletic gatherings, international correspondence among school children (including exchange of letters, drawings, handicraft, etc.), should be encouraged so as to put the young people of each country in the most direct contact possible with those of other countries.

"International exchanges of such kind, if supplemented and continued into the higher branches of education and carried out also in every other kind of training, by means of contact between pupils, apprentices, students and teachers, will have the effect of leading young people into habits of intellectual cooperation and thus supporting the League of Nations.

"In thus paving the way to mutual knowledge and understanding between peoples, education (in the home, in the school and in continuation courses) and training (literary, scientific, technical or professional) will effectively help in the organization of peace."[45]

The value of a coördinating committee for the unofficial organizations at the Institute in Paris has led to efforts to organize national liaison committees to coördinate all national forces directed toward realizing the aims of the international committee. This development is going forward, and the national coördinating committees have been charged by the international committee to establish relationships with the national committees of Intellectual Coöperation.[46]

This development is giving each country an organization in the form of a coördinating committee, that will represent a unified national opinion, and bring official and unofficial opinion into closer relationships. This network of relationships is bringing to the Institute of Intellectual Coöperation at Paris the corporate opinion of the world. The Institute, a member of the official group of international organizations, receives the unofficial opinion of the world and introduces

---

[45] International Association of League of Nation's Societies, *Tenth Plenary Congress, Proceedings and Resolutions,* 1926, pp. 48-49.

[46] League of Nations Institute of Intellectual Coöperation, *Neuvième Réunion des D légués des États auprès de l'Institut International de Coopération Intellectuelle, Annexe No. 1, au procès-verbal,* 1929, "Comité d'Entente des Grandes Associations Internationales," p. 6. Concerning the number of National Liaison Committees, a report of the meeting of the International Federation of League of Nations Societies in 1929 contains the following statement: "The Secretary commented [on] a report which he had prepared on this subject in accordance with a decision of the Prague meeting of the Committee. From this it appeared that liaison between the Education Committees of League of Nations Societies and the national sections of organizations represented in the International Liaison Committee which met in the Institute of Intellectual Coöperation existed in some 18 countries. The liaison was effected in some cases by *ad hoc* committees, but more generally through the education committees of League of Nations Societies coöpting the nominees of other organizations working for peace through the schools or through the adult education movement." (International Federations of League of Nations Societies, *Bulletin,* 1929, No. II, March-April, pp. 6-7.)

it into official channels from where it goes, in varying degrees, into official orders of the various countries.

A Motivating Purpose

A pedagogical doctrine which motivates the activity of the organizations discussed above is that to establish a safe world order the public schools must train the youth of the world in the spirit of international conciliation. This is to be done by teaching that international coöperation is the normal method of conducting world affairs and by developing a new mental attitude conducive to peace and opposed to war.

The international federations of educational organizations and the League of Nations Committee mentioned above have either been founded on this doctrine or have adopted it as an essential element of their program.

Upon reorganizing after the war the International Bureau of National Associations of Secondary School Teachers recognized the development of a new attitude as an essential part of the task of educators. This conviction, entertained by the Bureau from the beginning of its post-war activity, found expression in 1926 in a declaration adopted at the Congress of Geneva, which asserts the necessity of a new mental attitude if the ideal of peace is to be maintained and urges the responsibility of teachers above governments in this respect. The declaration reads:

"It is our belief that the work of Peace, such as the League of Nations is endeavoring to realize, will meet with constant difficulties unless educators—in particular, teachers in secondary schools, who train the intellectual élite of nations—shall have modified the attitude of peoples and have created in the world the new spirit which present humanity demands. It is our belief that educational reforms will be in danger of producing no results if imposed by governmental decrees. We believe that the aspirations of teachers and their professional experiences, finding expression in their congresses, should instigate the preparation of official texts."[47]

Likewise the World Federation of Education Associations in adopting the Herman-Jordan Plan accepted the following statement of the principle:

"As the history of the future shall be written in the schools of today, it is vital that the teacher lay in the minds of children the foundation of a sane and wholesome background from which to develop international amity and intelligent abhorrence of war."[48]

Also the International Federation of Teachers' Associations in its foundation statutes defined itself as an association to prepare for peace through the coöperation of peoples[49] and stated as the first principle of its program the doctrine that lasting peace has as its fundamental condition the education of the children of the world for international understanding:

"Program: (1) The International Federation of Teachers Associations holds that a lasting peace depends fundamentally upon the education of children of all countries for international understanding."[50]

In 1924, at its fourth session the attention of the League of Nations International Committee on Intellectual Coöpera-

[47] Bureau International des Fédérations d'Enseignement Secondaire, *Bulletin Internationale*, No. 25, June, 1929, "Dix Années de Vie Internationale (1919-1929)," pp. 31-32 (translated by the author).

[48] World Federation of Education Associations, *Proceedings of the Second Bienniel Conference*, 1927, pp. 194-195.

[49] Fédération Internationale des Association d'Instituteurs, *Bulletin* No. 1, July, 1927, p. 11.

"1.—Titre. Fédération Internationale des Associations d'Instituteurs, pour etablir la collaboration pédagogique et pour préparer la paix par la coöpération des peuples."

[50] Fédération Internationale des Association d'Instituteurs, *Bulletin* No. 1, July, 1927, p. 11 (translated by the author).

tion was called to the importance of the public school in a program of lasting peace. During this session the Argentine representative, M. Lugones, mentioned the fact that the Committee had devoted itself almost exclusively to European questions, and proposed to introduce a plan which "had a more general and even a more human interest," namely a plan for the same object that the League itself pursued— the avoidance of war.

Perhaps the most disturbing conclusion that could be drawn as a result of war, M. Lugones stated, was that public conscience was reconciled to a state of war. "A new public conscience must, therefore, be developed." The Committee, he urges, "should endeavor to bring about a change in the conception of public education, not only in the universities, but, above all, in the secondary schools and training schools for teachers." This development of a new public conscience might be effected through new attitudes in teaching history, geography, mathematics, the classics, and political economy.[51]

In the same year the Assembly of the League of Nations called attention of the States Members of the League to the "fundamental importance . . . of training the younger generation to regard international coöperation as the normal method of conducting world affairs," and to the desirability of further developing and encouraging efforts to educate the youth of all countries "in the ideals of peace and solidarity." The recommendations of the Sub-Committee of Experts summoned to consider this question, while emphasizing the importance of other influences, lay particular stress upon instruction in the public school and coöperation of voluntary organizations with the schools.

As for the practical application of this principle, a survey of the development and activity of the several organizations

---

[51] League of Nations International Committee on Intellectual Coöperation, *Minutes of Fourth Session,* 1924, p. 37.

concerned with international *rapprochement* through the lower schools reveals four points of common interest. These are (1) instruction in the existence and aims of the League of Nations; (2) an impartial or conciliatory approach to the teaching of history and kindred subjects; (3) a campaign against books containing elements of chauvinism or hatred; (4) direct and indirect contact of pupils (international exchanges and international correspondence). In the following discussion it is proposed to trace the interest in these points and indicate some of the results of this interest.

CHAPTER VI

TEACHING THE LEAGUE OF NATIONS IN THE SCHOOLS

THE IDEALS embodied in the Covenant of the League of Nations offered a field of instruction involving the principles underlying the statements above. This field, common to many nations, has been generally accepted as a hopeful medium for teaching the ideals of international coöperation and developing an attitude conducive to world peace.

Early Voluntary Initiative.—Among the suggestions for international coöperation which were forwarded by the Secretariat of the League to the International Committee on Intellectual Coöperation at its initial session was the proposal of the German Pacifist Students' Union (Berlin, August 5, 1921) that the League of Nations should invite States Members of the League to include instruction with regard to the League of Nations in their school curricula.[1] It was not until 1923, however, that the question of teaching the League in the schools was officially brought before States Members of the League. Meanwhile interest in the question had been stimulated in the several states from various quarters.

The education and propaganda committees of the several national League of Nations Societies in most instances from their beginning sought to enlist interest of school authorities and teachers in teaching the League in the schools. Moreover, educational authorities in at least two countries had before 1923 taken more or less effective steps to bring the League of Nations before the schools of the respective countries.

---

[1] League of Nations International Committee on Intellectual Coöperation, *Minutes of the First Session,* p. 44. Item No. 35.

On January 13, 1921, a little less than a month after the meeting of the first Assembly of the League, the Central Welsh Board, the authority for Intermediate Education in Wales, issued a circular to the head-teachers of the secondary schools suggesting instruction in the League in the secondary schools of Wales. The suggestion had no binding executive force, but it stimulated interest, and was the forerunner of active steps to encourage the teaching of the League and the spirit of international conciliation in the primary and secondary schools of Wales.[2] In the same year official interest was manifested in France. In August, 1921, the French Minister of Education, M. Léon Bérard, included the League of Nations in the syllabuses of civic instruction in the higher primary schools and normal schools of France.[3]

The Action of the League of Nations

The Assembly Resolutions.—In 1923 the question assumed international significance. In that year the League of Nations Assembly launched an active interest in teaching children and youth the principles of international coöperation. This interest has continued to grow and has become the nucleus about which the activities of other movements have centered. In September, 1923, Dame Edith Lyttelton, representative to the League of Nations Assembly from the British Empire, introduced in the Fourth Assembly of the League of

---

[2] See the report of Gwilym Davies, Director of the Advisory Education Committee of the Welsh League of Nations Union, League of Nations, *Educational Survey,* January, 1930, Vol. I, No. 2, pp. 92-100. The circular of the Board reads thus:

"The Board thinks it very desirable that the object and importance of the League of Nations should be brought to the notice of pupils in secondary schools. The subject may be most appropriately dealt with in connection with the history lessons and by occasional addresses at the opening of school. Very valuable suggestions are contained in the enclosed memorandum issued by the League of Nations Union, which the Board hopes will receive your most sympathetic consideration. The Board also suggests that a whole or half-day be devoted to a Peace Celebration on November 11th of each year." (P. 92.)

[3] League of Nations Document, A. 10, 1925, XII, p. 15.

9

Nations, a resolution to encourage instruction of children and youth in the existence and aims of the League of Nations. The resolution, adopted by the Assembly, made the following appeal:

"The Assembly urges the Governments of the States Members to arrange that the children and youth in their respective countries, where such teaching is not given, be made aware of the existence and aims of the League of Nations and the terms of the Covenant."[4]

Since the Assembly of the League of Nations was composed of representatives from more than fifty nations, the above resolution gave substantial publicity to the cause of teaching children and youth the principles of international coöperation. To the States Members of the League, the resolution was an official appeal. Sufficient sympathy was shown for the principles represented in the resolution that the Assembly, at its next meeting, September, 1924, passed the following resolution:

"Being convinced of the fundamental importance of familiarizing young people throughout the world with the principles and work of the League of Nations, and of training the younger generation to regard international coöperation as the normal method of conducting world affairs;

"In view of the resolutions adopted by the Fourth Assembly regarding the encouragement of contact between young people of different nationalities,[5] and concerning the instruction of youth in the ideals of the League of Nations:

"[The Assembly] is of the opinion that further steps should be taken to promote these objects;

"And therefore instructs the Secretariat to investigate the means by which efforts to promote contact and to educate the

---

[4] League of Nations, *Official Journal, Records of the Fourth Assembly, Plenary Meetings,* 1923, p. 109. For the second part of the resolution, proposed by the Chilean delegate, see below, p 203.

[5] See below, p. 203.

youth of all countries in the ideals of world peace and solidarity may be further developed and coördinated, and to furnish a report to the Sixth Assembly."[6]

The above resolution was of particular value in the field of training children and youth to view international coöperation as the normal method of conducting world affairs in that it initiated a movement that was soon to become increasingly organized and effective. The movement was the more organized and effective in that the Secretariat of the League of Nations was officially directed to inquire of the States Members of the League of Nations as to their activity regarding instruction of children and youth in the ideals of the League of Nations. Where the resolution of the Fourth Assembly (September, 1923) only asked the States Members to teach the rising generation the principles of international coöperation, the resolution of the Fifth Assembly (September, 1924) not only recommended that children and youth be taught that international coöperation is the normal method of conducting world affairs, but requested that governments report their progress in this matter to the League of Nations.

The efforts of the Secretariat to carry out the instruction of the Fifth Assembly concerning teaching to youth "ideals of world peace and solidarity" resulted in two reports of the Secretariat, compiled from material sent to the Secretariat by states and non-official organizations, describing what they were doing to carry out the provisions of the resolution of the Fifth Assembly quoted above. Forty-three states members of the League, one state not a member of the League, and fourteen non-official organizations sent reports to the Secretariat.[7] Among these reports a few were

---

[6] League of Nations, *Official Journal, Records of the Fifth Assembly, Plenary Meetings*, 1924, p. 143.

[7] League of Nations Documents A. 10, XII, 1925; A. 10(a) XII, 1925. The Associations replying were these: American School Citizenship League; Boy Scouts International Bureau; International Council of Girl Guides

mere acknowledgments of the Secretariat's inquiry. The great majority of the reports were favorable, and many indicated with varying degrees of precision what was being done in the respective countries.

The Sub-Committee of Experts.—After considering these reports the Sixth Assembly in September, 1925, passed the following resolution:

"The Assembly notes with satisfaction that most of the States Members of the League have acted on the resolutions adopted by the Fifth Assembly on the subject of instruction of youth in the ideals of the League of Nations and the encouragement of contact between young people of different nationalities. It expresses its satisfaction with the report prepared by the Secretary-General on this subject and considers that the report should be regarded as a first stage.

"It (the Assembly) therefore invites the Council:

(a) To consider the possibility of requesting all States Members of the League of Nations and non-member States to keep the Secretary-General informed of the progress made in their respective countries as regards the various points mentioned in the report and to forward to the Secretary-General all publications on this subject as soon as they appear.

(b) To instruct the Secretary-General to collect the information mentioned above. This information should be communicated from time to time to State Members of the League and to other States interested in the question.

(c) To forward the Secretary-General's report, together with the proposals submitted by the Chilean, Haitian, Polish and Uruguayan delegations,[8] to the Committee on Intellectual

---

Association; International Council of Women; International Federation of League of Nations Unions; International Federation of Secondary School Teachers; International Moral Education Congress; International Secretariat of the Catholic Youth; Universal Union of Jewish Youth; Junior Red Cross; International Inter-Scholar Correspondence; Y. M. C. A.; Y. W. C. A.; World Federation of Education Associations.

[8] These four proposals were presented to the Assembly that passed the above resolution. The proposals are as follows:

Chilean.—"The Assembly, considering that the education of the youth

Coöperation and to request it to consider the possibility of summoning a sub-committee of experts to consider the best methods of coördinating all official efforts designed to familiarize young people throughout the world with the principles and work of the League of Nations and to train the younger generation to regard international coöperation as the normal method of conducting world affairs."[9]

On September 26, 1925 the Council of the League of Nations passed a resolution accepting this decision of the

---

in a spirit of concord and international peace constitutes one of the most powerful safeguards of the work of the League of Nations,

And considering that the school can most effectively help to create a new spirit in future generations:

Invites the council:

To submit to careful consideration the replies already received by the Secretariat concerning the instruction of children and youth in the principles of peace and the ideals of the League of Nations, with a view to convening, if necessary, a conference of school teachers to study the best means of creating a spirit of world fraternity in schools." (League of Nations Document A. 83, 1925, XII.)

Haitian.—"With a view to moral disarmament, the League of Nations invites its members to undertake as far as possible the revision of their history manuals so as gradually to reduce the number of pages devoted to military events and especially those passages in which wars or conquests are justified and held up for admiration." (*Ibid.*)

Polish.—"In view of the profound influence which literature has on the education of the great mass of readers in general and of the youth in particular, the Second Committee (of the Assembly) invites the Committee on Intellectual Coöperation to consider the question of spreading universally the works of great literary artistic value of all nations whose spirit corresponds to the principles and aims of the League of Nations." (*Ibid.*)

Uruguayan.—"The Council is requested to authorize the Committee on Intellectual Coöperation to appoint a qualified person or persons to prepare documents for use as models or examples for the guidance of members of the teaching profession in explaining the organization, the aims, and the work of the League of Nations. After being examined and approved by the Committee on Intellectual Coöperation, these documents will be submitted to the Council of the League of Nations.

When the documents in question have received final approval, the Committee on Intellectual Coöperation will be asked to consider the best means of bringing them to the notice of such governments as may so request, and private educational establishments throughout the world." (*Ibid.*)

[9] League of Nations, *Records of the Sixth Assembly, Plenary Meetings,* 1925, p. 105.

Assembly.[10] Acting on these resolutions the Committee on Intellectual Coöperation, concluding that the League, though it had no compulsory powers, had the right to take steps to make itself better known, recommended the convening of a Committee of Experts composed of members experienced in educational work to consider how to make the League known and to develop the spirit of international coöperation.[11] Accordingly the Council of the League, in consultation with the chairman of the Committee on Intellectual Coöperation, appointed the Sub-Committee of Experts in 1926.[12]

The Sub-Committee of Experts at its meetings in 1926 and 1927[13] issued a series of recommendations and sugges-

---

[10] League of Nations Document A. 26, 1927, XII, p. 2.

[11] Ibid.

[12] Ibid. Following is a list of the names and positions of the Sub-Committee of Experts; Members of the Committee on Intellectual Coöperation: Professor Gilbert Murray (British), M. J. Destrée (Belgian), M. J. Casares (Spanish). Experts: M. Luis A. Baralt (Cuban), Professor and author of works on pedagogy; S. N. Chaturvedi, M.A. (India), "Licentiate of Teaching" at the University Allahabad, Director of a secondary school at Lucknow, sent to England by his government to study western systems of education; Madame Dreyfus-Barney (French), Vice President of the Peace Section of the International Council of Women, liaison officer between the International Council of Women and the International Institute of Intellectual Coöperation; Professor Giuseppe Gallavresi, Professor of History at the University of Milan, author of historical works and assessor for education at Milan; Professor Bogdan Gavrilovitch, former Rector of the University of Belgrade; Professor C. C. Kiritzesco, Director of Secondary Education at the Roumanian Ministry of Education; M. Rosset, Director of Primary Education of the Ministry of Education of France (to replace M. Lapie, Rector of the University of Paris, who died in 1926); Professor Peter Munch, author of several history manuals, former Minister, delegate of Denmark to the League of Nations; Professor Inazo Nitobe, Professor at the Imperial University of Tokyo, member of the Japanese Imperial Academy, member of the House of Peers; M. Arturo Pardo Correa, assistant professor of Pedagogy at the University of Santiago, Chile; Dr. W. Schellberg, counsellor of the Ministry of Education of Prussia. Representing the International Labor Office: M. Eastman, chief of the third section of the Research Division. Representing the International Institute of Intellectual Coöperation: Professor A. Simmern, Deputy Director. (League of Nations Document, C. I. C. I., 190, pp. 7-8.)

[13] In 1927 the recommendations of 1926 were slightly revised in content and in form in the light of replies received from governments and inter-

tions for teaching the ideals and activities of the League of Nations in the schools and developing the spirit of international coöperation. In 1927 and 1928 two further reports were compiled, comprising the replies of governments and non-official organizations concerning the application of the recommendations of the Assembly and the Sub-Committee of Experts.[14]

Information Centers.—Upon the recommendation of the Sub-Committee, approved by the Assembly in September, 1927, an educational Information Center was created with offices at Paris and Geneva, to make available to governments and interested organizations the progress of the work covered by the recommendations.[15] In 1928, with a view to making more generally available the information accumulated at the two centers, the Assembly provided funds for the publication, twice yearly, of the *Educational Survey*, to

---

national organizations to which they were submitted. (League of Nations Document A. 26, 1927, XII, p. 3.)

[14] League of Nations Document A. 30, 1928, XII, p. 1, Section A.

[15] The recommendation of the Sub-Committee reads:

"21. An official center should be established where information concerning the progress of the work covered by these recommendations would be available. (This office might have two sections, one established at Geneva, at the Secretariat of the International Committee on Intellectual Coöperation, the other at Paris, at the Institute of Intellectual Coöperation; the former would deal more especially with the action taken by Governments and official organizations, while the latter would keep in touch with the activities of private associations.)" (League of Nations International Committee on Intellectual Coöperation, Document 190, p. 21.)

These were organized in the course of the year 1927-1928. (League of Nations, *Official Journal, Special Supplement, No. 54, Records of the Eighth Ordinary Session of the Assembly, Plenary Meetings, Text of the Debates*, 1927, p. 134; League of Nations International Committee on Intellectual Coöperation, Document 190, pp. 32, 35.) One works with the League of Nations Secretariat at Geneva and receives the communications from States Members of the League; the other works with the Institute of Intellectual Coöperation and the "Comite d'Entente" at Paris, and receives the communications from non-official organizations. These two committees work together by exchanging duplicate records of the information gathered by their offices and collaborate in the publication of the *Educational Survey*. (League of Nations, *Educational Survey*, 1929, Vol. I, No. 1, p. 6.

consist of official documents and reports of authorities closely in touch with the progress of the points covered by the recommendations of the Sub-Committee of Experts.[16]

The reports presented in the League's *Educational Survey* and the series of reports compiled by the Secretariat of the League of Nations in response to the resolutions of the Assembly and the recommendations of the Experts constitute a fund of considerable detail concerning the activity of nations in behalf of teaching the League and its principles in the schools of the world.

Recommendations of the Sub-Committee of Experts.— The recommendations of the Sub-Committee of Experts, so far as they apply to instruction of children in the lower schools, cover four points: (1) the executive measures by which instruction in the League might be made general in all schools of a nation; (2) the place of the League in educational systems; (3) the material aids (books, films, etc.) which should furnish a basis of this instruction; (4) special preparation of teachers. The last point will be discussed later under the subject of the preparation of teachers to give instruction in the League.

Executive Machinery.—The resolutions of the Assembly concerning the instruction of children in the principles of the League called for official action. "Governments" were requested "to arrange that the children and youth . . . be made aware" of the existence and aims of the League. At least formal compliance with this request by issuing ministerial decrees was relatively easy in countries with centralized education departments under direct government supervision. This has been the most usual procedure in meeting the request of the Assembly, as will be noted later.

The Sub-Committee of Experts, realizing the necessity of voluntary coöperation on the part of schools and teach-

---

[16] League of Nations International Committee on Intellectual Coöperation, *Minutes of the Eleventh Session*, 1929, p. 73.

ers, recommended a different procedure. It suggested the convening of national educational conferences:

"In order to adapt these general recommendations to the particular needs of each country and to ensure the harmonious coöperation between the administrative authorities, teachers and voluntary associations, a national conference should be called in each, country by the Government, in consultation, as far as possible, with the National Committees on Intellectual Coöperation."[17]

This recommendation, as will be pointed out below, has not met with general acceptance.

In another section the recommendations called attention to the help which voluntary associations might confer in stimulating and supplementing the activity of educational authorities.[18] Both in countries in which instruction in the League has been declared compulsory by governmental authorities, and in countries whose educational program is not directed by a central governmental authority, the work of voluntary organizations has been largely responsible for the progress of the League in the schools. Governments and voluntary organizations have worked together in maintaining the actual program of instruction in the lower schools. The governments usually do their part by authorizing or ordering certain programs, or, at least, by acquiescing in whatever plans are pursued by the voluntary organizations. The voluntary organizations, in most cases, are largely responsible for the earliest supporting literature, teacher helps, and active public support.

The Position of the League in the Education of Youth.— Concerning the nature and method of instruction in the aims and existence of the League, the Sub-Committee of Experts made the following recommendations:

---

[17] League of Nations Document A. 26, 1927, XII, p. 8.
[18] League of Nations Document A. 26, 1927, XII, pp. 5-6, Section 11.

"All children and young people should, before completing their formal education, receive instruction suitable to their stage of intellectual development, in the aims and achievements of the League of Nations and, generally speaking, in the development of international coöperation. In view of the important part played by women in forming the character of the young, care should be taken in those countries where the education of boys and girls is different to see that this instruction is given to girls as well as boys.

"This instruction should begin in the primary school and should be continued to as late a stage as possible in the general education of the pupil.

"The exact place and time to be allotted to this instruction in the curriculum should be left to the decision of those normally responsible for such questions; but it should probably be correlated with the lessons in geography, history or civics or with moral instruction. The prominence given to the various aspects of the work of the League and the International Labour Organization will naturally vary according to the type of school.

"Provision for this instruction should be made for those who leave the ordinary schools for special schools of all types —agricultural, technical, commercial, military or naval—so that it may be continued to as late a stage as possible."[19]

In addition to regular curricular instruction, the Sub-Committee suggested further means of teaching the League or stimulating interest in it. It recommended that competent authorities might appoint special days for bringing the League before the attention of pupils, institute competitions on the League, place questions on the League on examinations, and facilitate the work of voluntary associations among school children out of school hours. These recommendations read:

"Competent authorities might further encourage the study of this subject in schools. . . .

---

[19] League of Nations Document A. 26, 1927, XII, p. 4.

"By appointing every year a day or half-day on which by suitable methods, definite ideas regarding the aims and achievements of the League would be impressed upon the minds of the pupils. This day might be made the occasion of a special celebration or even of a holiday, the reasons being explained by the teachers of the various classes;

"By instituting a competition open to the pupils in a particular school, district or country for the best essay on a subject connected with the League of Nations; . . .

"By facilitating the work of private associations among young people out of school hours;

"By arranging that, in examinations, questions on the League should be set whenever practicable."[20]

Materials of Instruction.—Concerning material to be used in this instruction the report of the Committee contains the following recommendation:

"The teacher should, if possible, have at his disposal to help him in his work:

(a) Literature giving an account of the principles and history of the League of Nations and its work;

(b) Material for visual instruction (pictorial illustrations, e.g., 'Images type Epinal,' lantern slides, cinematograph films, etc.). The slides and films for purposes of instruction concerning the existence and aims of the League of Nations should be exempt from customs duty. Governments might be asked to consider favorably the recommendations put forward by the International Cinematograph Congress of 1926;

(c) Reading matter for children of various ages."[21]

Further, under the division of *Books* the following recommendations are made:

"A special reference book giving an account of the work of the League of Nations and the International Labour Or-

---

[20] League of Nations Document A. 26, 1927, XII, pp. 4-5.
[21] *Ibid.*, p. 4.

ganization for the use of teachers should be prepared, which will probably assume a different form in various countries. The Secretary-General of the League of Nations should be asked to undertake, in coöperation with experts of his own choice, the preparation of that part of the reference book which deals with the organization and aims of the League of Nations. In any case all teachers who give this instruction should be provided with a copy of the Covenant and the 'International Charter of Labour,' with short explanations and concise bibliography.

"The Secretary-General might also be asked to examine the possibility of issuing periodical summaries specially prepared for the teaching profession and of forwarding them regularly to the leading educational reviews and journals and educational authorities.

"Scientific and learned societies, as well as authors and publishers of school-books, might be asked to see, in so far as the matter is within their province, that the League of Nations is given its due place. The history and work of the League should be treated adequately in all relevant text-books. It might be possible in some cases to reward meritorious action by means of honorary distinctions or prizes."[22]

The Assembly Resolutions and the Sub-Committee's Recommendations in Operation in the Several Nations

Only one country, Great Britain, had in 1930 complied with the recommendation to convene a national conference.[23] On June 18, 1927 the President of the Board of Education,

---

[22] League of Nations Document A. 26, 1927, XII, p. 6.

[23] League of Nations International Committee on Intellectual Coöperation, *Minutes of the Tenth Session,* 1928, p. 14. See also the report of replies of members of the International Federation of League of Nations Societies to question 6 ("National Education Conference—Experts' Recommendation No. 19. What steps have been taken with the Ministry of Education and the National Committee on Intellectual Coöperation?"), Mimeographed report, Madrid, May, 1929. The replies of Belgium, France, and Bulgaria indicated that the question is on the agenda of the Associations of the League of Nations Societies in these countries.

the Secretary of State for Scotland, and the Minister of
Education for Northern Ireland convened at Westminster
a conference of Representatives of Local Education Authorities in England and Wales, Scotland, and North Ireland for the purpose of seeing what could be done to comply
with the recommendations of the Sub-Committee of Experts.

Prior to this meeting, at the request of the President of
the Board of Education, representatives of eight important
British Associations of teachers prepared a statement of
what they considered the views of the teaching profession
concerning the place of the League in the schools of Britain.
This memorandum, *The Schools of Britain and the Peace of
the World*, commonly known as the *Declaration of the Teaching Profession*, endorsed the main issues of the Committee
of Experts; set forth opinions and suggestions concerning
the place and usefulness of teaching the League in the schools
and teacher training colleges; outlined the application of
League principles to the teaching of history, geography,
world civilization and patriotism; and approved extra-
curricular activities fostering interest in the League and
efforts to bring the League before the attention of teachers.
In conclusion, in the following statement it urged further
investigations by a national committee:

"We would urge that the matters discussed in this
memorandum—indeed, the whole question of the teaching of
the League of Nations in British schools of all types—should
be further, and as fully as possible, explored by a National
Committee including representatives of the administrative
authorities, the teaching profession and the League of Nations
Union."[24]

In response to the suggestion of the association of the
Education Committees, in June, 1927, the Annual Conference
in London set up a Joint Committee of Enquiry, composed

---

[24] British League of Nations Union, *Teachers and World Peace*, 1929,
pp. 15-16.

of representatives of educational authorities, the League of Nations Union, and six representative associations of teachers.[25] This committee in its report in 1929 made the following statement of the progress of League teaching in the schools of Great Britain:

"Twenty-one Authorities are found to have issued definite instructions 'that the aims and objects of the League of Nations should form a regular part of the instruction given to the children before they leave school.' Eighty-seven other Authorities have issued a circular recommending Head Teachers to apply for literature and either to attend meetings on the subject held in the neighborhood or to arrange special meetings. One hundred and forty-five Authorities give particulars of the way in which instruction about the League is, in their schools, included in the syllabus of other subjects, especially of History and Geography. In a few instances it is taken as a separate subject.

"One hundred and sixty-four Authorities report observance of Armistice Day and Empire Day with special reference to the League, and one hundred and fifty express their appreciation of occasional lectures by specialist speakers; some of these Authorities express a desire for more frequent visits of this kind. It is also clear from the replies that the League of Nations Union films have now been shown, with great effect to schools in many parts of the country."[26]

Because of the fact that in Great Britain no central authority dictates the material and nature of instruction, the extent to which the Assembly resolution and the Sub-Committee's recommendations were put into effect was necessarily dependent upon voluntary action of educational authorities and teachers. In States Members of the League in which somewhat similar freedom exists in school systems

---

[25] *Ibid.*, pp. 16-17.
[26] *Education and the League of Nations, Being a Report of the Joint Committee of Enquiry into the Teaching of the Aims and Achievements of the League of Nations,* London, 1929, pp. 14-15.

the question of instruction in the League has remained a matter of local concern, without the stimulus of a national conference.

In Switzerland, where education questions are within the competence of the cantons, the Federal Department of the Interior directed the attention of the Conference of Cantonal Directors of Education to the resolutions of the Assembly. At a meeting on October 20, 1924, the Conference of Educators appointed a committee of five to study the question and submit a report to the 1925 Conference. It was decided that the Cantonal Governments must decide for themselves the nature of their compliance with the Assembly resolutions.[27]

In 1929 twelve of the twenty-five cantons, in reply to an inquiry, stated that they had instituted teaching of the League in the public schools. A description of the program of instruction in the Canton of Neuchatel, which prescribes instruction in primary and secondary schools, throws some light upon the manner in which this canton goes into the matter.

"In primary schools," according to a report of a teacher at the École Normale of Le Locle, "the teaching mainly takes the form of special lessons on occasions such as the big meetings of the League (the Assembly, the Council, the International Labour Conference, meetings of the Health Committee, the Committee on Intellectual Coöperation, etc.). Lessons are also given on peace, the interdependence of nations, etc.

"In the secondary schools, lessons on the League form part of the curriculum in three subjects: (1) in civics, after the study of communal, cantonal and federal institutions, a number of lessons are given providing instruction on all the organs of the League, with charts and photographs of the Council and the Assembly, the present and the projected buildings, maps, etc., together with the main features of its work during

---

[27] League of Nations Document A. 10(a), 1925, XII, p. 9; League of Nations, *Educational Survey*, 1929, Vol. I, No. 1, p. 110.

the ten years of its existence; (2) in world history a study is made of the League's origin and work after instruction on the main phases of the war, its causes, war conditions, etc., and the League's future prospect; (3) in geography mention is made, in regard to each country, whether it is a Member of the League or not, its date of entry, whether it is a Member of the Council or the seat of an international organization, etc."[28]

In Germany, where the separate states determine matters of Education for themselves with more or less centralization in the case of each state, a Prussian decree in 1927 was the initial step in introducing instruction in the League into the German schools, according to a statement of the Councillor of the Prussian Ministry of Science, Art, and Education. On May 28, 1927, the Prussian Minister of Science, Art, and Education, issued the following decree:

"The instructions to be observed in framing the curricula of the higher schools in Prussia, the regulations regarding the intermediate schools in Prussia, and the instructions relating to the curricula for the upper classes of elementary schools already contain numerous directions with reference to the teaching of the League of Nations questions. Now that Germany is a member of the League, however, the schools should go still further and give full instruction in the character, work and aims of that institution. It is essential from the very nature of the League that instruction in this field should be inspired alike by an appreciation of the dignity of our own nation, by understanding and respect for foreign nations, and by a realization of the fact that the development of each individual nation is promoted by membership of an all embracing community. I direct that the subject should be given a suitable place in the programme of work and be dealt with in the above spirit in the higher classes of the elementary schools, in the intermediate and higher schools, in training colleges for teach-

---

[28] League of Nations, *Educational Survey*, 1930, Vol. I, No. 2, pp. 111-112.

ers, and in the training of candidates for the higher posts in the educational service."[29]

Speaking of the results of this decree in 1929, Dr. Wilhelm Schellberg, Councillor of the Prussian Ministry of Science, Art, and Education, said that it had given a strong and lasting impulse to the study of the subject in Prussian schools of every kind. Quoting from many reports made at the request of the Educational Administration he advances evidence that German teachers, even in occupied areas, were in 1929 actively interested in teaching the ideals of the League.

The position of the instruction in the curricula varied. In particular the reports advocated presenting the League not as an objective study of bare facts, but in connection with such subjects as religion, languages, history, geography and even natural sciences.[30] Dr. Schellberg ends his review with this observation:

"Even a cursory examination of the numerous reports must convince the most skeptical critic that the idea of introducing instruction regarding the League in the curricula of schools of all kinds is making very real progress. The authors of the reports are quite right when they point out that there has as yet been no time for tangible results to be achieved. Yet much has been done through the very fact that teachers as a body have been interested in the problem, that they recognize its importance, that they have seriously taken it up and are endeavoring to get a true understanding of it."[31]

Canada likewise lacks central education authority. Certain provinces, however, have made League teaching compulsory. A statement of Professor T. H. Soward, of the Department of History, University of British Columbia, describes the situation thus:

[29] League of Nations, *Educational Survey*, 1929, Vol. I, No. 1, p. 106.
[30] *Ibid.*, p. 112.
[31] *Ibid.*, p. 116.

"According to a survey made in 1928 by the League of Nations Societies in Canada, seven of the provinces make the League an object of study in their schools, some in secondary schools, some in both elementary and secondary schools. The two other provinces provide facilities for instructing the teacher and leave the use of his knowledge to his discretion. A valuable medium of information of League matters is a pamphlet prepared by educational experts for the League of Nations Society entitled 'A New World or the League of Nations.' Since its publication, 25,000 copies have been distributed, chiefly among teachers and students. In Nova Scotia, each high school student receives a copy from the Education Department. Manitoba requires every student in the second grade of high school to read it. British Columbia presents a copy to every student in junior matriculation grade (the junior matriculation examination admits students to the first year of the university), to every teacher of history in high schools and to every teacher in the senior grades of public school. British Columbia has also created a valuable precedent in making the League of Nations the subject of an obligatory question upon the junior matriculation examination in history. In June, 1929, some 2,100 students were required to answer the following questions, to which was assigned one quarter of the value of the paper:

" 'Account for the creation of the League of Nations. Do you think it has justified its existence? Give reasons for your answer.' "[32]

In Member States of the League maintaining a central educational authority with large powers in matters of curricula the Assembly resolution has been generally met by the issuing of a ministerial decree formally declaring League teaching compulsory at a certain point in the curricula. In many instances the history course is specified as the point of inclusion; frequently civics or geography are specified

---

[32] League of Nations, *Educational Survey*, 1930, Vol. I, No. 2, pp. 66-67. See also League of Nations Document A. 30, 1928, XII, pp. 3-4; A. 15, 1926, XII, p. 8.

also; occasionally law, religion, or morals is mentioned. In addition, certain voluntary procedures are recommended or sanctioned.

In France, it was pointed out above, as early as August, 1921, the Minister of Education included the League of Nations in the syllabuses of civics instruction for higher primary schools (second year) and history courses (third year). In the new programs of secondary education published in 1923 instruction in the League of Nations and international relations was included in philosophy and history syllabuses.[33] Since 1923 the Minister of Education has regularly addressed circulars to the teachers before November 11, requesting that on this day attention of school children be called to the principles of the League of Nations.

Recently the custom of celebrating a school "Peace Week" or a "League of Nations Week" has been voluntarily adopted in a number of elementary schools in France. This week, which centers around the celebration of armistice or goodwill day (May 18, the date of the first Hague Conference), is devoted to the teaching of peace through "reading, enrichment of vocabulary, French composition, history, geography, ethics and civics, arithmetic even, and singing, drawing and recitation."[34] Professor Max Hebert, director of the Teachers' Training College for the Côtes-du-Nord, Saint-Brieuc, France, writing in the League of Nations *Educational Survey*, January, 1930, gives an outline of a series of talks based upon the ethics items in the program for the week. These talks deal with justice, interdependence, havoc of war, war a crime, war orphans, Briand-Kellogg Pact, international campaign against tuberculosis and cancer, international coöperation in dealing with various epidemics, and the League of Nations.[35]

Belgium, since 1925, has made lessons on the League of

---

[33] League of Nations Document A. 10, 1925, XII, p. 15.
[34] League of Nations, *Educational Survey*, 1930, Vol. I, No. 2, p. 15.
[35] *Ibid.*, pp. 14–20.

Nations compulsory in history courses in secondary schools under governmental control[86] and has recommended that on memorable dates all teachers talk to their pupils on the efforts of the League to secure lasting peace. The Belgian government has, moreover, published syllabuses and synopses of lessons containing sufficient information to enable the teachers to conduct lessons on the League.[87]

In January, 1924, the Department of Education of Luxembourg enjoined upon the heads of schools, including industrial and commercial schools, to introduce into the modern history course lessons explaining the organization and aims of the League of Nations.[88] Likewise The Netherlands reported in 1926 that the inspectors had drawn the attention of the secondary schools to the fact that the teaching of history includes the origin, the foundation and the work of the League of Nations. A knowledge of these subjects is required by the leaving examination of the secondary schools of The Netherlands.[89]

Concerning instruction in the League in Austria, the Austrian Government reported in 1924:

"Official teaching in the higher classes of the primary schools (Volks-Schulen) and the higher primary and secondary schools (Burgher und Mittelschulen) are required to devote part of their lessons on history, constitutional law and, when occasion offers, geography, to the importance and working of the League of Nations."[40]

In 1928 the Hungarian Minister wrote,

"I am directed by my Government to inform you that children and young persons in Hungary are given instruction in

[86] Catholic schools in Belgium are not under the direction of governmental authority.

[87] League of Nations Document A. 10, 1925, XII, pp. 9-14. See also League of Nations, *Educational Survey*, 1930, Vol. I, No. 2, p. 62.

[88] League of Nations Document A. 10, 1925, XII, p. 22.

[89] League of Nations Document A. 15, 1926, XII, p. 11.

[40] League of Nations Document A. 10, 1925, XII, p. 9.

the existence and aims of the League of Nations by our teaching staffs in primary and secondary schools, . . . as a part of the courses in History and Geography."[41]

In Czechoslovakia a law of July 13, 1922, introduced a course on "Civic Instruction and Education" into the primary and higher primary schools. The syllabus for the course, issued in April, 1923, included instruction on the League. This instruction is given children of the sixth to the eighth school year in primary schools and children in all school years in the special courses given in higher primary schools, particularly under the headings "Humanity," "Mutual Relations between States," and "International Peace."[42]

The Minister of Education of Czechoslovakia also, on March 6, 1926, issued a Ministerial Decree providing for an annual half-hour lesson on peace in the schools of the nation, the League of Nations being suggested as a natural choice of subject. The decree, having called attention to the world movement in favor of peace after the war, culminating in the League of Nations, continues:

"On the basis of this fundamental conception of the League, most of the educational, religious and other organizations in all countries are endeavoring to awaken interest in the peace movement among all classes of the population.

"It is therefore indispensable that this tendency should be energetically encouraged in this country also. In this respect the schools have a most important duty to fulfill. In view of similar action taken in other countries, I am issuing instructions to the effect that in primary, higher primary, secondary and training schools, including training courses for apprentices, a lesson lasting half an hour should be devoted each year to acquainting pupils with the peace movement in civilized countries; this lesson should be given on March 28th, the anni-

---

[41] League of Nations Document A. 30, 1928, XII, p. 6.
[42] League of Nations Document A. 10, 1925, XII, p. 15.

versary of the birth of Jean Amos Komensky, or on March 27th if March 28th happens to be a Sunday. This lesson should be arranged as local circumstances permit, either for all the classes together or each class separately during the ordinary lessons. In the primary schools, only pupils in the higher classes are to attend this lesson.

"Although the subject of the lesson is left to the choice of the master in charge, the latter should in no case fail to mention, in connection with the history of the peace movement in general and the aims of the League of Nations in particular, the peaceful tendencies which have always been in evidence in the history of Czechoslovak civilization."[43]

Poland, which like Czechoslovakia was given sovereign status by the countries that evolved the League of Nations, expects to perpetuate the ideal of the League by teaching its principles in the schools of the Republic. Polish primary children are taught about the League of Nations, President Wilson's policy (the 13th of his 14 points), and the Treaty of Versailles in connection with the last period of Polish national history, the restoration of Poland. In the secondary schools the syllabus of the course on universal history has since 1925 been revised to include greater mention of the League.[44]

A number of Baltic countries have replied in similar terms. Norway has introduced instruction in the League in both her elementary and secondary schools in history, reading, and composition.[45] The Swedish government stated in 1926 that, generally, League of Nations principles were taught in all Swedish schools, correlated with lessons in history and civics.[46] Instruction begins in the highest form of the primary school, and is continued in the highest form of the "realskola" and the highest form of the gymnasium. A

[43] League of Nations Document A. 15, 1926, XII, p. 9.
[44] League of Nations, *Educational Survey*, 1929, Vol. I, No. 1, pp. 125-128; League of Nations Document A. 15, 1926, XII, p. 12.
[45] League of Nations, *Educational Survey*, 1929, Vol. I, No. 1, pp. 122-124.
[46] *Ibid.*, pp. 129-131.

circular forwarded in 1925 by the Danish Minister of Education to all school directors asked that, in addition to the teaching of the League which formed part of the history syllabus in the lycées and preparatory schools, special talks on the League be given in the primary and higher schools each year on the date of the opening of the Assembly.[47]

In 1925 Latvia reported to the League Secretariat that the Minister of Education, in compliance with the Assembly resolution, had recommended to the heads of primary and secondary schools that instruction on the League of Nations be given in history lessons in all secondary and commercial schools and in the upper classes of the primary schools.[48] In 1927 the government of Lithuania informed the Secretariat that Lithuania proposed to instruct all headmasters and teachers to refer in their history lessons to the work and aims of the League.[49]

A 1928 report from Finland reads as follows:

"From February 25, 1925, onwards, on which date the Finnish Board of Education circularized the headmasters of all primary schools asking them to take steps to bring the existence and aims of the League of Nations and the articles of the Covenant to the attention of children and youth, such instruction has each year become more general in the lycées and primary schools and also in the higher public and technical schools, high schools for the people and workers' colleges. . . .

"It is also taught in the course of religious instruction and geography lessons."[50]

In 1926 the Director of Political Affairs of Estonia stated,

"I am instructed by the Minister to inform you that in Estonia the aims of the League of Nations are explained to

---

[47] League of Nations Document A. 10(a), 1925, XII, pp. 6-7.

[48] League of Nations Document A. 15, 1926, XII, p. 11.

[49] League of Nations International Committee on Intellectual Coöperation, Document 190, p. 42.

[50] League of Nations Document A. 30, 1928, XII, p. 5.

the children during lessons on civics both in the primary and secondary schools. The curricula of the latter include a special subject called 'League of Nations.' "[51]

The Education Department of Albania reported in 1926 that it had "introduced into the curricula of the elementary and secondary schools special courses for the purpose of imbuing the youth of Albania with the lofty ideals of the League of Nations."[52] In 1927 a report from Italy showed that some teaching concerning the League of Nations was given in the elementary and secondary schools in connection with geography and history.[53]

In 1925 the Japanese government reported that instruction in the League of Nations was given to primary and secondary students through the course on morals. Because of the lack of qualifications of the primary teachers, the report stated, the instruction in primary grades was not very complete, but in the secondary school, text-books in history and geography contained chapters on the League of Nations. The interest of the teaching personnel was stimulated by the activities of the Japanese League of Nations Union.[54]

A statement sent in 1923 by the Minister of Education of Uruguay to the Minister of Foreign Affairs of his country stated that the Congress of Professors of Secondary and Primary Education of Uruguay had requested "the inclusion of the study of the constitution, aims, and work of the League of Nations in the program of civil instruction, which is obligatory in the fourth year of secondary education." This act was followed in 1925 by an order from the Minister of Foreign Affairs which recommended that the Minister of Education introduce instruction and propaganda

---

[51] League of Nations Document A. 15, 1926, XII, p. 9.
[52] Ibid., A. 15, 1926, XII, p. 6.
[53] League of Nations International Committee on Intellectual Coöperation, Document 190, 1927, p. 72.
[54] League of Nations Document A. 10, 1925, XII, p. 20.

regarding the League of Nations in the schools.[55]

In 1924 the Minister of Education of Haiti wrote to the League Secretariat as follows:

"I have taken the necessary steps to have introduced in the secondary schools and schools of law of the Republic, by professors of civic instruction, international law and constitutional law, a course which will include instruction regarding the development of the basic ideas which led to the creation of the League.

"The Department will shortly add to the programme of civic instruction special chapters devoted to the League of Nations."[56]

In New Zealand, according to the following report in the *Educational Survey* of the League of Nations, the teaching of the League is definitely provided for:

"The first mention of the League comes in the standard V. course. After the Napoleonic and great wars, which were described as 'two attempts to secure world-power,' the Treaty of Versailles, the League of Nations, and the Kellogg Pact are laid down for treatment. This is one of the nine sections in the year's course.

"In standard VI mention is made of the humanitarian and social work of the League, while in standard VII which at present scarcely exists, where there is provided a fairly comprehensive treatment of outstanding world movements and personages from 1603 onwards, we find mention of the League and the Mandate System among 'foreign movements affecting the British Empire.'

"It will be seen, then, that practically every child in the Dominion—for very few do not go through the primary schools—should hear at least something of the League, though in many cases it may be a very inadequate something.[57]

---

[55] League of Nations Document A. 10, 1925, XII, p. 24.
[56] *Ibid.*, p. 18.
[57] League of Nations, *Educational Survey*, 1929, Vol. I, No. 1, pp. 120-121.

Also in the new history syllabus directions for teaching history place emphasis on the League and its principles.[58]

Other replies, without specifying the method in which the League has been included in the curricula, have indicated that official decrees have stipulated that instruction shall be given in the schools. Thus the Roumanian Minister wrote to the League Secretariat in July, 1927:

"I have the honor to inform you that, as a further mark of its unshakable faith in the League of Nations, the Royal Government has decided that instruction shall be given regarding the aims, methods and future of the League throughout the whole Kingdom."[59]

Brazil, in 1925, requested the subdivisions of the Republic to "instruct all teachers in all the primary schools of the country to include in their syllabuses lectures not only on the existence of the League of Nations but also on the nature of its work, its mission and the great services which it has already rendered to civilization."[60] In the same year the Persian Government replied to the Secretariat's inquiry regarding the teaching of the League of Nations that instruction had been issued to the effect that Persian youth in higher and secondary schools should receive instruction on the League and the Covenant.[61]

In addition, a number of other countries replied to the Assembly resolution and the recommendations of the Sub-Committee of Experts more indefinitely to the effect that the necessary steps were being taken to comply with the request or that some effort would be made in that direction.[62]

---

[58] See below, p. 177.

[59] League of Nations International Committee on Intellectual Coöperation, Document 190, p. 43.

[60] League of Nations Document A. 10, 1925, XII, p. 14.

[61] *Ibid.*, p. 23.

[62] China (League of Nations Document A. 19, 1925, XII, p. 15); Siam (League of Nations International Committee on Intellectual Coöperation, Document 190, p. 44); Panama (League of Nations Document A. 10, 1925,

The United States has, of course, taken no official action on the resolutions of the Assembly or the recommendations of the Sub-Committee of Experts. Partisans of the League, however, have exerted influence on the schools through voluntary associations. Two nation-wide organizations have been especially active in placing League principles in the lower schools of the nation; the League of Nations Association and the American School Citizenship League.

The League of Nations Association has freely distributed printed material on the League of Nations, and much of it has reached the pupils in the lower schools. In particular, the Association has sponsored an annual competitive examination based upon the League. Sometimes whole classes participated in the contest, the local teacher sending the two best papers to the National Committee. Some teachers are planning to offer special courses on the League, others spend several weeks on teaching the League in history courses. The number of schools registering and the number of individual participants have substantially increased each year. Also the quality of the papers offered has improved.[63] For the third competition, March, 1929, 1,146 high schools registered, representing every state in the United States. The fourth competition, March, 1930, extended to 6,967 high schools.[64] The first prize in each instance has been a trip to Geneva and a first hand study of the League.

XII, p. 23); Cuba (League of Nations Committee on Intellectual Coöperation, Document 190, 1927, p. 58); Australia (League of Nations Document A. 19, 1925, XII, p. 9); Jugoslavia (League of Nations International Committee on Intellectual Coöperation, Document 190, 1927, pp. 79-80); Bolivia (League of Nations Document A. 19, 1925, XII, p. 14); India (League of Nations International Committee on Intellectual Coöperation, Document 190, 1927, pp. 69-71); Greece (League of Nations Document A. 19, 1925, XII, p. 18); South Africa (League of Nations Document A. 30, 1928, XII, p. 2).

[63] Report of the International Education Committee of the League of Nations Association, League of Nations, *Educational Survey*, 1929, Vol. I, No. 1, pp. 136-146.

[64] *La Coöpération Intellectuelle*, April, 1930, p. 163.

A very similar program that has obtained like results has been supported by the American School Citizenship League.[65]

LEAGUE LITERATURE IN THE SCHOOLS

The question of teaching the League of Nations in the schools called attention to the lack of information easily available to teachers and pupils. In the suggestions of the Sub-Committee of Experts in 1926 it was recommended in the passages quoted above that the Secretary-General of the League should coöperate in the publication of a special reference work on the organization and aims of the League and that greater attention be given to the need of text-books containing material on the League. This suggestion had already been put forward in 1922 by the International Federation of League of Nations Societies, in a communication to the Secretariat of the League.[66]

In 1928 the Council and the Assembly complied with Article 12 of the Sub-Committee's recommendations by authorizing the publication of a handbook for teachers. Accordingly, a handbook prepared by the Secretary-General of the League of Nations with expert assistance appeared in 1929. It gives in brief form the essentials of the organization and meaning of the League of Nations. The Assembly has recently (September, 1929) appropriated funds for the translation of this handbook into languages other than the official languages of the League of Nations, in order to make the handbook immediately available for the various language groups of the world.[67]

Meanwhile, in the several states, steps had been taken to

---

[65] League of Nations Document A. 10, 1925, XII, p. 33.

[66] League of Nations International Committee on Intellectual Coöperation, *Minutes of the First Session*, p. 46.

[67] League of Nations, *Educational Survey*, January, 1930, Vol. I, No. 2, p. 121, "Extract of Report of the Second Committee of the Assembly Concerning Intellectual Coöperation."

remedy the lack of literature on the League adapted for use in the schools. As the League became recognized as an historical fact, text-books—history texts in particular—naturally included factual information about it. Practically every country in its report to the Secretariat of the League has mentioned text-books containing material on the League which have been commonly adopted for school use. More significant of general interest and of willingness of states to comply in spirit as well as in letter with the request of the Assembly has been the action taken by states and voluntary organizations to supply information especially adapted to acquaint pupils in detail with the aims and activities of the League.

Official Measures.—In many instances governments, having authorized the teaching of the League in the schools, also authorized the preparation of pamphlets on the League for school use. Sometimes officials requested that text-books in use be revised by publishers to include League teaching or ordered the distribution of pamphlets issued by the League, voluntary associations, or individuals. This is particularly true in the instance of the smaller countries.

In Norway, in 1925, a small text-book published by the legal adviser to the Ministry of Foreign Affairs had been officially circulated to aid teachers in presenting the League to pupils.[68] In 1927 the Ministry of Education of Denmark had placed in all schools copies of the Covenant of the League of Nations, edited with explanations and pamphlets covering the annual activities of the League. It had also had prepared and issued to schools a special pamphlet entitled "The League of Nations—an Outline of its Origin and Aims."[69]

On the same date (1925) that the Board of Education of Finland addressed circular letters to directors of educational

---

[68] League of Nations Document A. 19(a), 1925, XII, p. 7.

[69] League of Nations International Committee on Intellectual Coöperation, Document 190, 1927, p. 57.

establishments urging the teaching of the League in all schools of Finland, it also addressed a circular to editors and publishers calling attention to the absence of League of Nations material in text-books. As a result of this communication, material on the League was included in new editions of several history texts.[70] In 1928 an official communication of the Finnish Delegate to the League of Nations stated:

"Latterly, an attempt has been made to remedy this [lack of publications on the League in the two languages of the country], publishers having brought out books on a fairly large scale suitable both for teachers and lecturers. For instance, during the last three years there have appeared in Finnish, in addition to Professeur Rafael Erich's important work on the judicial organization of the League of Nations, the following publications by the Secretariat of the League: *The League of Nations, Its Constitution and Organization; The League of Nations and Intellectual Coöperation; The Permanent Court of International Justice; The International Economic Conference at Geneva; The League of Nations: A survey.*

"It is intended that several of these works, and also a pamphlet now being published by the head of the Board of Education, *The School and the League of Nations,* shall be supplied to school libraries by the department. It is hoped in this way to evoke a keener interest than formerly and to create better conditions for the kind of teaching in question."[71]

In 1927 the Minister of Education of Estonia had revised special chapters on the League of Nations included in history and civics class-books used in primary and secondary schools.[72] In 1926, the Federal Chancellor of Austria stated that the Austrian Minister of Education had taken steps to ensure that text-books in primary and secondary schools

---

[70] League of Nations Document A. 15, 1926, XII, p. 10.
[71] League of Nations Document A. 30, 1928, XII, p. 5.
[72] League of Nations International Committee on Intellectual Coöperation, Document 190, 1927, p. 40.

should contain accounts of the existence and aims of the League of Nations.[73] In the same year the Albanian Government reported that the Education Department was publishing articles on the League in the *Educational Review* of Albania, and that a book for the benefit of schools was being prepared along the lines indicated by the Committee on Intellectual Coöperation.[74]

In 1926 also a ministerial order in Roumania placed upon the Permanent Board of Education and its advisory specialists the responsibility of seeing that the geography, history, and civics text-books contain, without fail, some reference to the League of Nations "treated in a manner suited to the grade and subject in question." The result was that every book of the above type published in 1927, contained a chapter on the League of Nations.[75]

In 1928, the Bulgarian Ministry of Education had published a pamphlet on the League of Nations designed for use of teachers ("The League of Nations—How to Instruct Pupils in the Work of the League of Nations and to Develop the Spirit of International Coöperation"). The pamphlet was distributed to all schools, accompanied by a special circular letter indicating how instruction in the League should be given.[76] Recently the Czechoslovak member of the International Committee on Intellectual Coöperation has stated that the Czechoslovak Ministry of Education will publish shortly, for wide circulation in the public schools, a translation of the League publication *The Aims and Organization of the League of Nations*. The pamphlet will contain notes and introduction adapted for Czechoslovak readers.[77]

In 1925 a pamphlet prepared by the Director of Public

---

[73] League of Nations Document A. 15, 1926, XII, pp. 3, 7.
[74] *Ibid.*, p. 3.
[75] League of Nations International Committee on Intellectual Coöperation, Document 190, 1927, p. 75.
[76] League of Nations Document A. 30, 1928, XII, p. 3.
[77] League of Nations, *Educational Survey*, 1930, Vol. I, No. 2, p. 75.

Instruction of the United Provinces of India, containing an account of the organization and activities of the League of Nations was being officially circulated to all English schools in the United Provinces. All headmasters were asked to use the text as a basis for informal lessons on the League of Nations and its aims.[78]

An official communication of Japan to the Secretariat of the League in 1925 stated that the Ministry of Education, at the instigation of partisans of the League and its ideals, had authorized the modification of school texts to include more adequate reference to the League and its ideals and to eradicate the chauvinistic spirit.[79]

The Provincial Government of British Columbia, Canada, proposed in 1925 to distribute copies of the Covenant of the League of Nations among the teachers of the province.[80] In 1926 Cuba, to cite a final example, reported that the "Junta de Superintendentes," which directs State Education, was preparing a pamphlet on the League of Nations for use in the schools.[81]

Efforts of Voluntary Organizations.—In addition to these official measures, active steps have been made by certain voluntary associations to introduce teaching material on the League into the public schools. In France the National Council of Women has been especially instrumental in supplying teachers and pupils with pamphlets on the League and in approaching publishers with requests that chapters on the League be included in school-books.[82] In some countries the national branches of the International Federation

---

[78] League of Nations Document A. 10(a), 1925, XII, p. 7.

[79] League of Nations Document A. 10, 1925, XII, p. 19.

[80] *Ibid.*, p. 14.

[81] League of Nations Document A. 15, 1926, XII, p. 9.

[82] League of Nations, *Educational Survey,* 1929, Vol. I, No. 1, pp. 91-92. In addition the Musée Pédagogique, an official institution, has received and circulated pamphlets on the League. Since 1926 it has included leaflets on the League of Nations in every parcel of books sent out by its circulating library. (*Ibid.*)

of University Women have been active in preparing and distributing school material on the League of Nations.[83]

League of Nations Societies have been particularly active. Almost all national unions have prepared League pamphlets for school use and have encouraged inclusion of League material in school text-books. In a number of instances publications of the League of Nations Societies have been more or less officially adopted by educational authorities and ministers of education because of their special adaptability to school use.

On the proposal of the League of Nations Association of Geneva, the Canton of Geneva in 1921 introduced a chapter entitled "The League of Nations" in the text-book of civics used by the pupils of the primary continuation classes and the institutions of secondary education.[84] In Norway the University Group for the League of Nations has worked since its foundation in 1925, to introduce teaching material on the League of Nations into the school. As a result booklets on the League of Nations suitable for teachers and advanced pupils and a brief *Bibliography of the League of Nations*, both prepared by the union, have been officially circulated in the schools through the Board of Education and the Foreign Office.[85]

Again, the Chargé d'Affaires of Greece reported in 1925 that a manual on the League of Nations had been prepared in that year by Professor Kouyeas, of Athens University, on the authority of the Greek League of Nations Society. This was to be distributed to the schools through the Ministry of Education.[86] In 1928 the Polish League of Nations Union, in order to assist in remedying the lack of Polish

---

[83] The Belgian and Bulgarian Associations especially note activity in behalf of the League as an important part of their program. (International Federation of University Women, *Report of the Council Meetings*, Vienna, July, 1927, pp. 34-35; Madrid, September, 1928, pp. 49, 55.)

[84] League of Nations, *Educational Survey*, 1930, Vol. I, No. 2, pp. 112-113.

[85] *Ibid.*, 1929, Vol. I, No. 1, p. 124.

[86] League of Nations Document A. 10, 1925, XII, p. 18.

11

literature on the League, appointed a special sub-committee to prepare three volumes on the League of Nations, one of them designed for use in the public schools. The cost of publication was being met by the Ministry of Education.[87] In Nova Scotia, each high school student receives from the Education Department a copy of the *League of Nations.* Manitoba requires all students of the second grade in high school to read it, and British Columbia presents a copy to all students in their junior matriculation grade and to teachers in senior grades of the public school.[88]

Finally, in Great Britain *The Declaration of the Teaching Profession* of the British teachers and the Report of the Joint Committee of Enquiry into the Teaching of the Aims and Achievements of the League of Nations recommend for use in the schools certain publications of the League of Nations Societies.[89]

PREPARATION OF TEACHERS

The effectiveness with which school children are made acquainted with the aims and work of the League depends upon the teacher's preparation and sympathy. The Sub-Committee of Experts, recognizing this fact, made the following recommendations concerning courses for teachers:

"As this instruction will be given by the regular teacher, special attention should be devoted to it in the training colleges, and questions on it should be set in training college examinations. Special courses should be organized for those teachers whose needs in this respect have not been met in the training colleges as well as for those who wish to study the subject further.

---

[87] League of Nations, *Educational Survey*, 1929, Vol. I, No. 1, p. 128.

[88] *Ibid.*, 1930, Vol. I, No. 2, pp. 66-67.

[89] British League of Nations Union, *Teachers and World Peace*, p. 15; *Education and the League of Nations, Being a Report of the Joint Committee of Enquiry into the Teaching of the Aims and Achievements of the League of Nations*, London, 1929, pp. 22, 27.

"The competent authorities might further encourage the study of this subject . . . by providing facilities for teachers to attend courses of instruction at Geneva and elsewhere."[90]

Essay competitions on the League were recommended in schools of all types, and particular attention was directed to the need of providing the teacher with literature.[91] The commentary of the Rapporteur further emphasized the point in the following passage under "Training of Teachers":

"The importance of training teachers and professors cannot be over-emphasized. It is perhaps in the colleges where most of the teachers for primary instruction are trained that the maximum effort should be made and maintained. If each of these student-teachers could be imbued at the training college with the conviction that international coöperation is the normal method of conducting world affairs, the fire of idealistic enthusiasm thus kindled would enlighten and inspire generations of children and thousands of citizens. The League of Nations cannot pay too much attention to those modest but indispensable helpers.

"The important part played in this respect by international teachers' associations should be emphasized."[92]

Official Measures—In complying with the Assembly resolution concerning the instruction of youth some States have given at least formal attention to preparation of teachers in the aims and work of the League. In the replies to the Assembly resolutions, some States specify that by official order the League of Nations has been included in the syllabuses of teacher training colleges. The point of inclusion is generally in the sociology, history, or civics course. This is true for France since 1921;[93] Belgium,[94] Denmark,[95]

[90] League of Nations Document A. 26, 1927, XII, p. 4.
[91] *Ibid.*   [92] *Ibid.*, p. 11.
[93] League of Nations Document A. 10, 1925, XII, p. 15.
[94] *Ibid.*, pp. 10, 12 ff., League of Nations International Committee on Intellectual Coöperation, Document 190, 1927, pp. 39, 46.
[95] League of Nations Document A. 30, 1928, XII, p. 4.

Greece,[96] and Roumania[97] since 1925;[98] and the Netherlands[99] since 1927. Also the Polish League of Nations University Federation reported in 1928 that at the suggestion of its Education Committee special compulsory courses on the League were to be established in the Polish Normal Schools for secondary teachers.[100]

In Czechoslovakia a ministerial decree of 1926 specifies for the training schools as well as primary and secondary schools that one lesson a year shall be devoted to the peace movement in civilized countries.[101] In other instances, in states not under central supervision (Germany,[102] Switzerland,[103] Canada,[104] Australia,[105] South Africa,[106] for example), certain districts have made instruction in the League obligatory at some point in the curricula of training colleges.

Voluntary Interest.—More general and more effective is the support given by voluntary associations, both educational associations and non-educational organs, working in coöperation with teachers and school authorities.

The most general method of acquainting teachers and teachers in training with the aims and activity of the League has been to distribute pamphlets on the League, especially adapted for the teacher's use. This, it was pointed out above, is an almost universal practice, either through official direction or, more frequently, through the interest of voluntary organizations which coöperate with educational authorities.

---

[96] *Ibid.*, 10(a), 1925, XII, p. 7.   [97] *Ibid.*, 15, 1926, XII, p. 13.

[98] League of Nations, *Educational Survey*, 1929, Vol. I, No. 1, pp. 106, 113.

[99] League of Nations Document A. 30, 1928, XII, p. 6.

[100] International Federation of League of Nations Societies, *Bulletin*, 1928, No. III, May-June, p. 65.

[101] League of Nations Document A. 15, 1926, XII, p. 9.

[102] League of Nations, *Educational Survey*, July, 1929, Vol. I, No. 1, p. 106.

[103] *Ibid.*, 1930, Vol. I, No. 2, p. 112.

[104] League of Nations Document A. 30, 1928, XII, p. 4.

[105] League of Nations, *Educational Survey*, 1930, Vol. I, No. 2, p. 122.

[106] League of Nations Document A. 30, 1928, XII, p. 2.

Similarly, lectures on the League constitute a common means of disseminating information and stimulating interest. Close coöperation of League of Nations Societies with teachers' organizations facilitate these arrangements. Also, in placing the League of Nations on programs of teachers' conferences, school authorities and voluntary teacher associations have encouraged the interest of teachers in teaching the League of Nations.[107]

League of Nations Summer Schools.—An interesting venture has been that of the League of Nations summer school for teachers. In a few instances national summer courses on the League have been organized. In England, for example, the League of Nations Union arranges each year a summer school on the subject of the League. This is held in August, alternating between Oxford and Cambridge. At these courses a large proportion of the students are teachers.[108] League of Nations Societies of Argentine, Belgium, and Holland stated in reply to the questionnaire of the International Federation in 1929 that they were attempting to organize League of Nations summer schools. In 1928 a holiday course for Norwegian teachers, on the subject of the League was held at the Nobel Institute.[109] In 1928 and 1929 the Association Française de la Paix par le Droit organized at Thonon, in France, a two weeks' course

---

[107] The *Bulletins* of the International Federation of League of Nations Societies afford numerous examples. See also League of Nations, *Educational Survey*, 1930, Vol. I, No. 2, p. 97 (Wales); *Ibid.*, pp. 110, 113 (Switzerland); *Ibid.*, 1929, Vol. I, No. 1, p. 101 (France); *Education and the League of Nations, the Report of the Joint Committee of Enquiry*, London, 1929, p. 15 (Great Britain).

The Belgian Ministry of Science and Arts, which has control over public education, has recently decreed that one of the four annual cantonal educational conferences should be devoted to the League of Nations. (League of Nations, *Educational Survey*, Vol. I, No. 2, p. 63.)

[108] *Education and the League of Nations, the Report of the Joint Committee of Enquiry*, London, 1929, p. 25; International League of Nations Societies, answers to the Questionnaire of April, 1929, Annex M. (Mimeographed copy.)

[109] League of Nations, *Educational Survey*, 1929, Vol. I, No. 1, p. 123.

for young women, chiefly teachers. The study dealt with the League of Nations and international conciliation.[110]

In addition, several international summer courses at Geneva have been arranged for teachers. The most widely supported is the International Federation of the League of Nations Societies summer school. In a resolution of the Warsaw Congress of the International Federation of the League of Nations Societies, 1925, the Congress recommended the organization of national summer schools on the League and coöperation of National Societies in organizing an international school at Geneva, supplementary to the one initiated by the British society.[111] As a result of the coöperation of the several societies, in the summer of 1926 the International Federation of League of Nations Societies organized a week of lectures at Geneva in the French language. These lectures, which have been continued and extended to a fortnight in duration, and are given also in German, are designed particularly for elementary and secondary teachers.

The plan of offering scholarships has greatly extended the influence of the courses. The scholarships are generally awarded as a result of a competitive examination or essay contest among teachers and teachers in training. Hence though comparatively few teachers or prospective teachers attend the training courses at Geneva, a large number acquire a better understanding of the League as a result of the competition.

In France in 1927 the competition was held only in the sixteen Normal Schools of the Academy of Paris. In 1928

---

[110] *La Coöpération Intellectuelle,* August, 1929, p. 525; International Bureau of Education, *Bulletin,* No. 12, June, 1929, p. 17.

[111] "4. That the National Societies be recommended to organize Summer Schools on the League in their own countries and to coöperate with the Federation in organizing at Geneva an International Summer School supplementary to that organized by the Geneva Institute of International Relations for English-Speaking Peoples." (International Federation of League of Nations Societies, *Report of the Ninth Assembly, Plenary Sessions,* 1925, p. 30.)

it was extended to the Academies of Aix, Dijon, Grenoble, and Lyon, thus interesting the students of forty Normal Schools. A special circular issued by the Minister of Education instructed the schools to organize these competitions, and suitable documentation was placed at the disposal of candidates.[112] The French Federation of League of Nations Societies estimated that the examination of 1929 would put into competition a thousand students belonging to the Normal Schools of some thirty French departments.[113] In Belgium the competition began to be held in 1928. Some 130 normal school students have taken part each year.[114] The United States offered a European trip as the first prize in a competitive examination held for the first time in 1929 in teachers colleges. In this contest 102 teachers colleges participated, one-third of the total number of colleges.[115]

Encouragement of interest in these examinations is one of the activities of a large number of national League of Nations Societies. At least eight countries sent scholarship holders to the League of Nations Summer School in 1928 and 1929. In most instances there was an increase in number in 1929.[116] In Belgium, Austria, and Poland, as well

---

[112] International Federation of League of Nations Societies, *Bulletin*, 1928, No. II, March-April, p. 97; League of Nations International Committee on Intellectual Coöperation, Document 190, 1927, p. 61.

[113] International Federation of League of Nations Societies, *Bulletin*, 1929, No. III, May-June, p. 42.

[114] *Bulletin*, 1929, No. IV, July-Sept., p. 15; *XIII Plenary Congress, Madrid, 1929, Proceedings and Resolutions*, p. 56; *Bulletin*, 1928, No. 11, March-April, p. 11.

[115] *Ibid.*, p. 33, Report of the United States League of Nations Associations, Inc.

[116] Belgium 4 (1928), 8 (1929); Bulgaria 1 (1928); Denmark 2 (1929); Prussia 1 (1928), 5 (1929); Wales 5 (1928); Holland 3 (1928), 5 (1929); Poland 2 (1929). (See the International Federation of League of Nations Societies Questionnaire of 1929, answers to question 7; International Federation of League of Nations Societies, *Bulletin*, 1928, No. II, p. 97, No. IV, p. 18; 1929, IV, p. 17; *La Coöpération Intellectuelle*, February 1929, p. 89.

France offered two scholarships in 1927. In 1929 it was estimated that scholarships and reductions in traveling expenses would enable fifty normal

as France, the Ministry of Education in each instance lent support to the scheme. In Poland the two scholarships, offered for the first time in 1929, were awarded by the Ministry of Education.[117] Since the competitive examination has been initiated, steps have been made to secure special rates for teachers and student teachers traveling to Geneva to study the League of Nations.[118]

In addition to the International Federation of League of Nations Societies Summer School, a special League of Nations summer course for teachers lasting one week has been conducted for three summers under the auspices of the International Bureau of Education at Geneva.[119] In 1929 a special course for teachers was also offered by the World Federation of Education Associations at its biennial Conference in Geneva.[120]

It has been pointed out that the League of Nations serves in the lower schools as a nucleus for teaching the principles of international coöperation. The activities touch such varied phases of human interest that many points of the school curricula offer opportunities for considering its work and its principles. The fact that ideals of international coöperation are exemplified in the organization of the League has been especially useful to the teaching program.

From the beginning of its existence efforts have been made to introduce instruction on the League into the schools. Since 1923 the League itself has been active in maintaining

students to attend the courses in Geneva. (International Federation of League of Nations Societies, *Bulletin*, 1928, No. IV, July-August, p. 18.) England has supported the Geneva Institute of International Relations rather than the International Federation of League of Nations Societies Summer School, sending every summer some 100 students, not limited to teachers or prospective teachers. (Answer to League of Nations Questionnaire, 1929, Annex M.)

[117] International Federation of League of Nations Societies, *Bulletin*, 1929, IV, p. 47.

[118] *Bulletin*, 1928, No. II, March-April, p. 14.

[119] International Bureau of Education, *Bulletin*, No. 13, September, 1929, pp. 5-6; *Bulletin*, No. 14, January, 1930, p. 7.

[120] *La Coöpération Intellectuelle*, July, 1929, p. 445.

and stimulating interest in its organization and activities. Through its Sub-Committee of Experts it has helped States and interested organizations to select methods of instruction in its principles and aims. It has also provided means of collecting and disseminating information regarding what is being done by the various countries to teach the League of Nations in the schools.

This support has reinforced the efforts of teachers' associations and other non-official organizations which have been active in furthering interest in the League of Nations through the lower schools. The result is that systematic and incidental instruction on the League is given in the schools of many countries of the world. Formal official and non-official declarations and programs of administrative organs have forced the issue more and more, and in view of the comparative lack of active opposition these measures are changing local indifference to active support.

Finally, because of the importance of the preparation and the attitude of the teacher, special efforts have been made to prepare the teacher more adequately to give instruction on the League. With the aggressive support of the League of Nations and voluntary organizations, and the consent or support of the States, the adequately prepared teacher occupies a relatively unrestricted position concerning the imparting of information and the development of attitudes regarding the League of Nations.

CHAPTER VII

HISTORY TEACHING AND TEXT-BOOK REVISION

Teaching the ideals of the League of Nations is not compatible with teaching history in a spirit of excessive nationalism. Hence it is natural that zeal for reform in history teaching in the lower schools should frequently be coupled with zeal for instruction of children in the existence and aims of the League of Nations. Reform in the teaching and writing of history has been one of the methods advocated for the development of a new attitude in world affairs.

Recognition of the Teaching of History as an Influence in International Understanding

Official Instructions.—In some instances ministers of education or other state officials have directed the attention of teachers to the importance of presenting history in an unprejudiced or conciliatory manner. After the war the Austrian Minister of Education and Under-Secretary of State gave instructions concerning use of old texts and the preparation of new ones. The following order of the Under-Secretary of State issued on September 10, 1929, concerns the teaching of history. It recommends (1) that the teacher should minimize the history of wars and reigning dynasties and emphasize instead economic and social developments and popular life; (2) that the recent war should be discussed with reserve, since full information concerning causes and events are lacking; (3) that in cultivating the national spirit one should guard against narrow nationalism; one should recognize the rights of ethnic groups and stress com-

munity of economic and intellectual interests as a reason
for national solidarity.

These provisions read:

"In general it is necessary to turn resolutely aside from
purely martial history. . . . What one will gain in restricting
military history may serve to develop the history of civilization: in particular stress will have to be laid in detail upon the
economic and social situation, on the intellectual movements.
Just as the teaching of history must cease to consider the wars
in themselves as an essential theme, likewise the history of
ruling dynasties must be curtailed. It will be a question of
replacing the history of states and of ruling families with their
wars, by a history of peoples and their life. . . . Naturally it
is not at all a question of diminishing the importance of great
monarchs or of illustrious statesmen. . . .

"In dealing with the world war, which the school neither can
nor should pass in silence, one must bear in mind that we do
not yet possess historical knowledge of this formidable event
in the scientific sense of the word. On the subject of the causes
or pretexts of the war, the development of the struggle and
its conclusion, so many questions, even from the simple point
of view of facts are still debated, that great reserve is enjoined upon the teacher. He will advance as facts only those
things which are generally admitted, but everything that is
the object of discussion and debate he will declare contro-
vertible and will indicate the arguments on both sides. . . .

"The separation of Austria, along with the non-German
peoples, from the former monarchy will naturally mean that
henceforth we shall no longer present our history as a part
of German history. . . .

"But in cultivating strongly and openly the national sentiment, it will be necessary to guard against a narrow nationalism. The great tasks of the future demand that the attitude
and the will be free in view of the *rapprochement* of peoples
grouped in national unities and conscious of themselves. To
attain this end there is no better means than to awaken

the youth to the community of interest in work and life that
peoples form from the economic and intellectual point of view,
a community which cannot prosper except through an intelligent collaboration of all its members."[1]

A broader purpose in teaching history is emphasized in
the instructions to teachers included in the history syllabus
of the secondary schools of Poland, as revised in 1925. Polish
teachers are counselled to consider history as a means of
extending the pupil's consciousness in civic, national and
international relations. The instructions read:

"The teaching of historical science should form a starting-
point from which the pupil may progress to a knowledge of
the principles of civic life, to a sure realization that he is
linked by indissoluble ties to his country and to all mankind,
to an understanding of the spirit of Polish culture, and, finally,
to the ideal of the Polish citizen to be identified with the larger
ideal of humanity."[2]

Of similar import is the following extract from the decree
of the Minister of Education of the State of Brunswick,
made effective in 1928:

"Children must be initiated, in their history lessons, not
only into the history of their country—the evolution of the
German nation—but must be given a general view of history
as a whole, so that nation, country, humanity form the necessary complement of each other in their minds. They must
understand that each nation is an integral part of humanity

---

[1] Quoted by Dr. Karl Brockhausen of the University of Vienna, who
undertook the investigation of post-war school books in Austria for the
Carnegie Foundation for Peace. (Carnegie Foundation for International
Peace, *Enquête sur les Livres Scolaires d'Après Guerre,* 1923, pp. 286-287.)
Translated by the author.
[2] Quoted by F. Sokal, Minister Plenipotentiary, Delegate to the League
of Nations, in an official communication to the Secretariat of the League.
League of Nations Document A. 15, 1926, XII, p. 12.

and only acquires its full value with the help of advancing universal culture."[3]

In Hungary the scientific spirit is urged. Professor Horvath, Director of the Inter-University Office of Hungary, quotes the following instructions concerning the teaching of history—the first for normal schools and the second for secondary schools:

"I. 1. The teaching of history should be absolutely objective.—2. The facts and the events should be judged in the spirit of the period to which they belong.—3. The teacher shall avoid all useless and inconsiderate generalizations; he shall be impartial without exaggerating, and by his example he shall teach the love and respect of justice."

"II. The most effective remedy for all erroneous teaching is impartiality and respect for scientific truth. It is evident that this quality is especially important in the teaching of history. The teacher will constantly guard against formulating personal opinions and introducing current prejudices into his teaching."[4]

In New Zealand the instructions to teachers assume a consciously pacifist note. Recently, according to a statement of Professor Airey, of University College, Auckland,

"to the original statement [in the introduction to the history syllabus of the primary schools] that the pupil 'must be so taught that it shall be his joy and pride to play his part, however humble it may be in the advancement of New Zealand and the Empire' has been added 'and in the promotion of peace, well-being, and happiness among the nations.' "[5]

In the appendix to the syllabus is the following extract:

---

[3] Translated in the *Bulletin of the International Bureau of Education*, Year IV, No. 1, January, 1930, p. 30.

[4] Carnegie Foundation for International Peace, *Enquête sur les Livres Scolaires d'Après Guerre*, 1927, pp. 208, 209. (Translated by the author).

[5] League of Nations, *Educational Survey*, 1929, Vol. I, No. 1, p. 121.

"The narrow nationalistic interpretation of history should be avoided; international jealousies should not be aroused—a fatally easy course; but there should be sedulously cultivated a strong faith in a more peaceful, harmonious and prosperous world. Frequent reference should be made in the higher classes to the constitution and activities of the League of Nations, and to some at least of the disputes that it settled. One of the teacher's main aims should be to implant in the minds of his pupils a detestation of war as a means of settling international differences. On no account should too great emphasis be laid on achievements in war. At the same time these should not be ignored, nor should there be anything but the highest praise for those who sacrificed their lives for their country's freedom. Every opportunity that occurs through annual commemorations, such as Anzac Day, Armistice Day, Trafalgar Day, should be utilized to inculcate in the minds of the young love of country and a desire to promote peace among the nations."[6]

It is not to be expected that a ministerial order can effect a reform in the spirit of history teaching in the public schools, or that such a decree is an index to current practice. One cannot suppose that teachers of Hungary will regard the recent events in a purely objective, impartial, and scientific spirit.[7] The instructions to teachers in the history syllabus of New Zealand, Professor Airey points out, are misleading if considered in isolation, apart from the intense imperialistic trend of public opinion. The directions quoted above do argue, however, that public educational authorities recognize the teaching of history in the public schools as a possible force in international conciliation or international discord, and that because of personal interest or the force of public opinion they feel obligated to declare that history

---

[6] *Ibid.*

[7] Professor Horvath concludes from his investigation that Hungarian school-books, while expressing a spirit by no means reconciled to the Treaty of Trianon, have refused to be the instrument of political demands. (Carnegie Foundation for International Peace, *op. cit.,* Vol. II, pp. 201-231.)

shall be taught in an unprejudiced or conciliatory spirit or in a manner to develop the sense of world unity.

Action of National Associations of Teachers.—National bodies of teachers have given expression to similar views. In 1924 a meeting of the Syndicat National des Institutrices et des Instituteurs, representing some 78,000 French teachers, attacked the subject of history teaching in the primary schools of France. It was proposed that the teaching of history should be suppressed altogether in the lower elementary schools. The session rejected this proposal, but urged a conciliatory spirit in teaching. At the close of the session the Syndicat National passed a resolution urging international federations of teachers

"to make every effort, in all countries, to displace the nationalistic point of view in history teaching by the human and fraternal point of view conducive to close relationships of peoples."[8]

At its Congress in Strassbourg in 1926 the Syndicat National voted unanimously a declaration against text-books written in a spirit that might implant or perpetuate germs of hatred or misunderstanding with respect to other nations. Concerning the spirit of teaching in general the declaration asserts that it should contribute towards peace and an appreciation of the interdependence of peoples.

"Teachers," declares the resolution, "will endeavor to teach their pupils that they have obligations to fulfill, not only towards family and country, but also towards the peoples of the world; that there exists among the various peoples an interdependence that is constantly increasing; that civilization is the common work of all peoples, including those that history has most harshly put in opposition.

---

[8] Quoted by J. Prudhomeaux, *Pour la Paix par l'École, ce qui a été fait en France pour lutter contre les livres scolaires contraires au rapprochement des peuples,* p. 13. (Translated by the author.)

"They will give to their pupils, along with the consciousness of this community of interests, the desire of maintaining and developing it; in their teaching, they will avoid all statements capable of confusing the desire for peace."[9]

The National Union of Teachers in Sweden (Folkskollararförbund) in a report to the International Federation of Teachers Associations in 1928 pointed out that it considered the absence of material of antagonistic import in school books and in teaching only a negative step in international conciliation.[10] A more positive step should be that of making known the heroes and ideals of other peoples and their contributions to the spiritual and economic advancement of humanity. Consequently, as one of its aims in education for peace it included "propaganda among teachers to convince them of the necessity of educational reform and to bring them to accept the ideal of the reconciliation of peoples." In this connection, under the head of *history*, the Union announced the following aim:

"*In history.* Pupils should be taught to know, admire, and love the heroes and great men of other peoples. The origin of wars should be explained, and justice should be rendered to everyone, even to former enemies."[11]

It was stated above that the Declaration of the Teaching Profession of Great Britain concerning teaching the principles of the League of Nations in British Schools was subscribed to in 1927 by eight important associations of British teachers.[12] The Declaration makes the following statements concerning the aims in teaching history:

---

[9] Fédération Internationale des Associations d'Instituteurs, *Bulletin* No. 3, March 1928, p. 16. Report of the Syndicat National des Institutrices et des Instituteurs. (Translated by the author.)

[10] For this gain in Sweden it gave credit to the activity of the School Association for Peace (Skolornas Fredsforening). Federation Internationale des Associations des Instituteurs, *Bulletin*, No. 3, March, 1928, p. 30.

[11] *Ibid.* (Translated by the author.)

[12] See above, p. 145.

(Under *The School Curriculum*) "The study of international coöperation in the modern world should develop from those studies of modern history and geography which form part of the general school education of every boy and girl."

(Under *History*) "Where the teachers understand the facts in question, realize their importance, and are eager to teach them, most will be taught in history lessons. The history of England, or of Scotland, will then be presented in its proper relation to the history of the world. Only so can British children fully appreciate the League of Nations as a fruit long ripened on the tree of time. Particularly in the teaching of modern history 'the growing sense of the interdependence of communities, as shown, for example, in the work of the League of Nations, should receive due prominence,' to quote the Consultative Committee of the Board of Education in their recent report on the education of the adolescent. But the new material should not be confined to the history of the last seven, or the last seventy, years."[18]

In these declarations national groups of teachers consciously turn their backs upon excessive glorification of nationality in teaching history and embrace the spirit of truth as opposed to chauvinism, a sense of the interdependence of nations, and a positive appreciation of the contributions of foreign nations to the advance of civilization.

Action of International Organizations.—The teaching of history has been included also in the agenda of international educational organizations as a means of international conciliation.

At its organization in 1923 the World Federation of Education Associations called attention to the importance of history in the school curriculum as a means of promoting international respect, coöperation, and good-will.[14] At the

---

[18] British League of Nations Union, *Teachers and World Peace*, 1929, pp. 10, 11.

[14] *World Conference on Education*, 1923, pp. 7, 19. Published by the National Education Association.

12

next meeting, 1925, the following resolution was passed:

"That the World Federation of Education Associations prepare a statement of the ideals which should obtain in history and history teaching. Such statement should emphasize the necessity for an impartial treatment of international intercourse. A frank admission of shortcomings should accompany the claim of services rendered to the cause of human welfare in each country. In proceeding from national to world history emphasis should be laid upon progress from conflict to conciliation."[15]

At this Conference a Committee was appointed to investigate the teaching of history, a phase of the Herman-Jordan Peace Plan endorsed by the Federation. The Committee reported at the second biennial conference in 1927 the following recommendations concerning the teaching of history and the preparation of textbooks:

"1. The truth should be taught in preference to nationalistic propaganda.

"2. Teachers of history and textbooks on the subject of history should divert the emphasis from the glorification of war to a study of the pursuits of peace.

"3. Textbooks in history should be written by international committees of historians instead of by individuals.

"4. Textbooks in history should aim to develop significant world movements, rather than national movements, with the development centering around great personalities.

"5. There should be included in these books abundant material to indicate the lot of the common people during the war time.

"6. The extensive use of carefully selected periodicals should be increased to develop in the pupils the habit of keeping up with the times.

"7. All history should be built around great personalities.

---

[15] *World Federation of Education Associations,* First Biennial Conference, 1925, Vol. II, p. 915.

"8. True patriotism includes a fair criticism of one's own country."[16]

The International Bureau of National Associations of Secondary Teachers considered the question at its meeting in Geneva in 1926. It concluded (1) that the primary aim of history teaching in secondary education was an impartial consideration of human events; (2) that the teaching of national history should be considered a valuable means in the formation of future citizenship, but that in presenting national history systematic glorification of nationality must be sedulously avoided; (3) that the economic order and the interdependence of peoples should receive stress, particularly in the upper grades of secondary instruction. The following resolutions were adopted:

"A. History.—1. The study of history in secondary schools has for its essential aim neither moral instruction of pupils nor, exclusively, the training of the intellect by the study of the evolution of humanity; it proposes above all to comprehend and to make plain events and men in order that they may be judged with complete impartiality.

"2. The teaching of history may and should be conceived in all countries as the most efficient means of forming the future citizen, and to this end national history should be taken as the center of instruction, especially in the lower grades, but on explicit condition that it does not lead, consciously or not, to the systematic glorification of country, and especially that it does not regularly depreciate all other countries.

"3. The study of history in secondary schools should, especially in the higher grades lay stress upon the phenomena of the economic order and upon the interdependence which is forced upon all civilized nations; it must also make clear the movement for human solidarity and the rôle of international

---

[16] World Federation of Education Associations, *Proceedings of the Second Biennial Conference*, 1927, p. 350.

organisms concerned with this movement, among others the League of Nations, which should occupy in this study the place which its importance and activity warrant."[17]

Finally, the action of the International Committee of Historical Sciences should be mentioned as evidence of the interest of professional historians and teachers of history. At its first meeting, in 1927, the International Committee of Historical Sciences voted to create a sub-committee on the teaching of history.[18] In the following year at Oslo the International Congress of Historical Sciences was held under the auspices of the International Committee of Historical Sciences. One of its sections dealt with the teaching of history. A report on the investigation of nationalism in history textbooks, which had been prepared jointly by committees of the World Alliance for Promoting International Friendship through the Churches and the Universal Christian Conference on Life, was distributed to the members of the Congress for the particular use of the section on the teaching of History.[19] In the consideration of the aims of instruction in history the Congress passed a resolution that history should contribute to a better understanding among peoples."[20]

At the meeting at Venice in 1929 the International Committee of Historical Sciences decided to retain the Committee engaged in the study of the teaching of history. This Committee since the meeting at Oslo has been engaged in collecting information concerning the teaching of history in

[17] Bureau International des Fédérations Nationales du Personnel de l'Enseignement Secondaire Public, *Bulletin International*, No. 25, June, 1929, pp. 29-30. (Translated by the author.)

[18] *American Historical Review*, July, 1927, Vol. 32, p. 947.

[19] *Ibid.*, Vol. 34, pp. 270-271; *La Coöpération Intellectuelle*, July, 1929, pp. 75-76: Michel Lheritier, "Comment Organiser le Prochain Congres International des Sciences Historiques?"

[20] Bureau International des Fédération Nationales du Personnel de l'Enseignement Secondaire Public, *Bulletin International*, March, 1929, p. 46.

the primary schools of the several countries with a view to a comparative study of curricula, manuals, and administration.[21]

SCHOOL BOOKS AND INTERNATIONAL CONCILIATION

Closely linked with the question of reform in the teaching of history is, as indicated in the preceding pages, the question of the international attitudes displayed in school books. In their efforts to establish an active program in the lower schools for the instruction of children and youth in the principles of international coöperation interested individuals, organizations, and governments have stressed the importance of textbooks.

The Carnegie Investigation.—The interest in new books and the revision of old ones received its primary post-war impetus from an investigation made by the European division of the Carnegie Foundation for International Peace. The Executive committee of this organization, in collaboration with representatives of the Comité français de la Division de l'Économie Politique et de l'Historie of the University of Paris, met in 1921 to see what could be done to continue the work of peace that had been interrupted by the War.

After discussion it was agreed to define the work to be attempted as follows:

"Examination was to be made of the school books in history, geography, morals, and civics, and of anthologies and readers intended for pupils in the primary and secondary schools, to discover whether the points of view embodied in them were good or objectionable so far as the *rapprochement* of people was concerned. For each country, a collaborator, chosen preferably from the teaching profession, was to be charged with collecting and examining the books of his country. If

---

[21] *La Coöperation Intellectuelle,* July, 1929, pp. 75-76; *Ibid.,* p. 407; *Ibid.,* March, 1930, p. 129.

the importance of the school literature to be studied so demanded, several investigators might be requested for a single nation. A joint report would then be compiled with the aid of the particular reports."[22]

The work of the Carnegie Foundation was started in 1921, and in 1923 the first volume was circulated. It contained reports on the textbooks of the lower schools of France, Belgium, Germany, Austria, Great Britain, Italy, and Bulgaria.[23] This report added to and increased the interest that had been created in the countries where the investigations had been under way since 1921. The second volume, covering the investigations made in Albania, Belgium, Flanders, Esthonia, Finland, Greece, Hungary, Ireland, Lithuania, Luxembourg, Poland, Roumania, the Kingdom of the Serbs, Croats and Slavs, Russia, Czechoslovakia, and Turkey, appeared in 1927.[24] The subsequent discussions and activity of significant national and international organizations bear testimony to the increasing importance attached by edu-

---

[22] Carnegie Foundation for International Peace, *Enquête sur les Livres Scolaires d'Après Guerre*, 1923, Vol. I, pp. 2-3 (translated by the author). The question is not new. As early as 1893, for instance, the Universal Peace Congress recommended the revision of history manuals in the following resolution passed in its Fifth session:

"The Congress welcomes the formation of an International Universities Committee, recently organized at Paris, as an important step towards enlisting the coöperation of educational institutions and forces in the work of peace. It is of the opinion that it is most desirable that there should be such a revision of manuals of instruction as will eliminate false and misleading representations of the nature of war, and inculcate the true principles lying at the basis of social order, and which should govern the nations in their relations one to another; and it further expresses the wish that there should be established in the universities departments for instruction in the principles of international unity and concord." (*Fifth Universal Peace Congress*, p. 294, Chicago, 1893.) In 1912 the School Peace League of Great Britain and Ireland had as one of its two special committees a committee to study the question of history teaching and textbooks used in the schools. (*The Peace Yearbook*, 1912, pp. 101-102.) See above, p. xxvi.

[23] Carnegie Foundation for International Peace, *Enquête sur les Livres Scolaires d'Après Guerre*, Vol. I.

[24] *Ibid.*, Vol. II, 1927.

cators and pacifists to the question of international attitudes in textbooks.

Interest of International Educational Organizations.—In
the same year that the first volume of the Carnegie Foundation Report appeared, the organizing meeting of the World
Federation of Education Associations passed a resolution
"that the International Education Association undertake
at once a study of the ways and means to assist national
educational bodies to see that the preparation of textbooks
and other methods of instruction employed by their countries is governed by fairness and good-will."[25]

It was mentioned above that upon adopting the Herman-
Jordan Plan as a part of its program at this meeting the
Federation appointed a committee to investigate history
teaching and textbooks. This committee has been retained
at the two succeeding meetings to work in coöperation with
local committees upon a plan adopted at the Toronto Conference in 1927, which includes a comparative study of the
history textbooks in the several countries.[26]

In June, 1926, one of the most significant international
organizations of teachers, the International Federation of
Teachers' Associations, originated, as was mentioned above,
out of a movement against chauvinistic school-texts.[27]

The Carnegie investigation stimulated the French Syndicat National des Institutrices et Instituteurs to a campaign against textbooks containing passages likely to
provoke or perpetuate international ill-will. The Syndicat
invited German and Dutch national organizations of teachers to join with it in an organized campaign for good-will
through the schools. As a result the International Federation of Teachers was formed. From its foundation the ques-

[25] *World Conference on Education,* June 28-July 6, 1923, p. 7.

[26] World Federation of Education Associations, *Proceedings of the Second
Biennial Conference,* 1927, p. 230.

[27] See above, p. 117. See Fédération Internationale des Associations
d'Instituteurs, *Bulletin,* No. 3, 1928, p. 16.

tion of the elimination of hatred and error from school-texts has been an issue of the organization.[28]

At its Congress in Berlin in April, 1928, the first definite resolution of the Federation concerning concerted action in textbook revision was adopted. The member associations were urged to conduct simultaneously a campaign against school books likely to arouse or establish national prejudices, and to encourage the editions of books of conciliatory or impartial nature. In such concerted action the member associations would have the advantage of coöperation of other associations through the secretariat of the Federation. The resolution reads as follows:

"The Federation recommends to the member associations not only to conduct simultaneously a campaign against belligerent works, which instead of seeking historical truth seek to develop a blind hatred and aimless mistrust, but also to study in their congresses the means of encouraging the publication of school books, especially texts in reading, history, geography, and civics—written in a spirit of international fairness. To this end the associations will have the advantage of requesting information from other associations, through the intermediary of a Secretariat, so that children may be given a true conception of the civilization of foreign nations."[29]

Succeeding meetings have reasserted belief in the importance which attaches to the consideration of school-texts in a program of international conciliation.[30] The meeting of the Executive Bureau of the Federation in September, 1929, suggested the following formula governing the spirit of history textbooks:

"In history texts, do not simplify the causes of wars for fear of disclosing the truth; indicate the complexity of these

---

[28] *Bulletin* No. 1, 1927, p. 7.
[29] Fédération Internationale des Association d'Instituteurs, *Bulletin*, No. 4, 1928, p. 10. (Translated by the author.)
[30] *Bulletin*, No. 5, 1928, p. 4; No. 7, 1929, p. 23.

causes in making clear the responsibility of peoples, establish the idea that in every case (even when one speaks of national honor) arbitration is worthy of everyone and is efficacious in the maintenance of peace."[31]

Certain national members of the Federation, as will be pointed out below, have been active in coöperating with the international program of the Federation in the matter of school-texts.

The International Bureau of National Associations of Secondary Teachers has likewise endorsed international coöperation in preparation and revision of school books. At its eleventh Congress, November, 1929, the Bureau unanimously voted its approval of a proposal concerning school book revision, formulated by the president of the Netherlands Association.[32]

The proposal was advanced as a more practicable measure than that endorsed by the League of Nations Committee on Intellectual Coöperation, which is described later,[33] since it provided a more definite organism of control. Its provisions are the following:

(1) That in each country there be established an organ to deal with what foreign school books teach concerning that country.

(2) That in each country there be created a permanent

---

[31] Fédération International des Associations d'Instituteurs, *Bulletin* No. 8, 1929, p. 9. (Translated by the author.)

[32] The attention of the author of the proposal (M. Buurveld) had been called to the question by a letter received from the Hungarian Committee for the revision of school books, pointing out misstatements concerning Hungary in the Netherlands school books. An organization in the Netherlands having similar interests—"Holland Abroad"—had recently published an account of their findings concerning the treatment of the Netherlands in foreign school books. (Bureau International des Fédérations Nationales du Personnel de l'Enseignement Secondaire Public, *Bulletin International*, November, 1929, pp. 111-119. For a brief statement from the "Holland Abroad" association concerning its work see also International Committee on Intellectual Coöperation, *Minutes of the Sixth Session*, pp. 37-38.)

[33] See below, pp. 192-195.

collaboration between this organ, the National Committee on Intellectual Coöperation (where one exists), and international organizations of teachers. Circumstances would determine which of these three organizations would eventually communicate with the foreign country in question and the method of communication (with editors, with authors, or with national organizations).

(3) That in each country a national center be established to receive the books of other countries and furnish information to other countries.[34]

Finally, the International Bureau of Education has also supported the investigation of school text-books as a means of promoting international understanding. It was mentioned above that the International Bureau of Education since 1925 has been compiling information concerning children's literature contributing to international goodwill. In 1925 also it assumed the work of the International Bureau of Moral Education, one aspect of which had been, since 1922, the question of history teaching and history text-books as forces in moral education.[35]

In 1927 the Bureau organized an international Conference of educators at Prague under the patronage of President Masaryk and the Minister of Public Education of Czechoslovakia. Eighteen countries were represented by delegates or reports. This Conference, which designated itself "La Paix par l'École," was arranged and conducted for the sole purpose of discussing the promotion of peace through the schools.[36] In the course of its meetings the

---

[34] Bureau International des Fédérations Nationales du Personnel de l'Enseignement Secondaire Public, *Bulletin International*, November, 1929, pp. 117-119.

[35] "The Work of the International Bureau of Education," *School and Society*, March 26, 1927, Vol. 25, pp. 370-371. Statement of Pierre Bovet, Director of the Bureau.

[36] See the report of the meeting, *La Paix par l'École, Travaux de la Conference Internationale tenue à Prague du 16 au 20 Avril, 1927.* Edited by Pierre Bovet.

question of school books in the program of peace received consideration. Dr. Kawerau, Director of Schools of Berlin, proposed that the Conference support the recommendations concerning text-books which the Education Committee of the Alliance des Églises had adopted at its meeting at Berne in 1926.

These recommendations set forth points that should govern the authors of history text-books and guide authorities in charge of selecting them. They read:

"1. Elminate every statement the falsity of which can be established. Omission of essential facts, even though they may be detrimental to one's own nation, must be considered contrary to truth.

"2. Oppose a double standard (that something which in the case of another people would be styled barbarity may be in one's own people a work of civilization). Recognize the good elsewhere than at home.

"3. Oppose generalizations, especially when it is a question of blaming races or entire peoples.

"4. Be cautious when discussing the war.

"5. Deal in a positive manner with the problem of the League of Nations."[37]

At the close of the Conference at Prague the following resolutions were adopted concerning school text-books. They conclude with an approval of the general spirit of the recommendations adopted at Berne:

"School books hold today an important place in teaching. They exercise great influence on the child. It is indispensable that they also be permeated with the spirit of international co-operation.

"The variety of situations in the several countries prohibits the laying down of fixed standards of procedure, but the Conference congratulates the professional groups of teachers on

---

[37] *Pa Paix par l'École. Travaux de la Conférence Internationale tenue à Prague, du 16 au 20 Avril, 1927*, p. 22. (Translated by the author.)

their initiative and their success in attacking this problem.

"The Conference has noted with satisfaction the results of the meeting of the Alliance of Practical Christianity at Berne, and it approves, in their suggestion and their general tenor, the standards which this meeting laid down for the preparation of history text books."[38]

The Interest of the League of Nations.—In September, 1925, the Sixth Assembly of the League of Nations accepted the following proposal of the Haitian government:

"With a view to moral disarmament, the League of Nations invites its members to undertake as far as possible the revision of their history manuals so as gradually to reduce the number of pages devoted to military events and especially those passages in which wars of conquests are justified and held up for admiration."[39]

This proposal was forwarded to the States Members along with the Secretariat's report concerning steps taken by the several governments to make the League of Nations known in the schools of their respective countries.[40]

In the preceding month the Sixth Session of the International Committee on Intellectual Coöperation had considered the proposal of the Spanish representative, which had been presented at the preceding session, May, 1925.[41] The proposal suggested that unfair representation of one country in the school texts of another country might be remedied through the coöperation of the National Committees of International Coöperation in the countries concerned, stipulating, however, that the request for emendation should be confined to questions of definitely established fact concerning the country's material and cultural life and

---

[38] *Ibid.,* pp. 145-146. (Translated by the author.)

[39] League of Nations Document A. 83, 1925, XII, p. 5.

[40] See above, p. 136, note 8.

[41] League of Nations International Committee on Intellectual Coöperation, *Minutes of the Fifth Session,* 1925, p. 29.

development. The Committee in the following resolution adopted the proposal:

"The Committee on Intellectual Coöperation, considering that one of the most effective methods of bringing about the intellectual *rapprochement* of peoples would be to delete or modify passages in school text-books of a nature to convey to the young wrong impressions leading to an essential misunderstanding of other countries;

"Being convinced that it will be unable to postpone for long the consideration of this problem, which has been brought before it since its creation in the form of suggestions both from its own members and from outside, and realizing at the same time the difficulties which attend any attempt to undertake an enterprise of this kind on a large scale;

"Requests the coöperation of the National Committees in trying, on a limited scale in the first instance, the following procedure, whose extreme elasticity seems of a nature to obviate any risk of wounding national susceptibilities:

"(a) When a National Committee thinks it desirable that foreign text concerning its country and intended for use in schools should be amended for the reasons indicated in the present resolution, it shall make a request to this effect to the National Committee of the country where the text is in use, at the same time submitting, if necessary, a draft emendation on the desired lines, together with a brief statement of the reasons.

"(b) National Committees on receiving a request of this kind, shall decide in the first instance whether the request should be accepted and shall then determine what representation of a friendly and private nature, if any, should be made to the authors or publishers with a view to the proposed emendation. If these representations are successful, the Committee shall notify the Committee making the application and the International Committee; if not, it shall not be obliged to give any explanation either of the reasons for its failure or of its failure or of its own refusal to take action.

"(c) Requests for emendation shall refer exclusively to questions of definitely established fact regarding the geography or civilization of a country, its material conditions of life, natural resources, customs of the inhabitants, scientific, artistic and economic development, contribution to international culture and the welfare of humanity, etc.

"It is strictly prohibited to make or accept applications for emendation referring to personal views of a moral, political or religious order.

"(d) All the National Committees will at the same time be requested to specify the publications most suitable for giving foreigners a knowledge of the history, civilization and present position of their country."[42]

This proposal was approved by the Sub-Committee of Experts on the Instruction of Youth in the following recommendation on the subject of school text-books:

"Those in charge of educational institutions should be asked to use their influence to ensure that text-books in general should not be written in such a way as to conflict with the spirit of mutual conciliation and coöperation. In this respect, history text-books should be the subject of particular care. It is desirable that, in every country, incitements to hatred of the foreigner should be eliminated and every effort made to arrive at a better comprehension of what one nation owes to another. The Casares proposal, adopted by the Committee on Intellectual Coöperation, provides the best method of correcting definite misstatements."[43]

This proposal, though it has elicited statements of approval from a few National Committees,[44] has apparently

---

[42] League of Nations International Committee on Intellectual Coöperation, *Minutes of the Sixth Session,* 1925, p. 15.

[43] League of Nations Document A. 26, 1927, XII, p. 6.

[44] Reports of the Committee on Intellectual Coöperation quote the replies from four National Committees to the Casares Proposal: the Australian, Danish, Roumanian, and Italian National Committees. The replies are merely expressions of interest or approbation. (League of Nations, International Committee on Intellectual Coöperation, *Minutes of*

resulted in no concrete action. In view of the fact that its practicability has not been demonstrated, the president of the Netherlands group of secondary teachers advanced the proposal described above providing for special national organisms to deal with school text-books in their international relations.

INVESTIGATIONS UNDERTAKEN IN SEVERAL COUNTRIES

National Associations of Teachers.—In several countries various organizations have made the investigation of school books a part of their program for promoting international good will. In addition to the work sponsored by the Carnegie Foundation for Peace referred to above, numerous national investigations have proceded from various quarters. Probably the most decisive and thorough action has been that of the French teachers, of which Professor J. Prudhommeaux has made an interesting study (*Pour la Paix par l'École: ce qui a été fait en France pour lutter contre les livres scolaires contraires au rapprochement des peuples, 1923-1928.*[45]

The teachers of France were stimulated by the first volume of the Carnegie Report which appeared in 1923; and in June, 1924, there appeared in one of the teachers' organs an article entitled "Contre l'Enseignement de la Haine Entres les Peuples."[46] This article was well documented and contained many citations taken from school books. It criticized severely the narrow nationalism contained in the books, but the tenor of the article was approved by the teachers' federation in whose publication it appeared (La Fédération Unitaire de l'Enseignement Laique).[47]

---

the *Eighth Session*, 1926, pp. 47-48; *Minutes of the Ninth Session*, 1927, p. 54.)

[45] Published in 1928. Nîmes. Édition de la Paix par le Droit, 38 pages.

[46] *L'Émancipation*, June 22, 1924, supplement of L' École Émancipé. Cited by J. Prudhommeaux, *op. cit.*, p. 7.

[47] Composed of some five or six thousand members belonging to some fifty departmental organizations. Prudhommeaux, *op. cit.*, p. 7.

Following a meeting in which the report was discussed (with the result that it was decided to invite labor syndicates and other organizations to assist in boycotting books containing elements contrary to international goodwill), the Federation addressed a communication to the principal editors of school books. The communication contained the report against the teaching of international hatred, and declared the intention of the Federation to suppress the use of books not conducive to sentiments of justice and international solidarity.

A few months before this communication was sent to the editors, a very active group of teachers, a member of the Federation, incited by the appearance of new chauvinistic school books, passed resolutions in their local organization stating that their organization was boycotting and would continue to boycott school books that were inherently chauvinistic.[48] The publishers assumed various attitudes; some remained silent, others used evasive arguments, but, in time, most of them were ready to make concessions.[49]

In 1926 the more powerful teachers' organization, the Syndicat National des Institutrices et des Instituteurs, entered active protest against school books containing passages likely to develop or perpetuate international ill-will. The Syndicat National, as was mentioned above, had already, in 1924, declared its support of a conciliatory attitude in teaching history. In 1926, Prudhommeaux points out, it declared itself, with its constituent membership of 78,000 teachers, vigorously opposed to prejudiced representations in school books and other publications and specified in particular opposition to anti-German propaganda. It publicly denounced twenty-six reading and history books.[50]

---

[48] J. Prudhommeaux, *Pour la Paix par l'École*, p. 9.

[49] See the replies from publishers quoted by Prudhommeaux, *op. cit.*, pp. 9-10.

[50] Three histories of France, five histories of the World War, eighteen readers. See Prudhommeaux, *op. cit.*, p. 14.

The result of the campaign has been that since the close of 1927 local groups in a number of departments of France have agreed to boycott certain books condemned by the Syndicat National. Since great freedom exists in the choice of school books, the lists vary in the several instances.[51] Naturally as a consequence of this action authors and editors have revised or discontinued objectionable texts, and the production of new books for school use has been stimulated.[52]

National organizations in other countries have directed their attention to school books in a less vigorous manner. In Germany the General Association of German Teachers (Deutsche Lehrerverein, 154,000 members),[53] which in 1926

---

[51] Prudhommeaux specifies some ten departments in which one or more books were boycotted. *Ibid.,* pp. 22-25.

[52] Prudhommeaux, *op. cit.,* pp. 21-38. As an example of the revision effected by the teachers. Prudhommeaux cites, among others, the following passages from the same series of books, dealing with the same phase of the World War:

(From the 1921 edition)—"C'était un trés méchant homme, .le kaiser Guillaume II! Au lieu de dire à son peuple que le progrès ne se réalise que par le travail, que le honheur n'est que dans la bonté, l'honnêteté, la justice, il lui disait: Voyez la France, si riche! si belle! . . . Voyez ses paturages, ses vignobles, ses moissons, ses usines! . . . Armés jusqu'aux dents, nous pénétrerons chez les Français pacifiques et nous prendrons leurs biens; et leurs biens deviendront votre bien. Les Allemands avides écountèrent leur empereur. Brusquement, sur un signe de Guillaume, la plus affreuse des guerres éclata, et le monde fut à feu et à sang!

"L'horrible carnage commença en Belgique: assassinats! pillages! incendies!" (Gauthier et Deschamps, *Histoire de France,* p. 91.)

(From the 1926 edition)—"La Grande Guerre, commencee en 1914, dura 50 mois. Elle a ruiné l'Europe; dix millons d'hommes périrent! Sur ces dix millions, la France compte 1,500,000 Français!

"Au mois de juillet 1914, les Autrichiens envahirent la Servie. Pour défendre ses protégés serbes, la Russie mobilisa. L'Allemagne, alliée de l'Autrich, déclara la guerre à la Russie (er août 1914). A la France, aliée de la Russie, l'Allemagne, délara la guerre (3 août 1914). Puis l'Angleterre déclara la guerre à l'Allemagne. (P. 124.)"

One editor voluntarily destroyed eleven thousand copies of Fournier's *Pour Notre France,* which had been criticized by the Syndicat National. *Ibid.,* p. 36.

[53] Fédération Internationale des Associations d'Instituteurs, *Bulletin* No. 7, June, 1929, p. 3.

affiliated with the French Syndicat National in forming the International Federation of Associations of Teachers to secure peace through the schools, works in the interest of school books. German teachers have less freedom than French teachers in the selection of school books. Hence the German Association has to pursue a policy different from that of the Syndicat National of France. It proposes, according to its statement in the official *Bulletin* of the International Federation, to use its influence to bring about the adoption of books of less objectional nationalistic import as the present supply of more chauvinistic books is exhausted.[54]

Likewise the Swedish member of the International Federation of Associations of Teachers (Folkskollararforbund, 5,000 members)[55] states as part of its active program the revision of text-books. A statement of its aims and activity in the *Bulletin* of the International Federation, March, 1928, reads thus:

"In brief, our program of education for peace is to follow two chief aims:

First, propaganda among teachers to convince them of the necessity of educational reform and to induce them to accept the ideal of the reconciliation of peoples. In the second place, revised editions and new editions of school books, including readers for use in schools, and all measures useful in the education of children, with a view to making them understand and love their sister nations."[56]

Other National Voluntary Organizations.—Another organization in Sweden which has considered the revision of school books as a part of its program is the School Association for Peace (Skolornas Fredsforening). In 1923, at

---

[54] Fédération Internationale des Associations d'Instituteurs, *Bulletin* No. 1, July, 1927, p. 10; No. 8, 1929, p. 7.

[55] *Bulletin* No. 7, June, 1929, p. 3.

[56] Fédération Internationale des Associations d'Instituteurs, *Bulletin* No. 3, March, 1928, p. 30. (Translated by the author.)

Malmo, it considered the question along with other points, in the conference with the Norwegian and Danish peace societies.[57]

A second instance of coöperation among the northern countries in this aim is the work of the Norden, a federation of groups representing the four Northern countries. According to reports of the Norwegian Association of University Women and the Norwegian University Group for the League of Nations Union, the national Associations of the Norden coöperate in examining text-books to eliminate passages calculated to offend one of the other nations. A committee of university professors and school teachers serves as the examining committee. Each Association communicates its views to the Association of the country where a revision of texts is desired.[58]

A somewhat similar example of coöperation among a group of nations is found in the instance of the Institute of Pacific Relations. It has published a preliminary investigation of the history and geography text-books of Australia, Canada, New Zealand, the United States, and Japan, which points out in the case of each country the amount of space devoted to the other countries and to economic and military questions. It makes no criticism, however, of particular books. The work merely proposes to be a starting point for a more intensive investigation.[59]

In several instances the national groups of the International Federation of University Women have undertaken investigations of studies of school books in use in their respective countries. In 1927 the Belgian, Bulgarian, and

---

[57] *Ibid.*, p. 30; Report of the International Conference at Prague, *La Paix par l'École*, 1927, p. 127.

[58] International Federation of University Women, *Report of the Council Meeting*, July, 1927, p. 24, report of the Norwegian Association; League of Nations, *Educational Survey*, Vol. I, No. 1, p. 124, statement of the president of the Norwegian University Group for the League of Nations.

[59] Institute of Pacific Relations, Second General Session, July 15-19, 1927, *A Preliminary Text-book Study, Honolulu, Hawaii, June, 1927*.

Polish Federations reported the revision of text-books, as a point of their agenda.[60] In 1926 the American Association of University Women undertook an investigation of history text-books in use in the United States. In this investigation the World Federation of Education Associations coöperated. The result was the publication in 1929 of the *Report of the Committee on United States History Text-books used in the Schools of the United States*. It briefly describes history books commonly in use and concludes that on the whole the faults of text-books in use are sins of omission.[61]

Official Interest.—Finally, three instances may be cited in which official orders in small countries have recognized the demands of public opinion with reference to the spirit of school text-books. In 1926 the Director of the Ministry of Foreign Affairs of Latvia made the following statement in a report to the Secretariat of the League of Nations:

"The revision of school text-books is entrusted to a special committee attached to the Ministry of Education. Its duty is to examine all text-books published in Latvia from a scientific, educational and practical point of view. It also ensures that text-books shall contain nothing of a nature to rouse hatred between the social classes, and especially between nations."[62]

In 1926 a circular issued by the Belgian Minister of Education advised the teachers that it had been decided to ban from every establishment under state control all works which spread race hatred and hostility among nations.[63] Again, according to a statement of Professor Josef Susta

---

[60] International Federation of University Women, *Report of the Council Meeting, Vienna, 1927*, pp. 22, 35, 51-52.

[61] American Association of University Women, *Report of the Committee on United States History Text-books used in the Schools of the United States*, 15 pp.

[62] League of Nations Document A. 15, 1926, XII, p. 11.

[63] League of Nations International Committee on Intellectual Coöperation, Document 190, 1927, p. 47; Bureau International des Fédérations Nationales du Personnel de l'Enseignement Secondaire Public, *Bulletin International*, No. 26, November, 1929, p. 119.

of Charles University, Prague, a Czechoslovak ministerial
order of July 3, 1928, makes the following statement concerning the rewriting of text-books:

"School books must encourage national and religious tolera-
tion, develop the spirit of peace, inspire respect for international treaties, and emphasize the spiritual solidarity of all
peoples: in short, they should inculcate a true human spirit
into the pupils."[64]

It has been shown that during the last decade public
opinion in educational matters has strongly asserted the
importance of international attitudes in the teaching of history and the preparation of school text-books. The teaching
of history is conceived as a force in the formation of ideals
and judgment and in the establishment of a proper basis for
international relations. The value of history in developing
national consciousness is not ignored. The teaching of history
in the primary grades, in particular, is recognized as an
opportunity for forming the ideals of the future citizen of a
country and for impressing national obligations. The national consciousness excessively developed, however, is contrary to the spirit of scientific truth and breeds and
perpetuates international misunderstandings. With reference
to the primary grades especially emphasis is placed upon
elimination of traditional misrepresentations of other countries, traditional chauvinism, and glorification of war.

In the upper grades objectivity, or the impartial, scientific
attitude in presenting events, is the criterion. The teaching
of history is regarded as a field for developing judgment
and a respect for truth. The pupil is to be taught to ascer-
tain facts even though they are unfavorable to national
pride.

Much emphasis is placed upon the teaching of history
to develop sentiments of international solidarity. History

---

[64] League of Nations, *Educational Survey*, Vol. I, No. 2, p. 75.

should be presented in its full significance, taking into account the mutual interdependence of national groups. The pupil should form a just estimation of the contributions of other nations to civilization in addition to a due appreciation of the contributions of his own country. The several national cultures should be regarded as integral parts of a universal culture, and history should be presented in such manner as to develop in the pupil a sense of his obligation to well-being among nations as well as to national advantage.

From several quarters have come proposals of international coöperation in the preparation of school books in conformity with the standards described above. These suggestions, it has been shown, have met with approval chiefly in theory. Local interest, however, has resulted in definite local measures; action on the part of national groups in investigating the international attitudes displayed in school books has been general.

In this aspect of educational thought two points have stood out: (1) interest in international *rapprochement* through the schools and (2) interest in encouraging scientific accuracy and liberal culture. Books and attitudes in teaching are regarded as factors in forming the public opinion of the future, and it is demanded that they should not be opposed to international conciliation. Moreover, chauvinism is branded contrary to truth, and the ignoring of the contributions of other nations to world civilization is declared a mark of intellectual narrowness. In the latter point of view lies the important gain in education.

CHAPTER VIII

SCHOOL CONTACTS AND INTERNATIONAL FRIENDSHIP

THE INTEREST IN INTER-SCHOOL CONTACTS

Interest of the League of Nations.—In 1923 the attention of the States Members of the League of Nations was directed to the importance of the international contact of young people of school age. A resolution concerning the promotion of international contacts among youth was proposed by the Chilean delegate and adopted by the Fourth Assembly along with the resolution concerning the instruction of youth in the existence and aims of the League. The resolution reads:

> "The Assembly, considering the importance of encouraging contact between the younger generations of different nationalities, invites the Governments of the States Members of the League of Nations to grant all possible facilities for travel by land or by water: (a) to groups of students at higher or secondary educational institutions; (b) to groups of Boy Scouts or Girl Guides belonging to a registered national association of any State Member of the League, when such groups are traveling from the territory of one State Member of the League either through or to the territory of another State Member."[1]

As in the case of the resolution concerning instruction in the League, the Assembly in the following year adopted a resolution reinforcing its former recommendation concerning the promotion of contacts. It urged that the states take further steps to promote international contacts between youth and that the Secretariat investigate the means of further encouraging and coördinating existing efforts.

[1] League of Nations Document A. 10, 1925, XII, p. 2.

In 1927 the Sub-Committee of Experts summoned to consider the two questions returned the following recommendations concerning the development of contacts:

"The following methods of encouraging direct contacts between young people would be valuable; (a) Interchange of individual children between families. (b) International camps for children and international holiday colonies. (c) Group excursions under competent leaders. (d) Congresses and other gatherings, as may be appropriate. (e) Interchange of pupils between schools of different countries. Some coördination of the standards of school-work in different countries might greatly facilitate these exchanges. Governments should be urged to examine this question without delay. (f) Vacation courses."[2]

Finally, in 1928, the Assembly again directed the attention of States Members of the League to the question of school exchanges, in the following more definite resolution:

"The Assembly requests the State Members to take into consideration the need for the systematic organization of the exchange of children in secondary schools during the summer holidays with a view to developing the spirit of peace and international coöperation, for which purpose the existing University Offices should be utilized or special organizations created.

"Convinced that the International exchange of school children would greatly promote mutual understanding among peoples, the Assembly recommends that arrangements be made between different countries on this subject, and it begs the Committee on Intellectual Coöperation to instruct the International Institute of Intellectual Coöperation and the Secretariat of the League to facilitate the execution of such arrangements."[3]

---

[2] League of Nations Document A. 26, 1927, XII, pp. 7-8.

[3] League of Nations, *Official Journal, Special Supplement No. 64, Records of the Ninth Ordinary Session of the Assembly, Plenary Meetings, Text of the Debates,* p. 134.

In compliance with this resolution, the International Committee on Intellectual Coöperation appealed in 1929 to the International Institute of Intellectual Coöperation to facilitate the realization of the arrangements called for by the Assembly resolution.[4]

The interest thus officially formulated in the resolutions of the League of Nations and its Committee is the expression of an increasing general interest in the international contacts of young people as a means of promoting good-will between nations.

Interest of Voluntary Organizations.—After the war a number of interested groups urged the importance of contacts between children of school age. Among non-scholastic organizations were the two mentioned in the Assembly resolutions, each of which by the nature of its activities encouraged group travel. In 1919 the Girl Guides created an International Council, among whose duties was the encouragement of international contacts through international conferences, or World Camps.[5] Similarly, in 1920, the organization of Boy Scouts established an International Council having among its functions the promotion of contacts between groups of different nationalities.[6] Other international and national associations and a number of exchange bureaus, mostly of local nature and of post-war origin, have encouraged interchanges of various kinds between children of school age.

The "Comité d'Entente," the coördinating committee for the principal international organizations interested in teaching the youth of the world the principles of international understanding, has included pupil exchanges in its declaration of principles. Concerning the value of pupil contacts in

---

[4] League of Nations International Committee on Intellectual Coöperation, *Minutes of the Eleventh Session,* 1929, p. 63.

[5] League of Nations Document A. 10, 1925, XII, p. 34.

[6] *Ibid.*

promoting international good-will, the Committee says in its
Declaration of Principles:

"It is expedient likewise to place the youth of each country
in contact as direct as possible with the youth of other countries, in all ways such as trips abroad, periods of study, camps,
exchange of letters, drawing, school books, etc. . . .

"These international interchanges, completed, prolonged in
every degree and order of instruction through contacts between
pupils, young apprentices, students, teachers, are useful in
orientating young people in methods of intellectual coöperation
and in assisting the work of the League of Nations."[7]

Among the organizations represented by the "Comité
d'Entente" are the international federations of teachers' associations. The interest of these organizations deserves
particular mention, because of their direct contact with
schools and administrative authorities.

The World Federation of Education Associations in its
successive conferences has endorsed international contacts
among pupils, without undertaking active measures for
realizing them.[8] The International Bureau of National Associations of Secondary Teachers has manifested a more
practical interest by acting as an intermediary between its
national members and numerous exchange organs and vacation camps and residences. According to a statement of the
Bureau in 1929 it was in that year in touch with some thirty
exchange committees and vacation camps and residences outside of France.[9]

---

[7] League of Nations Institute of International Intellectual Coöperation,
*Neuvième Réunion des Délégués des États Auprès de l'Institut Inter-
national Coöperation Intellectuelle, Annexe No. 1, au procs-verbal*
"Comité d'Entente des Grandes Associations Internationales," 1929, p. 5.
(Translated by the author.)

[8] World Federation of Education Associations, *Proceedings of the First
Biennial Conference*, 1925, Vol. II, p. 914; *Proceedings of the Second
Biennial Conference*, 1927, pp. 792-793.

[9] Bureau International des Fédérations Nationales du Personnel de
l'Enseignement Secondaire Public, *Bulletin International*, No. 24, March,
1929, pp. 7-8.

The International Federation of Teachers from the moment of its foundation made the interchange of teachers and pupils an essential aim. The statutes of organization (1927) specify teacher and pupil exchange as one of the means by which the Federation will achieve its aim of lasting peace among peoples. Section 2 of the "methods of activity" states that the Federation creates

"2. A service of exchange of teachers and pupils, of magazines and corporative publications, and of transportation facilities."[10]

At its first Congress, held in Berlin, in 1928, the Federation passed resolutions asking the several national members to institute and control a Committee of Exchange and Travel, and to send to the International Secretariat the provisions of these committees.[11] The resolutions of the Congress of 1929 again emphasized the value of international interchange, recommending it in all of its forms, and re-

---

[10] Fédération Internationale des Associations d'Instituteurs, *Bulletin Trimestriel*, No. 1, July, 1927, p. 11. (Translated by the author.)

[11] Resolution number 2 reads:

"Chaque Association envoie au Secretariat les conditions materielles dans lesquelles un service d'échange et de voyage peut être organisé méthodiquement.

"Chaque Association institue dans son sein—et fonctionnant sous son controle—un Comité d'échanges et de voyages."

Resolution number 3 deals with the same subject:

"La F. I. A. I. recommande aux autorités officielles de divers pays de faciliter les relations internationales entre les instituteurs, autant dans un but pédagogique que dans un but pacifique; et pour cela, d'accorder des reductions sur les tarifs de chemin de fer, et de bateau, sur les frais de passeport; de consentir aux indemnités aux instituteurs utilisant les voyages à l'étranger pour y étudier de problème professionel; d'échanger des instituteurs aves les écoles normales étrangères, ou des les y detacher; de donner le tarif le plus favorable aux instituteurs voyageant en groupe avec leurs élèves.

"La F. I. A. I. charge le Secretariat de soumettre cette resolution aux divers gouvernements par l'intermediare de l'Institut International de Coopération Intellectuelle et d'engager les demarches pour la faire aboutir." (Fédération Internationale des Associations d'Instituteurs, *Bulletin Trimestriel*, No. 1, July, 1928, p. 9.)

questing the several national Associations to approach the respective governments concerning the appropriation of budgets to insure interchanges.[12]

The interest voiced in the various resolutions quoted above is evidently an interest in a movement in its initial stages. Hence one may expect to find only fragmentary and more or less isolated steps in realization of the aims expressed.

National Official Interest.—In a few instances international interchange of school children has been given official encouragement. In the discussion of university exchanges mention was made of the treaties of exchange concluded by France and Belgium since 1919.[13] With one exception the provisions extend to the lower schools. The French treaties with Belgium, Italy, Norway, Poland, Luxembourg, and Czechoslovakia provide that duly accredited work done by the pupils in the schools of a contracting country will be recognized as the equivalence of studies done in France and vice versa. The Belgium treaty with Luxembourg has the same provision. In the French treaties with Italy and Norway the clauses concerning exchange in the lower schools are restricted specifically to the secondary schools.[14]

Official encouragement of interchange of school children is also given in France through the activity of the National University Office, which is an official organ, and through the official sanction that has been accorded the voluntary Franco-German Interchange Committee described below. The Roumanian Government maintains a joint committee composed of representatives from the departments of Education, Foreign Affairs, and Transportation, for the purpose of encouraging contacts with young people of other

---

[12] Fédération Internationale des Associations d'Instituteurs, *Bulletin Trimestriel*, No. 6, April, 1929, p. 49.

[13] See above, p. 79.

[14] League of Nations Institute of Intellectual Coöperation, *Bulletin for University Relations*, 1928, No. 2, pp. 99, 142.

countries.[15] In July, 1929, according to a statement in a *Bulletin* of the International Bureau of Education, the Director of secondary education in Berlin, Dr. Heyn, spent several days in Paris arranging with the Ministry of Education and the National Office of French Universities and Schools for exchanges of secondary school children.[16] For the most part, however, school interchanges are arranged by voluntary organizations working in connection with the schools.

THE FORMS OF INTER-SCHOOL CONTACTS

Direct Exchanges.—Of the different forms of inter-school contacts perhaps the most fundamental in its value is direct exchange of children between families of different countries. A report of the director of the National University Office of France,[17] in 1923-1924, states that the Office, with the subvention of the Franco-British Association, realized this type of exchange for 1,500 English and French school children between 1918 and 1923.[18] The exchange period was from two to six months.

Since 1926 the Franco-German Committee of Inter-school Exchange (Comité des échanges interscolaire Franco-Allemagne) has effected direct exchanges of school children of French and German families during the vacation period. This committee was established in 1926 by the Comité Français de Secours aux Enfants, and, as was mentioned above, has the patronage of the French Minister of Education.

---

[15] League of Nations International Committee on Intellectual Coöperation, Document 190, p. 76.

[16] International Bureau of Education, *Bulletin,* January, 1930, pp. 30-31.

[17] Office National des Universités et Écoles. The Office is concerned chiefly with university relations. See above pp. 7 ff.

[18] *Rapport sur l'Expansion Universitaire et Scientifique de la France et l'Activité de l'Office National des Universités en 1923 et 1924,* p. 16. The report of the office for 1928-1929 complains that for 220 English requests there were only 80 French requests. (*Rapport du Directeur sur l'Activité de l'Office des Universités en 1928-1929,* p. 19.) The report of 1925-1926 (page 20) attributes the difference in demands to the rate of exchange.

Each year the Minister of Education has sent a circular to the Rectors of Academies urging them to make known to all the schools of France the activities of the Committee. Two German organizations work in close collaboration with the Committee: the Deutsche Liga fur Menschenrechte und the Deutsch-Französischer Schüleraustauschdienst.

During the first year of its activity the Committee realized 40 exchanges; in 1927, 115; and in 1928, 265. During 1928, 262 applications for exchange were received by the Committee from French pupils (254 boys, 38 girls). Among these applications were those of 31 pupils who had participated in previous exchanges. The applications came from 63 departments, and even from Algeria.[19]

At the international conference La Paix par l'École, at Prague, 1927, the secretary of the Fellowship of Reconciliation mentioned the work of the Fellowship in arranging gratuitously exchanges of this kind between school children of Germany and Czechoslovakia. In 1928 it placed almost 300 children.[20]

Group Visits.—Group visits, chiefly brief vacation contacts, are more frequent. Again, the French National University Office has been active in encouraging contacts of this nature. School children visiting France during vacations in the company of teachers are given lodging in French lycées. In 1923-1924, according to a report of the Office, the French lycées received some 400 English school children during the Easter vacation.[21] In 1925-1926 during the Easter vacation and long vacation more than 500 were received.[22] In 1928-1929 during the Easter vacation 484

---

[19] Bureau International des Fédérations Nationales du Personnel de l'Enseignement Secondaire Public, *Bulletin International*, June, 1929, pp. 65-67.

[20] *La Paix par l'École*, p. 24. Edited by Pierre Bovet.

[21] *Rapport sur l'Expansion Universitaire et Scientifique de la France et l'Activité de l'Office National des Universités en 1923 et 1924*, p. 16.

[22] *Rapport sur l'Activité de l'Office National des Universités et Écoles Françaises*, 1925-1926, p. 20.

school children were received from England, Germany, Holland, and Czechoslovakia.[23]

The Norden Society performs a similar service for Norway, Sweden, and Denmark, acting through its School Journey Bureau, which was established in Copenhagen in 1923.[24]

In addition, numerous private ventures of more or less occasional nature may be cited.[25] Among these are the four "good-will expeditions" of school boys which have occurred between the Scandinavian countries and America;[26] an exchange of visits between some two dozen school boys each of Chatham, England, and Bremen, Germany, during two successive summers, 1928 and 1929;[27] and the international gatherings of French, German and English pupils in 1927, 1928, and 1929. These last are of particular interest. The series of three international gatherings have been held through private initiative in successive years in France (Bierville), Germany (Freiburg in Breisgau), and England (Petersfield). Groups of 50 French, 50 German and 50 English school children between the ages of 12 and 16 have

---

[23] *Ibid.*, 1928-1929, p. 4.

[24] League of Nations Document A. 10(a), 1925, XII, pp. 8-9; League of Nations International Committee on Intellectual Coöperation, Document 190, 1927, p. 61. (Reports of the Norden Society.)

[25] In addition to the ones mentioned above one may cite the following: exchanges recently arranged by the Deutscher Philologen Verband between German pupils and pupils of the Nordic countries and Holland (Bureau International des Fédération Nationales du Personnel de l'Enseignement Secondaire Public, *Bulletin International,* March, 1929, p. 7); English-German exchanges solicited by the School Journey Association (*London Times, Educational Supplement,* August 13, 1927, p. 377; *School and Society,* March 16, 1929, pp. 63-65; *School Life,* February, 1930, p. 102); the visit of 450 Scotch pupils to Geneva, 1929 (Bulletin of the International Bureau of Education, January, 1930, Year IV, No. 1, p. 16).

[26] *Bulletin* of the International Bureau of Education, Year IV, No. 1, 1930, pp. 32-33; *Journal of American Association of University Women,* October, 1929, p. 11.

[27] *London Times, Educational Supplement,* June 15, 1929, p. 273; Bulletin of the International Bureau of Education, Year IV, No. 1, January, 1930, p. 22.

assembled each year for two weeks of friendly intercourse and language study under the direction of leaders from the three countries.[28]

INTERNATIONAL CORRESPONDENCE

A form of contact between school children of different nationalities which is much more widespread in practice and offers possibilities of more unlimited development, is found in international inter-school correspondence. This activity embraces two types in extensive use at present (1930) : collective, or group, correspondence and individual exchange of letters by school children of different nationalities. Since 1919 these two forms of inter-school correspondence have been very actively encouraged by school organizations and other voluntary associations both as a means of promoting international good-will among school children and as a means of enlivening curricula studies, particularly foreign language study and geography.

Group Correspondence.—Group correspondence among children is directed chiefly through the Junior Red Cross. It began at the close of the World War and in 1923 was established on an international basis through the Secretariat of the International Junior Red Cross.[29] The Junior Red Cross promotes correspondence between groups in the schools and the exchange of portfolios, gifts, magazines, school work, etc., leaving individual correspondence to other international organizations.[30] In this work it performs

[28] *London Times, Educational Supplement*, August 10, 1929, p. 356; *Ibid.*, August 27, 1927, p. 394; *Bulletin* of the International Bureau of Education, No. 13, September, 1929, p. 22; *School Life*, December, 1929, p. 69; League of Nations, *Educational Survey*, 1929, Vol. I, No. 1, pp. 65-70.

[29] Statement of Everett B. Sackett, Assistant Director of the International Junior Red Cross, "La Croix Rouge de la Jeunesse et la Correspondance Scolaire Internationale," *La Coöpération Intellectuelle*, August, 1929, p. 515.

[30] Bulletin de la Correspondance Scolaire Internationale, 1930, p. 11, published by the Institute of Intellectual Coöperation; *La Coöpération Intellectuelle*, August, 1929, p. 516.

definitely a school function, since the class-room is the unit of correspondence.[31] Group correspondence under the direction of the Junior Red Cross holds certain advantages over individual correspondence. It eliminates to a large extent postal difficulties, affords closer supervision, and, most important of all, eliminates the barrier of language difficulties, since the Society maintains translation offices.

A chart sent by the Director-General of the Junior Red Cross to the League of Nations Secretariat in 1925 represents the activity of the organization for 1924 and 1925.[32] In 1924, thirty-nine countries were engaged in correspondence, in two hundred different combinations; in 1925 forty-six countries were linked in two hundred and fifty-nine different combinations. Each contact, in turn, represents many schools, in each of which a whole class, or even the whole school participated.[33] In 1929 fifty-five countries were engaging in this form of intercourse, twenty-nine of them in correspondence with ten or more foreign countries. The exchanges ranged from one or two in number in some instances to 618 in the case of exchanges between Japan and the United States.[34]

Individual Correspondence.—The more direct form of correspondence, exchange of letters between two pupils, originated before the World War and has received decided stimulus since the war. Particularly during the two years 1928-1929 significant development in international organization took place.

The movement began at the close of the nineteenth century, according to a statement of Charles Garnier, director of the French International Bureau of Inter-School Correspondence. In 1894 Professor Mieille, a teacher of modern languages in France, established contacts in

[31] League of Nations Document A. 10, 1925, XII, p. 42.
[32] See chart, opposite page 214.
[33] League of Nations Document A. 10, 1925, XII, p. 42.
[34] E. B. Sackett, *op. cit.*, p. 516.
14

Germany and England for the purpose of promoting the exchange of letters between school children in French, German, and English languages; and by 1900 the practice was well established.[35]

After the World War the work was revived in France by M. de Lapradelle, Professor in the Faculty of Law of Paris and Delegate to the Hague Court of Justice, who established in 1919 the French Bureau of International Inter-School Correspondence. In 1921 activity of the Bureau extended to five countries and involved 16,773 exchanges; in 1923, sixteen countries, involving 17,900 exchanges. In 1925, 31,543 exchanges took place; but in 1926, because of the increased cost of postage the number dropped to 4,350. In 1927-1928 the number of exchanges increased again, reaching 32,110.[36]

In England International Inter-School Correspondence began under the auspices of the *Review of Reviews*, which collaborated with Professor Mieille's plan. In 1914, the Modern Language Association assumed supervision of the exchange of letters between pupils and has continued to direct the work. In 1929 a number of organizations in England were engaged in promoting international inter-school correspondence. Nine of these organizations have recently accepted the Modern Language Association bureau as the central organization for England.[37]

According to the authority of the director of the Roumanian Bureau of Inter-School Correspondence, international inter-school correspondence was begun in Rou-

---

[35] *La Paix par l'École* (edited by Pierre Bovet), p. 90; World Federation of Education Associations, *Second Biennial Conference*, 1927, p. 233.

[36] *La Coöpération Intellectuelle*, August, 1929, pp. 506-508, report of Charles M. Garnier of the French Bureau of International Inter-School Correspondence, made at the meeting of experts on International Inter-School Correspondence, 1929 (see below, p. 215); League of Nations Document A. 10, 1925, XII, pp. 42-43; *La Paix par l'École*, p. 91.

[37] *La Coöpération Intellectuelle*, August, 1929, pp. 508-509; report of F. Renfield, Secretary of the Modern Language Association, made at the meeting of the Committee of Experts on International Inter-School Correspondence; *Bulletin de la Correspondance Scolaire Internationale*, pp. 8-9.

LIGUE DES SOCIÉTÉS DE LA CROIX-ROUGE

SECTION DE LA CROIX ROUGE DE LA JEUNESSE
Echange de Correspondance Inter-scolaire

-1ᵉʳ JANVIER 1924.-

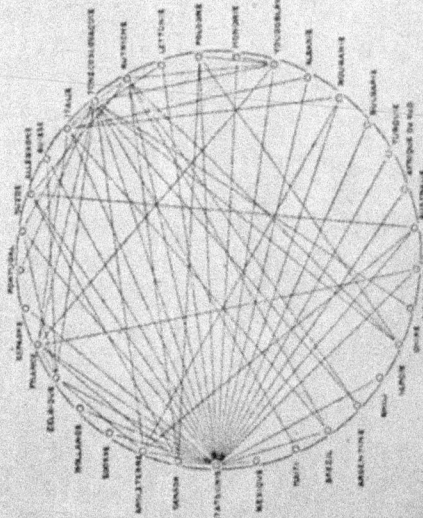

39 PAYS
200 COMBINAISONS

-1ᵉʳ JANVIER 1925.-

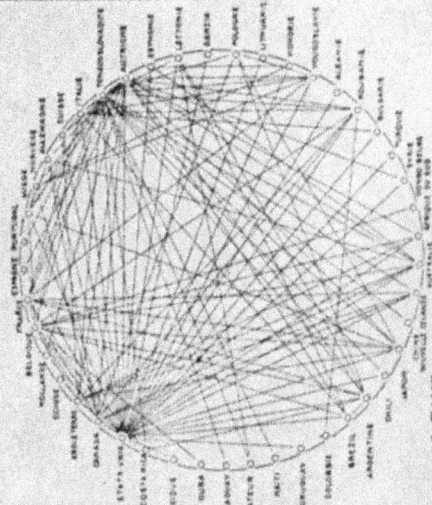

46 PAYS
259 COMBINAISONS

mania in 1906, and after a long lapse appeared again in 1922 and has received increasing encouragement both official and unofficial.[38] In the United States international inter-school correspondence seems to have begun in 1919 through the coöperation of Dr. Roehm, of Peabody College, with the French Bureau.[39] Other countries, as the international meeting of experts of international school correspondence discussed below indicates, have manifested more or less active interest. In a few instances, esperanto has been encouraged as a medium of inter-school correspondence.[40]

The Permanent International Committee on Correspondence.—In 1928 individual correspondence received added stimulus through the action of the League of Nations International Committee on Intellectual Coöperation. In 1928 the Sub-Committee of University Relations of the International Committee on Intellectual Coöperation authorized the Institute of Intellectual Coöperation to organize a meeting of experts to consider the question of international inter-school correspondence.[41] Accordingly thirteen experts, representing active organizations in the field of inter-school correspondence or other forms of pupil contact in seven countries met at the Institute on May 27-28, 1929.[42] At this meeting the permanent Committee on International Inter-school Correspondence was established to deal with individual correspondence.[43]

[38] *La Coöpération Intellectuelle,* August, 1929, pp. 513-515.

[39] See League of Nations Document A. 10, 1925, XII, p. 43; Charles M. Garnier, "Le Bureau de Correspondance Scolaire Internationale," *La Paix par l'École,* p. 89; Alice Wilson, Director of the World League of International Education Associations, report at the meeting of experts, *La Coöpération Intellectuelle,* 1929, pp. 504-506.

[40] *La Paix par l'École,* pp. 93-98, Report of a German School; pp. 99-100, Report of a Bulgarian School.

[41] League of Nations Document C. 57, 1929, p. 1.

[42] *Ibid.,* pp. 1-2.

[43] *Bulletin de la Correspondance Scolaire Internationale,* No. 1, January, 1930, p. 4. Published at the Institute of Intellectual Coöperation.

In the course of the meeting the Committee voted the following resolutions:

"1. The meeting requests the International Institute of Intellectual Coöperation to ask the proper authorities in each country to encourage the formation of international inter-school correspondence offices, and, where such already exist, to help them by mentioning them in the official *Educational Review* and by encouraging the work of teachers who interest themselves in the matter.

"2. In the interest of international coöperation the meeting recommends that a national center for international inter-school correspondence should be set up in every country.

"Certain National Committees on Intellectual Coöperation seem eminently qualified to undertake this duty.

"3. With a view to increasing the value of letters exchanged by way of international inter-school correspondence, the meeting calls the attention of directors of international inter-school correspondence offices and members of the teaching profession to a point of capital importance, namely, that it is just as necessary that those wishing to take part in the correspondence should be able to write their native tongue fluently and correctly as that they should be to some extent able to express themselves in a foreign tongue.

"The meeting is of the opinion that the classifications A, B, and C, indicating the capacities of pupils on the enrollment-lists, should refer, not to their knowledge of the foreign tongue, but to character and intelligence combined with their standard in the mother-tongue.

"4. The meeting decides to form a Permanent International Inter-School Correspondence Committee. . . .

"The meeting requests the International Institute of Intellectual Coöperation to detail one of its officials to act as Secretary to the Committee.

"It shall be the duty of the Secretariat of the Permanent Committee to collect and circulate information relating to the practical work done in the matter of international inter-school correspondence, to publish an information bulletin and to organize periodical international meetings."[44]

Acting upon the request contained in the resolutions of the Committee on International Correspondence, in 1929 the Sub-Committee on University Relations of the International Committee on Intellectual Coöperation authorized the following procedure:

"The Sub-Committee . . . authorizes the Institute to ask the authorities concerned in each country to encourage the foundation and activities of international inter-school correspondence offices. It authorizes the Director to appoint an official of the Institute to act as Secretary of the Permanent Committee set up by the meeting in all matters coming within the Institute's range of work."[45]

This official support of the League of Nations has strengthened the interest in international inter-school correspondence, having given recognition and authority to the program. Since 1929, in compliance with the request of the Institute, the National Committees on International Intellectual Coöperation of Germany, Spain, United States, Italy, and Holland have agreed to serve as liaison Committees to develop and coördinate efforts for international inter-school correspondence in the respective countries.[46]

In England, since 1929, the Modern Language Association, acting through its secretary, serves as a liaison center for nine organizations in Great Britain conducting international correspondence.[47] In France, as was mentioned

[44] League of Nations International Committee on Intellectual Coöperation, *Report of the Committee on the work of its Eleventh Plenary Session,* 1929, pp. 10-11.

[45] League of Nations International Committee on Intellectual Coöperation, *Minutes of the Eleventh Session,* 1929, p. 88.

[46] *Bulletin de la Correspondance Scolaire Internationale,* No. 1, January, 1930, pp. 8, 12.

[47] *Ibid.,* pp. 8-9.

above, the Bureau of International Inter-School Correspondence of the Musée Pédagogique has been serving in this
capacity for a number of years.[48] At present also Finland
is making efforts to establish a central national committee.[49]
In these efforts of official and voluntary organizations to
promote international contacts of school children directly
through exchanges and group visits and indirectly through
correspondence, one finds an interesting effort to encourage
in pupils a sentiment of international good-will. The international exchange of school children must, because of inherent difficulties of economic and psychological nature, remain restricted to a comparatively few pupils of the upper
grades. International correspondence, which has in greater
measure demonstrated its practicability and effectiveness,
offers possibility of extensive expansion and is a factor of
potential significance in the broadening of interest and the
motivation of studies. Hence the establishment of the
Permanent International Committee to coördinate international school correspondence and direct its development
is a point of considerable importance in international education relations.

Conclusion

In the course of this study the extensive voluntary organization and official action to promote international
understanding through the schools have been described.

An important feature of the organization to further international educational relations is the central position which
the League of Nations' Committee on Intellectual Coöperation and its executive organ, the International Institute, have
come to occupy. In an investigative capacity, the Committee
has undertaken to study, chiefly through its Institute of
Intellectual Coöperation, the problems of international inter-
school relationships and international studies. As an ad-

---

[48] *Ibid.*, p. 12; League of Nations Document A. 10, 1925, XII, pp. 42-43.
[49] *Ibid.*, p. 8.

visory body of the League it has brought these problems of international educational relationships before governments, universities, and other organizations of States Members of the League.

As a coördinating force it has brought into co-operative relations important national and international organizations pursuing similar interests. The annual meetings of directors of national university offices, representatives of Institutions for the Scientific Study of International Affairs, and representatives of the International Federations of Students are convened by the Institute of the Committee. Also, as a result of a common interest in teaching the ideals of the League of Nations, a group of international organizations, working under the direction of the Institute, have evolved an international liaison committee to encourage the teaching of international coöperation in the schools. In a similar way the permanent committee on International Inter-School Correspondence has been established through its influence.

With reference to the higher institutions of study the efforts to further international understanding have been directed chiefly toward the extension of international interchange of professors and students and the encouragement of schools and courses for the study of international problems and foreign cultures. During the decade since the war private interest, official measures, and voluntary organization have contributed to increased development in each of these fields of inter-school relationships.

In the lower schools definite teaching programs have been evolved and supported. It has been shown that educational activity of the decade since 1919 has been marked by the increasing importance attached to the lower schools as a medium of promoting international understanding. An essential function of education in the lower schools has been held to be the formation of a new mental attitude conducive to world peace and opposed to war. In consequence systematic effort has been made "to train the younger generation to regard international coöperation as the normal method of conducting world affairs," to teach the League of Nations as an example of international coöperation in the conduct of world affairs, to eliminate elements of chauvinism and international prejudices from school text-books and methods of teaching, and to present history in a manner to develop sentiments of international solidarity by emphasizing the mutual interdependence of national groups.

In general the effort directed to the promotion of international understanding through both higher and lower schools has at its basis the conception that international conciliation must result from a mutual appreciation among nations of the several national civilizations and an understanding of the international problems arising from the differences in these civilizations.

BIBLIOGRAPHY

I. GENERAL

Abbott, Edith, *Immigration—Select Documents and Case Problems*. Chicago. 1924.

Abel, James F., *Major Trends of Education in Other Countries*. Bulletin 1928, No. 13, Department of the Interior, Bureau of Education (Advance Sheets from the Biennial Survey of Education in the U. S. 1924-1926). Washington, 1928.

American Association of University Women, *Report of the Committee on United States History Text-books used in the Schools of the United States*. Reprinted from the Proceedings of the Biennial Convention. New Orleans, Louisiana. 1929.

American National Red Cross, *School Correspondence Plan of The American Junior Red Cross*. A. R. C. 621, Washington, D. C.

Anderson, Hendrick C., *World Conscience—An International Society for the Creation of a World Center*. Rome.

Andrews, Fannie Fern, *American School Citizenship League*. (An eleven year survey of activities of the "American School Peace League" from 1908-1919.) Boston. 1919.

Angel, Norman, *The Great Illusion*. New York. 1913.

Anon., *Education and the League of Nations, Being the Report of the Joint Committee of Enquiry into the Teaching of the Aims and Achievements of the League of Nations*. Hamilton House, London. 1929.

Anon., "International Conference on Education," *Nature*, 30: 363-5, August 14, 1884.

Anon., "International Education," *Independent*, 65; 1258-1259. November 26, 1908.

Anon., *The Manuale Scholarium* (An original account of life in the Mediaeval University translated from the Latin by Robert Francis Seybolt). Cambridge. 1921.

Barnard, Henry (editor), *American Journal of Education*, 31 volumes. 1855-1881.

Beach, Charles F., Jr., "Educational Reciprocity," *North American Review*, 183:611-612. October 5, 1906.

Bosanquet, Bernard, *Social and International Ideals*. London. 1917.

Bourgeois, Léon, *L'Oeuvre de la Société des Nations*, 1920-23, Paris. 1923.

Bourgeois, Léon, *Pour La Société des Nations*. Paris. 1910.

Bourne, Randolph Silliman (compiler), *Toward an Enduring Peace*. American Association for International Conciliation. New York. 1916.

Bridgman, Raymond L., *World Organization*. Boston. 1905.

British League of Nations Union, *Teachers and World Peace*. London. 1929.

Brunet, René, *The New German Constitution*. Translated from the French by Joseph Gollomb, 1922.

Bryce, James, *International Relations*. New York. 1922.

Burns, C. Delisle, *A Short History of International Intercourse*. New York. 1926.

Burns, C. Delisle, *The Morality of Nations*. London. 1915.

Butler, Nicholas Murray, *The International Mind*. New York. 1912.

Capes, W. W., *University Life in Ancient Athens*. London. 1877.

Cloyd, David E., *Modern Education in Europe and the Orient*. New York. 1917.

Compayré, Gabriel, *Abelard and the Origin and Early History of the Universities*. New York. 1893.

Crafts, Wilber Fish, *A Primer of Internationalism*. Washington, International Reform Bureau. 1908.

Cubberley, E. P., *History of Education*. New York. 1920.

Davidson, Thomas, *Education of the Greek Peoples*. New York. 1917.

Davis, George B., *Outlines of International Law*. New York. 1887.

Deburgh, W. G., *The Legacy of the Ancient World*. London. 1924.

Dowling, Evaline (editor), *World Friendship*. Los Angeles School Publication, No. 145.

Drane, A. T., *Christian Schools and Scholars*. New York. 1910.

Estournelles de Constant, Baron D' (Paul Henri Benjamin), "The Next Step—International Conciliation," *Outlook* 86:147-151, May 25, 1907.

Fairchild, Henry Pratt, *A World Movement and American Significance*. New York. 1920.

Fairchild, Henry Pratt, *The Melting-Pot Mistake*. Boston.

Fisher, Irving, *America's Interest in World Peace*. New York.

Fought, H. W.; Hope, A. H., etc., *Comparative Education*. New York. 1927.

Fouillée, Alfred, *Education from a National Standpoint* (translated by W. J. Green). New York. 1892.

Freeman, Kenneth J., *Schools of Hellas*. London. 1907.

Garnett, James Clerk Maxwell, *Education and World Citizenship*. Cambridge. 1921.

Graves, F. P., *A History of Education During the Middle Ages* New York. 1909.

Graves, F. P., *A History of Education during the Middle Ages and the Transition to Modern Times*. New York. 1910.

Gulliver, Lucile, *The Friendship of Nations*. Boston. 1912.

Harris, W. T., "The Belgian International Congress of Educators," *Education* 1:623-632, July, 1881.

Hart, Albert Bushnell, *School Books and International Prejudices*. International Conciliation Pamphlet, No. 38. 1911.

Haskins, Charles H., *The Rise of Universities*. New York. 1923.

Hughes, R. E., *The Making of Citizens*. New York. 1906.

Institute of Pacific Relations, Second General Session, July 15-9, 1927. *A Preliminary Text-Book Study*, Honolulu. 1927.

Kallen, Horace Meyer, *The Structure of Lasting Peace.* Boston. 1918.

Kandel, I. L. (editor) *Educational Yearbook.* International Institute of Teachers College, Columbia University. New York. 1924-1928.

Kasson, Frank H., "Chicago and the Congress of Education," *Education,* 14:32-36, September, 1893.

Kennedy, J., "Rhodes Scholarships," *School and Society,* 9:763-767, June 28, 1919.

Kentaro, Kaneko, "For a Better Understanding between the East and the West," *Independent,* 63:251. August 1, 1907.

Kerschensteiner, George, *Education for Citizenship* (translated by A. J. Pressland from the fourth edition). New York. 1911.

Kilpatrick, William Heard, *Education for a Changing Civilization.* New York. 1926.

Lips, Julius Ernst, *Die internationale Studentenbewegung nach dem Kriege* ("La Confédération Internationale des Étudiants"). Leipzig. 1921.

Lochner, Louis P., *Internationalism among Universities,* World Peace Foundation Pamphlets Series, Vol. III, no. 7, part I. July, 1913.

Lochner, Louis P., "The Cosmopolitan Club Movement," *International Conciliation,* No. 61, December, 1912, pp. 1-14.

Lowe, L. S., "The Possibility of Intellectual Coöperation between North and South America," *International Conciliation,* No. 6, April, 1908, pp. 3-15.

Lyte, H. C. M., *History of the University of Oxford to 1530.* London. 1886.

Maltby, Margaret (editor), *History of the Fellowships awarded by the American Association of University Women 1889-1929, With the Vitas of the Fellows.* Washington. 1930.

Matter, M., *Histoire de L'École d'Alexandrie Comparée Aux Principales Écoles Contemporines,* second edition, 3 vols. Paris. 1840.

Mead, Lucia Ames, *Educational Organizations Promoting International Friendship*. World Peace Foundation Pamphlet Series, Vol. II, no. 6, part IV, pp. 3-6. July, 1912.

Monroe, Paul, *A Text-book in the History of Education*. New York. 1906.

Monroe, Paul, editor, *Cyclopedia of Education*. 5 Vols. New York. 1911-13.

Monroe, Paul, *Essays on Comparative Education*. New York. 1927.

Moon, Parker Thomas, *Syllabus on International Relations*. New York. 1925.

Moore, Ernest Carroll, *What the War Teaches About Education*. New York. 1919.

Mott, John R., *La Fédération Universelle des Associations Chrétiennes d' Étudiants, les Origines, l'Oeuvre Accomplie dans le premier Quart de Siècle, 1895-1920, l'Oeuvre Projetée*. Geneva. 1921.

Munro, D. C., *The Medieval Student: Translations and Reprints*. Vol: II, no. 3. Philadelphia. 1903.

Neumann, George Bradford, *International Attitudes of High School Students*. Teachers College Contribution to Education No. 239. New York.

Norton, Arthur B., *Readings in the History of Education*. Cambridge. 1909.

Oldham, Reta, *Some Problems of Interchange*, Occasional Paper No. VI. International Federation of University Women.

Prudhommeaux, J., *Pour La Paix par L'École: ce qui a été fait en France pour lutter contre les livres Scolaires Contraires au rapprochement des peuples, 1923-1928*. Deuxiéme Édition, Nîmes, 1928.

Rait, R. S., *Life in a Medieval University*. Cambridge. 1912.

Rashdall, H., *The Universities of Europe in the Middle Ages*. 3 vols. Oxford. 1895.

Rathenau, Walter, *The New Society*. Translated by Arthur Windham. New York. 1921.

Reisner, Edward H., *Nationalism and Education Since 1789.*
New York. 1923.

Remme, Karl, *Die Hochschulen Deutschlands, Ausgabe für
Ausländer.* Berlin, Akademischer Auskunftsamt. 1926.

Robertson, David Allen, "International Educational Relations
of the United States," *Educational Record,* Vol. 6, No. 2,
1925, pp. 91-150; Vol. 7, No. 1, pp. 46-59. January,
1926.

Rogers, Robert W., *The Basis of World Order.* Boston. 1918.

Root, Elihu, *Addresses on International Subjects.* Cambridge.
1916.

Rouse, Ruth, *Rebuilding Europe,* Student Christian Movement. London. 1925.

Ryan, W. Carson, Jr., "Edinburgh Conference of the World
Federation of Education Associations," *School and
Society,* 22:249-259, August 29, 1925.

Scott, Jonathan French, *The Menace of Nationalism in
Education.* London. 1926.

Scott, W., *World Education.* Cambridge. 1912.

Sisson, Edward O., *Educating for Freedom.* New York. 1925.

Smith, Anna T., "The Educational Congress at Paris." *Education,* 21:124-126, October, 1900.

Smith, Frank Webster, *Historical Development of Secondary
Education from Prehistoric Times to the Christian Era.*
New York. 1916.

Smith, Henry Lester and Chamberlain, Leo Martin, *An Analysis of the Attitude of American Educators and Others
toward a Program of Education for World Friendship and
Understanding.* Bulletin of the School of Education
Indiana University. Bloomington, Indiana, 1929.

Smith, Margaret, "International Congress of Education, at
Le Havre," *Education,* 6:178, December 1885.

Snedden, David, *Civic Education.* New York. 1922.

Sproul, Robert C., *The International House at the University
of California.* Pamphlet of International House, New
York. 1928.

Staniford, Peter, *Comparative Education.* London. 1918.

Thwing, Charles Franklin, *The Training of Men for the World's Future*. New York. 1916.

Tolman, William H., "International Student Associations," *Educational Review*, 5:363-9, April, 1893.

Townsend, W. T., *The Great Schoolmen of the Middle Ages*. New York. 1905.

Viallate, Achille, *Economic Imperialism and International Relations during the last Fifty Years*. New York. 1923.

Volkmann, Hellmut, *Die Deutsche Studentenschaft in ihrer Entwicklung seit 1919*. Leipzig, Quelle & Meyer. 1925.

Walden, John W. H., *The Universities of Ancient Greece*. New York. 1909.

Walsh, Edmund A., *The History and Nature of International Relations*. New York. 1922.

Walters, Raymond, *Educational Jottings Abroad*. New York. 1924.

Washburne, Carleton and Stearns, Myron M., *New Schools in the Old World*. New York. 1926.

Waterman, Richard, Jr., "International Educational Congresses of 1893," *Education Review*, 6:158-166, September, 1893.

Wellons, Ralph Dillingham, *The Organizations set up for the Control of Missions Union Higher Educational Institutions*. New York. 1927.

Wheeler, W. R., King, H. H., and Davidson, A.B., *The Foreign Student in America*. New York. 1925.

Wilson, Woodrow, *Guarantees of Peace*. New York. 1919.

Wilson, Woodrow, *In our First Year of the War*. New York. 1918.

Wilson, Woodrow, *International Ideals*. New York. 1919.

Wilson, Woodrow, *Speeches and Addresses made during the President's European Visit, December 14, 1918 to February 14, 1919*. New York.

Wilson, Woodrow, *Why We are at War*. New York. 1917.

Woellner, Fredric P., *Education for Citizenship in a Democracy*. New York. 1923.

World's Student Christian Federation, *An Adventure in International Friendship*. Geneva. 1929.

World's Student Christian Federation, *Student Hostels, Foyers, Clubs, and Similar Institutions*. Geneva. 1930.

The World Student Christian Federation, International Student Service, *Student Service in Five Countries*. Geneva. 1929.

Zimmern, Alfred, *Learning and Leadership: A Study of the Needs and Possibilities of International Intellectual Coöperation*. Geneva. 1927.

II. LEAGUE OF NATIONS DOCUMENTS

League of Nations Assembly:

Les Travaux de La Commission Internationale de Coöpération Intellectuelle. Rapport. (Second Committee.) Geneva. 1922.

L'Organization du travail intellectuel. (Second Committee.) Geneva. 1920.

Records of the Assembly. (Records of the First ten Assemblies.) Geneva. 1920-29.

Validity in all States, on a basis of reciprocity of certain secondary education diplomas. Letter from M. Quinones de Leon, Spanish representative on the council. Geneva. 1923.

Work of the Committee on Intellectual Coöperation. Report presented to the Assembly by the Fifth Committee. Geneva. 1923.

Work of the Committee on Intellectual Coöperation. Report of the Second Committee to the Fifth Assembly. Geneva. 1924.

Work of the Committee on Intellectual Coöperation. Fifth Meeting, 1924. Geneva. 1924.

Work of the International Committee on Intellectual Coöperation. Report of the second committee to the Sixth Assembly. Geneva. 1925.

Work of the International Committee on Intellectual Co-operation. Resolutions. (Sixth Meeting, 1925.) Geneva. 1925.

League of Nations Committee on International Intellectual Coöperation:

An Appeal Made on Behalf of Intellectual Workers of Hungary. Geneva. 1924.

Bulletin of the International University Information Office, first year, numbers 1 and 2. Geneva. January, April, 1924.

Conditions of Life and Work of Musicians. Report of W. Martin. Vol. 1, Brochure No. 3, Vol. II, Brochure No. 3. First Series. Geneva. 1923.

Educational Survey. Vol. I, Nos. 1, 2. 1929-1930.

Enquête sur la Situation du Travail Intellectualle. Observations sur la Methode d'une Statistique de la Vie Intellectuelle. Julien Luchaire. Brochure No. 1, Première Série. Geneva. 1923.

Exposé Documentaire sur l'État de la Vie Intellectuelle en Autriche. Lausanne. 1922.

How to make the League of Nations known and to develop the Spirit of International Coöperation. Geneva. 1927.

Intellectual Life in the Various Countries: Inquiries Into the Conditions of Intellectual Life. Second Series, pamphlets Nos. 6-13, 16, 19-21, 24-25, 28-31, 33-41.

Les Échanges Internationaux de Publications. Rapport par O. de Halecki. Brochure No. 3 bis. Première Série. Geneva. 1923.

List of National Committees on Intellectual Coöperation. Geneva. 1926.

Memorandum by Madame Curie, member of the Committee, on the Question of International Scholarships for the Advancement of the Sciences and the Development of Laboratories. Geneva. 1926.

15

Minutes of the first nine sessions. Geneva. 1922-1927.

Minutes of the tenth plenary session. Geneva. August 10, 1928.

Note provisoire sur l'état de la vie intellectuelle en Pologne soumis au conseil par la commission de coöpération intellectuelle. Geneva. 1922.

Observations Sur Quelques Problèmes de L'Organization Intellectuelle Internationale. Julien Luchaire. Brochure No. 2. Première Série. Geneva. 1923.

Sub-Committee of Experts for the Instruction of Children and Youth in the Existence and Aims of the League of Nations. Geneva. 1926; 1927.

League of Nations Committee on International Intellectual Cooperation, Institute of Intellectual Coöperation:

Bulletin de la Correspondance Scolaire Internationale. Paris, No. 1, January, 1930. Published by Secretariat of the Permanent Committee on International Inter-School Correspondence.

Bulletin of the International University Information Office. Geneva. 1924, No. 5. 1-4; 1925; Nos. 1-6, 1926, Nos. 1-5.

Bulletin for University Relations. Geneva. 1926.

Handbook of Institutions for the Scientific Study of International Relations. Paris, 1929.

Handbook of University Exchanges in Europe. Paris. 1928. 1929.

Holiday Courses in Europe. 1928, 1929, 1930.

La Coöpération Intellectuelle, Published Monthly: January, 1929-April, 1930.

Neuvième Réunion des Délégués des États Auprès de L'Institut International de Coöpération Intellectuelle, March, 20, 1929, Annexe No. 1, au procès-verbal, "Comité d'Entente des Grandes Associations Internationales." 1929.

Statistique Intellectuelle de la France. 1923-1924. Compiled by Tatiana Beresovski-Chestov. Published under the auspices of the Institute of Intellectual Coöperation and the Institute of Statistics of the University of Paris. Paris, 1926.

League of Nations Council:

Association Française pour La Société des Nations, Création d'un Bureau Internationale pour Les Relations Intellectuelle et d'Education. Lettre en date du 8. Juillet, 1920. Geneva. 1920.

Committee on Intellectual Coöperation. Extract from the minutes of the thirty-fifth session of the council, tenth meeting. Geneva. 1925.

Foundation of International Institute of Intellectual Coöperation—Offer of French Government, Geneva. 1924.

Foundation of an International Institute of Intellectual Coöperation, Report by M. de Jouvenel—Adopted by Council, September, 1924. Geneva, 1924.

L'Organization du Travail Intellectuelle. Rapport presenté par M. Léon Bourgeois . . . adopté par le conseil Le 2 Septembre, 1921. Geneva. 1921.

Résolutions adoptées par le conseil européen de la Dotation Carnegie. Geneva. 1920.

Union des Associations Internationales University Internationale. (Lettre en date du 19 Aout, 1920.) London. 1921.

Université dont la création est projetée par l'union des associations internationales à Bruxelles. Geneva. 1920.

Work of Committee on Intellectual Coöperation. Report by de Jouvenel. Geneva. 1924.

League of Nations Secretariat:

Application de L'article 24 du Pacte concernant les Bureaux Internationaux. Memorandum 1921. Geneva. 1921.

Bureau International d'Assistance. Note 1921. Geneva. 1921.

Illustrated Album of the League of Nations. Printed by Atar. Geneva. 1926.

International Institute of Intellectual Coöperation. 1925. Geneva. 1925.

L'Activité Éducative et L'organization du Travail Intellectuelle Accomplies par L'Union des Associations Internationales. Memoire 1921. Geneva. 1921.

L'Utilité d'un Organisme Technique pour Le Travail Intellectuelle. Memoire 1921. Geneva. 1921.

The League of Nations and Intellectual Coöperation. Revised Edition. Information Section of the League of Nations Secretariat. Geneva. 1927.

Miscellaneous League Documents:

League of Nations Handbook of International Organizations (Associations, Bureaux, Committees, etc.). Geneva. 1926.

League of Nations. Monthly summary of the League of Nations. Vols. 1-7. Geneva. 1921-28.

League of Nations. Official Journal. Vols. 1-9. Geneva. 1920-1928.

League of Nations Treaty Series; Publication of Treaties and International Engagements Registered with the Secretariat of the League of Nations. Vol. 1, 1920 —Vol. LV, 1926. London. 1920-1926.

Publications de la Societe des Nations, I. B. Minorities, 1927. I. B. 2.

III. MISCELLANEOUS DOCUMENTS: BULLETINS, HANDBOOKS, MINUTES AND REPORTS

American-Scandinavian Foundation, *Sixteenth Annual Report.* New York, 1929.

Association for the International Interchange of Students. *First Annual Report,* 1909-1910. Edited by Henry W. Crees, London. 1910.

Second Annual Report, 1911. Edited by Henry W. Crees. London. 1911.

Third Annual Report, 1912. Containing the Report

of the First International Conference at the Termination of the Experimental Period, 1909-1912. Edited by Henry Crees. December, 1912. London.

Bureau international des fédérations d'instituteurs. Session de 1913. Reunion de Bruxelles. Journal des instituteurs. Brussels. 1913.

Bureau International des Fédérations Nationals du Personnel de L'Enseignement Secondaire Public, Bulletin International, March, June, November, 1929, No. 24, 25, 26. Cahours, Imprimerie Coneslant. 1929.

Dix Années de Vie Internationale, 1919-1929. Cahors, Imprimerie Coneslant. 1929.

Carnegie Foundation:

A Manual of Public Benefactions of Andrew Carnegie. New York, 1919.

Carnegie Endowment for International Peace: Division of Intercourse and Education. Annual Report of the Director for the year 1927. New York, 1928.

Carnegie Endowment for International Peace. Division of Intercourse and Education. Enquête sur les livres scolaires d'après guerre. Paris, 1923-27. 2 vols.

English Speaking Union. Landmark, January, 1919, May-December, 1919, January, 1920-July, 1930. List of Members, London, 1920.

Fédération International des Associations d'Instituteures, Bulletin Trimestriel, Nos. 1-8, July, 1927. November, 1929. Paris.

Guggenheim Foundation: Reports of the Secretary and Treasurer, 1927, and Reports of the Educational Advisory Board and Treasurer's Report, 1925-26. John Simon Guggenheim Memorial Foundation. 1926.

Institute of International Education:

A Decade of International Fellowships, by Theodosia Hewlett, New York, January, 1930.

Annual Reports of the Director, New York, 1920-1929. Fellowships and Scholarships Open to American Students *for Study in Foreign Countries,* New York, 1923, 1925, 1929.

Fellowships and Scholarships Open to Foreign Students for Study in the United States. New York, 1923, 1925, 1929.

Institute of International Education. Bulletin No. 5, *Guide Book for Foreign Students in the United States.* New York. 1921.

Institute of International Education; Its Origin, Organization, and Activities. Ninth series, Bulletin No. 1. New York, 1928.

News Bulletin, New York, 1928, 1929. Published Monthly.

The problem of Fellowships for Foreign Students in American Universities and Fellowships for American Students in Foreign Universities, Fifth Series, Bulletin No. 1, 1924.

Instituto Cultural Argentino-Norteamericano. *Estatutos del Instituto Cultural Argentino Norteamericano.* Buenos Aires. 1928.

Memoria y Balance del Primer Ejercicio Terminado en 30 de Abril de 1929. Buenos Aires, 1929. (35 pp.)

International Bureau of Education:

Bulletin, Nos. 11-14, March, 1929. January, 1930. Geneva.

Children's Books and International Good-Will, Report and Book List, 1929, 80 pp.

La Paix L'École Travaux de la Conférence Internationale tenue à Prague du 16 au 20 avril, 1927. Publication of the International Bureau of Education. Edited by Pierre Bovet, 1927.

International Confederation of Students, *Year Book,* 1927-1928, 1929 (French edition), Brussels, 1928, 1929.

International Federation of League of Nations Societies, *Bulletin,* Nos. 1-2, 1924; Nos. 1-5, 1925; Nos. 1-5,

1926; Nos. 1-5, 1927; Nos. 1-5, 1928; Nos. 1-5, 1929.

Assemblies, Nos. 6-9, 1922-1925.

Plenary Congresses, Nos. 10-13, 1926-1929.

Questionnaire on the Work of Education and Liaison Committees Replies, Brussels Secretariat, 1929.

International Federation of University Women:

Reports of the First, Second, Third, Fourth and Fifth Conferences, 1920, 1922, 1924, 1926, and 1929. *Bulletin,* Nos. 7, 9, 10.

National Students Federation of the United States of America. *Year Book,* 1926, 1928, 1928-1929.

International Polity Summer School (Old Jordans Hostel Beaconsfield Under the Auspices of the Garton Foundation, July 17 to 27, 1914.) London, 1915.

Office National des Universités et Écoles Françaises:

Rapport sur L'Expansion Universitaire et Scientifique de la France et LActivité de l'Office National des Universités en 1923 et 1924. By Charles Petit-Dutaillis, Director of the Office. Bibliotheque du l'Office National des Universités et Écoles Françaises. Tome II. Paris, 1925.

Rapport sur l'Activité de l'Office National des Universités et Écoles Françaises. By Charles Petit-Dutaillis, Director of the Office.

Pan-American Educational Conference, Los Angeles, 1922:

Inauguration ceremonies of Rufus Bernhard von Kleinsmid. Los Angeles. 1922.

Pan-Pacific Union:

Documentary Information Compiled by the Division of Intellectual Coöperation of the Pan-American Union for the Information of the Delegates to the Inter-

American Congress of Rectors, Deans and Educators, to be Held at Havana, Cuba, on February 20, 1930. Washington, 1929.

First Pan-Pacific Educational Conference, Official Bulletin, August 11, 1921.

Proceedings of the First Pan-Pacific Conference on Education, Rehabilitation, Reclamation, and Recreation. Held at Honolulu, Hawaii, April 11-16, 1927. Washington, 1927.

Report of the Activities of the Pan-American Union, 1923-27. Washington, 1928.

Report of the Governments of the Republics, Members of the Pan-American Union on the Work of the Union since the close of the Fourth International Conference of American States, Covering the Period, 1910-1923.

Special Handbook for the Use of Delegates to the Fifth International Conference of American States. Washington. 1922.

Special Handbook for the Use of Delegates to the Sixth International Conference of American States. Washington, 1927.

Peace Organizations:

Fifth Universal Peace Congress, Chicago, 1893. The American Peace Society, Boston, 1893.

The Peace Year Book, 1911, 1912. National Peace Council. London.

Proceedings of the International Conference on Education. Edited by Richard Cowper. London, 1884.

Rockefeller Foundations. *Rockefeller Foundation Annual Report,* 1913-14. New York. 1915.

Royal Institute of International Affairs:

Directory of Societies and Organizations in Great Britain Concerned with the Study of International Affairs. Compiled by Stephen A. Heald. Published under the joint auspices of the Royal Institute of International

Affairs and the Information Service on International
Affairs. London, 1929.

Society for the propagation of the Gospel in Foreign Parts:
Two Hundred Years of the S. P. G. London, 1901.

Universities Bureau of the British Empire:
*Report of the Second Congress of the Universities of the
Empire, 1921.* London. 1921.
Yearbook of the Universities of the Empire, 1914-1930.
London.

Union of International Associations:
Annuaire de La Vie Internationale. 1 ᵉʳ série, 1908-1909;
2 ᵉᵐᵉ série, 1910-1911. Office Central des Associa-
tions Internationales. Brussels. 1908-1911.
*Congres des Associations Internationales. Rapport No. 1.
L'Organization Internationale et Les Associations
Internationales.* P. Otlet. Office Central des Institu-
tions Internationales. Brussels. 1910.
*La troisième session de congres mondial des Associations
Internationales—Les Congres de 1915 à San Fran-
cisco.* Publication No. 81. Union des Associations In-
ternational, Office Central. Brussels. 1914.
*L'Union des Associations Internationales Constitution du
Centre International Congress Mondial. Publication
No. 24 a.* Office Central des Associations Interna-
tionales. Brussels. 1912.
Office Central des Associations Internationales. Publica-
tion No. 25 a. 1912.
Sur La Création d'une Université Internationale. P. Otlet.
Publication No. 90. Union des Association Internationales. Brussels. 1920.
*The Union of International Associations: A World Cen-
ter*—Publication No. 60. Central Office of Interna-
tional Associations. Brussels. 1914.

U. S. Bureau of Education:

A Handbook of Educational Associations and Foundations in the United States. U. S. Bureau of Education. Bulletin, 1926. No. 16. Washington. 1926.

Annual Report of the Department of Interior, Report of the U. S. Commissioner of Education. 1904. Vol. II.

Report of the Commissioner of Education. 1915.

U. S. Sixtieth Congress, Second Session, House of Representatives, *Document No. 1275.*

World Federation of Education Associations:

World Conference on Education Held Under the Auspices of the National Education Association of the United States, June 28 to July 6, 1923, in San Francisco. Published by the National Education Association, 1923.

World Education, Proceedings of the First Biennial Conference of Educational Associations Held at Edinburgh, July 20 to July 27, 1925. 2 vols. Edinburgh. 1925.

World Federation of Education Associations, Proceedings of the Second Biennial Conference Held at Toronto, Canada. August. 1927.

INDEX